D0438724

IMAGES OF THE WEST

IMAGES OF THE WEST

Responses to the Canadian Prairies

R. Douglas Francis

Western Producer Prairie Books
Saskatoon, Saskatchewan

Copyright © 1989 by R. Douglas Francis
Western Producer Prairie Books
Saskatoon, Saskatchewan

All rights reserved. No part of this publication may be reproduced, stored in a retrieval system, or transmitted, in any form or by any means, electronic, mechanical, photocopying, recording, or otherwise, without the prior written permission of the publisher.

Jacket design by John Luckhurst/GDL
Jacket illustration: "A Prairie Sunset" (1915) by C. W. Jefferys. Courtesy Art Gallery of Ontario, Toronto. Gift of Mrs. K. W. Helm, daughter of C. W. Jefferys, Kneeland, California, 1980. Photograph by Carlo Catenazzi, AGO. With the permission of the estate of C. W. Jefferys.

Printed and bound in Canada
96 95 94 93 92 91 90 89   8 7 6 5 4 3 2 1

The publisher acknowledges the support received for this publication from the Canada Council.

Western Producer Prairie Books is a unique publishing venture located in the middle of western Canada and owned by a group of prairie farmers who are members of the Saskatchewan Wheat Pool. From the first book in 1954, a reprint of a serial originally carried in the weekly newspaper *The Western Producer*, to the book before you now, the tradition of providing enjoyable and informative reading for all Canadians is continued.

Canadian Cataloguing in Publication Data

Francis, R. D. (R. Douglas), 1944–
    Images of the West : changing perceptions of the
Prairies, 1690–1960

    Includes bibliographical references.
    ISBN: 0-88833-274-2

1. Prairie Provinces – History – Sources. 2.
Prairie Provinces – Description and travel.
I. Title.
FC3237.F736 1989   971.2   C89-098129-9
F1060.F736 1989

The credits appearing on pages x to xiv of the Acknowledgements are hereby made part of this copyright page.

To Barbara

*who has shared with the experience
of seeing the prairies through western eyes.*

CONTENTS

ACKNOWLEDGEMENTS

I am indebted to a number of people who provided assistance and support during the completion of this book. I want to thank the various libraries, archives and art galleries that helped me in locating material and that granted me permission to use the visual and written sources for the book. In particular I would like to thank the librarians and archivists at the Glenbow-Alberta Institute and at the University of Calgary Archives and Special Collections where a good deal of my research was completed in a friendly and helpful atmosphere. The University of Calgary provided me with a research grant at the initial stages of the project, and with a Killam Resident Fellowship which gave me release time from teaching and administrative responsibilities for an academic term to complete the writing of the book. My fellow Canadian historians in the History Department provided moral support and an interest in the project. The secretarial staff—Liesbeth von Wolzogen, Marjory McLean, Joyce Woods, Olga Leskiw and Laureen Quapp—willingly typed different drafts of the text. Gordon and Sylvia Jones of Calgary kindly allowed me the use of their cabin during the writing of the book.

Gerald Friesen, George Melnyk, and Doug Owram read a draft of the manuscript under short notice and amid busy schedules of their own, and offered constructive criticism. Ramsay Derry, a freelance editor, worked with me in the final stages of the book and offered his usual expertise in suggesting ways to improve the book.

At the press, Rob Sanders, formerly of Western Producer Prairie Books, initially accepted the project for publication, while Jane McHughen, Editorial Director, has seen it through to completion. She has been unfailing in her effort to keep me on schedule. Don Ward did a fine job of editing the manuscript and making helpful suggestions on the selection of the excerpts and images to include.

I would like to thank my parents, who have always shown an interest in my work, and to thank my children—Marc, Myla and Michael—for their patience and understanding when I have been preoccupied with "images." Finally, I want to thank sincerely my wife, Barbara—to whom this book is dedicated—for her ideas, time, and patience in the completion of this book. Only I am responsible for the limitations and shortcomings of the book that still remain.

Extracts from the following works have been reprinted with permission:

"The Alberta Homestead," in Edith Fowke and R. Johnston, eds., *More Folk Songs of Canada* (Waterloo: Waterloo Music, 1967). Reprinted by permission of Waterloo Music, Waterloo, Ontario.

"Alberta Land," in Leonora M. Pauls, "The English Language Folk and Traditional Songs of Alberta" (M. Mus., University of Calgary, 1981). Reprinted by permission of Leonora Pauls.

As For Me and My House and *The Lamp at Noon* by Sinclair Ross, used by permission of the Canadian Publishers, McClelland and Stewart, Toronto.

Black Night Window by John Newlove, used by permission of the Canadian Publishers, McClelland and Stewart, Toronto.

"A Century of Plain and Parkland" by W. L. Morton, with the permission of G. Margaret Morton, literary executrix of the estate of W. L. Morton.

David Thompson's Narrative of His Explorations in Western America, with the permission of The Champlain Society, Toronto.

Fruits of the Earth and *Settlers of the Marsh* by F. P. Grove, used by permission of the Canadian Publishers, McClelland and Stewart, Toronto.

Gully Farm by Mary Hiemstra, used by permission of the Canadian Publishers, McClelland and Stewart, Toronto.

"Harvest" by Jessie Louise Hetherington and "Manitoba" by Jonathan Hughes Arnett, in Margaret A. MacLeod, *Songs of Old Manitoba* (Toronto: Ryerson Press, 1959). Reprinted by permission of McGraw-Hill Ryerson Limited, Toronto.

"In Open Prairie" by Kenneth McRobbie, with the permission of the author.

"Into the World" by Frans van Waeterstadt, translated by and reprinted with the permission of Herman Ganzevoort.

Journals and Letters of Pierre Gaultier de Varennes de La Vérendrye, with the permission of The Champlain Society, Toronto.

The Kelsey Papers, A. G. Doughty and C. Martin, eds., with the permission of the National Archives of Canada and the Deputy Keeper of the Records, Public Record Office of Northern Ireland.

Letter from a Danish immigrant in "Scandinavian Experiences on the Prairies, 1890–1920: The Fredericksens of Nokomis," with the permission of Jorgen Dahlie.

"Letters from a Barr Colonist" by Alice Rendell, with the permission of the Historical Society of Alberta.

Narrative of the Canadian Red River Exploring Expedition of 1857 and of the Assiniboine and Saskatchewan Exploring Expedition of 1858 by Henry Youle Hind, with the permission of Hurtig Publishers Ltd., Edmonton.

"Not a Penny in the World" in *The Pioneer Years 1895–1914* by Barry Broadfoot. Copyright © 1976 by Barry Broadfoot. Published by Doubleday Canada Ltd. Reprinted by permission of Doubleday Canada Ltd.

Ocean to Ocean by George M. Grant, with the permission of Hurtig Publishers Ltd., Edmonton.

"On Viewing the Grave of the Murdered Scout" by George F. Crofton, with the permission of the Historical Society of Alberta.

The Papers of the Palliser Expedition 1857–60, Irene Spry, ed., with the permission of The Champlain Society, Toronto.

"A Peigan Myth" by Claude Mélançon, translated by David Ellis, with the permission of Gage Educational Publishing Company, a Division of Canada Publishing Corporation.

"Poor Little Girls of Ontario," collected by Edith Fowke. Reprinted by permission of Edith Fowke.

"The Prairie: A State of Mind" by Henry Kreisel, with the permission of the author.

"A Prairie Sampler" by Dorothy Livesay, with the permission of *MOSAIC*.

Rupert Brooke in Canada, S. Martin and R. Hall, eds., with the permission of the editors.

Saskatchewan by Edward McCourt, with the permission of Macmillan of Canada Ltd., a Division of Canada Publishing Corporation.

"Saskatchewan," from the singing of T. Rogers, in R. D. Francis and H. Gonzevoort, eds., *The Dirty Thirties in Prairie Canada* (Vancouver: Tantalus Research Ltd., 1980). Reprinted by permission of Tim and Patti Rogers, Calgary.

"Seeing an Unliterary Landscape" by W. L. Morton, with the permission of G. Margaret Morton, literary executrix of the estate of W. L. Morton and *MOSAIC*.

"Sources" by Margaret Laurence, with the permission of *MOSAIC*.

Sowing Seeds in Danny by Nellie McClung, with the permission of the estate of Nellie McClung.

Who Has Seen the Wind by W. O. Mitchell, used by permission of Macmillan of Canada, a Division of Canada Publishing Corporation.

The Wild North Land by William Butler, with the permission of Hurtig Publishers Ltd., Edmonton.

Wolf Willow by Wallace Stegner, used by permission of Macmillan of Canada, a Division of Canada Publishing Corporation.

The author and publisher gratefully acknowledge permission to include illustrative material.

William Armstrong, *Fort Garry* (C–10514). Courtesy National Archives of Canada.

"Canada West: Contentment, Abundant . . ." (NA–3818–3, back cover) and "Canada West: Homes for Millions" (NA–3818–2, front cover), *Canada West* magazine (1921). Courtesy Glenbow Archives, Calgary.

"Canada West: Canada–The New Homeland" (NF–37–1, from PAM 971.2, C212c, c.2, front cover), *Canada West* magazine (1930). Courtesy Glenbow Archives, Calgary.

Corps of Royal Engineers, *Survey Camp on North Antler River* (C–73303). Photograph courtesy National Archives of Canada/RCMP.

Reta Cowley, *Potash Plant with Wolf Willows*. Courtesy of the artist and the Mackenzie Art Gallery, Regina. Gift of the Art Gallery Society. Photographed by Don Hall, AV Services, University of Regina.

Maureen Enns, *Sky Hill*. Courtesy of the artist.

Ivan Eyre, *Black Sun*. Collection of Winnipeg Art Gallery. Donated by the late Mary H. Acheson in memory of her mother, the late Helen E. Acheson. Photographed by Ernest Mayer, Winnipeg Art Gallery.

"Fertile Canada" (NA–789–128) and "The Only Drawback" (NA–789–129) in *Canada, The Granary of the World* (Canada Department of the Interior, 1903). Courtesy Glenbow Archives, Calgary.

"Fur Rivalry and Exploration," map reprinted from P. Cornell, J. Hamelin, F. Ouellet, and M. Trudel, *Canada: Unity in Diversity* (Toronto: Holt, Rinehart and Winston, 1967).

Sydney Prior Hall, *The Beginnings of Calgary, Alberta* (C–13025), *Lord Lorne Interviewing a Settler on the Prairies* (C–12900), and *The Prairie* (C–13023). Courtesy National Archives of Canada.

Humphrey Lloyd Hime, *Encampment on the Red River* (C–4572) and *The Prairie Looking West* (C–17443). Photograph courtesy National Archives of Canada.

W. G. R. Hind, *Buffalo Magnified by Mirage* (M460). Courtesy McCord Museum of Canadian History, Montreal. *Oxen with Red River Cart*. Courtesy National Gallery of Canada, Ottawa, with the permission of Mr. D. T. Hind. *Roadside Scene with Three Houses, Manitoba* (T–31491). Courtesy Metropolitan Toronto Library.

Robert Hurley, *Sunset* and *Winter Scene*. Reproduced from *Sky Painter* (Saskatoon: Western Producer Prairie Books, 1973). *Untitled [sunset]* (67.1.26). Collection of the Mendel Art Gallery, Saskatoon. Courtesy Western Producer Prairie Books, Saskatoon.

"I Have a Message," G. L. Dodds (R–B2462). Courtesy Saskatchewan Archives Board.

C. W. Jefferys, *A Prairie Town*. Courtesy of Mr. Anthony Allen, Edmonton. *Wheat Stacks on the Prairies*. Courtesy Government of Ontario Art Collection, Queen's Park, Toronto. Photographed by T. E. Moore Photography, Toronto. With the permission of the Estate of C. W. Jefferys.

George Jenkins, *The Old Toal Place*. Courtesy of the artist and the Mendel Art Gallery, Saskatoon.

Henri Julien, *The Sweet Grass Hills* (59.40.14). Courtesy Glenbow Museum, Calgary.

Paul Kane, *Assiniboine Hunting Buffalo* (6920). Courtesy National Gallery of Canada, Ottawa. Transferred from Parliament of Canada, 1955. Photographed by L. V. Cave, Ottawa, 1969. *Big Snake, a Blackfoot Chief* (22). Courtesy National Gallery of Canada, Ottawa. Transferred from Parliament of Canada, 1888. *Buffaloes at Sunset* (6919). Courtesy National Gallery of Canada, Ottawa. Transferred from Parliament of Canada, 1955. *Kee-akee-ka-saa-ka-wow (The Man that gives the War Whoop)* (912.1.42) and *A Prairie on Fire* (912.1.39). Courtesy Royal Ontario Museum, Toronto.

Gus Kenderdine, *Land of Promise*. Collection of the University of Saskatchewan. Gift of Dr. W. C. Murray.

Illingworth Kerr, *Chinook Country*. Private Collection, Calgary. *Prairie Sky*. Courtesy Amoco Canada Petroleum Company Ltd. Corporate Art Collection. *Straw Stacks, March Thaw* (62.116.1). Courtesy Glenbow Museum, Calgary, with the permission of the Estate of Illingworth Kerr.

Dorothy Knowles, *The River*. Courtesy of the artist and the Mendel Art Gallery, Saskatoon.

William Kurelek, *Dinnertime on the Prairies*. Courtesy McMaster University Art Gallery, Hamilton. *Not Going Back to Pick Up a Cloak*. Courtesy The Isaacs Gallery, Toronto, Canadian Art Galleries Ltd., Calgary, and Rork Hilford, Calgary. *Who Has Seen the Wind*. Courtesy The Isaacs Gallery, Toronto, with special assistance from Hurtig Publishers.

Kenneth Lockhead, *Return to Humanity*. Courtesy of Johanna Mitchell, Saskatoon.

Macleod, Alberta: Where Nature is making a Big City (NA-789-127, cover). Fort Macleod Industrial Commissioner, 1912. Courtesy Glenbow Archives, Calgary.

Lucius O'Brien, *Oat Harvest* (6466). Courtesy National Gallery of Canada, Ottawa.

"Palliser's Triangle," map reprinted from *Images of the Plains: The Role of Human Nature in Settlement*, edited by Brian W. Blouet and Merlin P. Lawson, by permission of the University of Nebraska Press. Copyright © 1975 by the University of Nebraska Press.

Peter Rindisbacher, *Blackfeet Hunting on Horseback*. Courtesy Amon Carter Museum, Fort Worth, Texas. *Indian Taking Scalp* and *The Murder of David Tully and Family*. Courtesy of the West Point Museum collections, United States Military Academy, West Point, New York.

Otto Rogers, *Sunset Stillness* (67.9). Courtesy of the artist and the Mendel Art Gallery, Saskatoon.

Edward Roper, *Some Prairie Flowers and a Prairie Dog* (C-11036) and *Sulky Ploughing Near Carberry Mountain, Manitoba* (C-11033). Courtesy National Archives of Canada.

Harry Savage, *Partridge Hill Road Series*. Courtesy of the artist, with special assistance from The University of Alberta Press.

F. B. Schell, *A Prairie Stream* (C-82954). In *Picturesque Canada*, vol. 1 (Toronto, 1882). Courtesy National Archives of Canada.

Inglis Sheldon-Williams, *The Fire Guard* (24-1) and *The Landmark* (16-7). Collection of the Norman Mackenzie Art Gallery, Regina. Photographed by Brigden's, Regina. *Man Ploughing with Two Horses* (S-W.65.58-154). Courtesy Glenbow Museum, Calgary.

Peter Stevens, *Prairie: Time and Place*. Courtesy of the artist and the Mendel Art Gallery, Saskatoon.

Frederick Verner, *Bison Foraging in Blizzard* (3589-4/Vo56), *Buffalo Grazing under a Moonrise* (3592-2/Vo69), *Indian Warrior Overlooking an Encampment* (3588-3/Vo79), *The Last Buffalo*, and *Sioux Encampment at Sunset* (3591-3/Vo62). Courtesy The Pagurian Corporation Limited, Toronto.

Capt. Henry Warre, *Fort Ellice on the Assiniboine River*. Courtesy American Antiquarian Society, Worcester, Mass.

Western Canada: The Granary of the British Empire (NA-789-126, cover). Canadian Pacific Railway, 1908. Courtesy Glenbow Archives, Calgary.

The author has made every effort to obtain permission to reprint material still in copyright. The publisher would be pleased to hear from anyone who has details about uncredited material and will make corrections to subsequent editions of this book.

INTRODUCTION

My first image of the Canadian West was from a picture on a calendar in our farmhouse in southern Ontario. The image was of a field of golden wheat blowing in the wind under a sunny and azure sky. I assumed from my southern Ontario perspective, where wheat fields were always framed by rows of trees or shrubs, that this field of prairie wheat was only a focused picture and that beyond the eye of the camera stood the trees and shrubs and lush vegetation. I could not imagine a landscape of only earth and sky, what novelist W. O. Mitchell describes in *Who Has Seen the Wind* as "the least common denominator of nature, the skeleton requirements simply, of land and sky—Saskatchewan prairie." My first image of the West, like the images of earlier writers and artists described in this book, was shaped by images outside the region.

My study of Canadian history at university widened my perspective of the prairies to include an appreciation of the people who had populated the West—the native people, the English- and French-speaking fur traders, the Métis, the settlers from the rest of Canada, and immigrants from the four corners of the earth. I learned about the history of western protest, from the Riel Rebellions of 1869 and 1885 to the agrarian reform movements of the 1920s, from the political protest of the 1930s as manifested in the CCF and Social Credit to "Diefenbakerism" in the 1950s. I equated the prairies with protest, radicalism, and discontent. I had the typical central-Canadian image of the West as the unhappy child of Confederation with little cause to complain. I would have agreed with historian Ed Rea's summation of the popular impressions of the Canadian prairie:

> To most Canadians the Prairie provinces are a curious region, peopled with farmers complaining about the weather or wheat prices, and convinced they have been victimized by "eastern interests" who manipulate a complex tariff structure to exploit the West. On the infrequent occasions when they think of the Prairies, the images that are conjured up are those of vast fields of waving, golden grain and strong taciturn men who braved the wilderness (and the winter wind at Portage and Main).

Then I had occasion to travel west in the summer of 1967 while working on the Canadian Pacific Railway. I remember leaving busy Union Station in Toronto and travelling up through the cottage country of central Ontario and across the rugged precambrian shield with its endless rocks, lakes, trees, and muskeg. Then came that magical moment as we left Kenora and northern Ontario and entered the prairies near Winnipeg. It was a beautiful late summer's day; the wheat fields were shimmering under an open sky. It was my calendar image recreated before my eyes, my inner and outer images reconciled.

In 1976 I came to teach at the University of Calgary. In my first year in the History Department I was conscripted to teach a course on "Rural Society in Prairie Canada." While I had grown up in the rural society of southern Ontario, I soon discovered that that experience only reinforced how different were the rural societies of Ontario and the prairies. I had to shift my focus – and hence my images – of the West to that of the West itself. I learned to see the prairies through western eyes. I came to appreciate the western perspective, and to see that beyond the physical landscape existed a landscape of the mind shaped by the myths, stories, and attitudes of its people. I began to see the mythic West described in this book.

I combined my newly-acquired interest in western Canadian history with my long-time interest in intellectual history when I was given the opportunity to teach a course on "Images of the Canadian West." Here I studied how people over time had pictured the West, and to realize that their ideas or images of the West shaped the region as much as, if not more than, the decisions of politicians, the intricate workings of the economy, and the daily activities of its people. I understood what Robert Kroetsch, the poet and novelist, meant when he said: "In a sense we [westerners] haven't got an identity until somebody tells our story. The fiction makes us real." It is people's perception over time, both in literary and historical sources, that have shaped the region and given it meaning – its images.

What I offer here in this book is a look at the changing images of the West through the variety of sources in which they were expressed. I have drawn upon the extensive and good work already done on aspects of the imagery of the West – detailed studies of images in particular periods, such as Douglas Owram's *The Promise of Eden* (1980), which examines the ideal of the West as promoted by an influential group of national expansionists on the eve of Confederation; or studies from the perspective of a particular group, such as Ronald Rees's *Land of Earth and Sky* (1984), which discusses the prairie artists' perception of the West. What is new and different is my examination of the changing images of the West over the entire three centuries of exploration and settlement by the white man. This broad perspective includes not only such traditional historical sources as fur traders' journals, reports of scientific expeditions, travelogues, government immigration propaganda, booster literature of towns and cities, but also art, literature, songs, and poetry. I have, for example, found images in the poetry of Robert Stead as well as the journal of the explorer David Thompson, in the art of C. W. Jefferys as well as the immigration propaganda distributed by the Canadian government and the Canadian Pacific Railway Company. The book brings together these various sources to show that a particular image predominated at a period of time irregardless of the medium through which it was expressed, since the image reflected the prevailing belief about the West at the time. Inevitably, I have had to sacrifice depth for brevity, to sketch the images in broad strokes rather than in minute detail. The book is, therefore, meant more for the general reader than for the specialist, but I hope will be of interest to anyone wishing to understand this unique and fascinating region of Canada.

Each chapter deals with a dominant image of the West in a particular era in the historical evolution of the region. These images overlap, however, since ideas are never clear cut. New ideas or perceptions evolve out of previous ones, and only replace them gradually. No sooner is one image established than it is challenged and eventually replaced by another. Furthermore, one image does not predominate to the exclusion of all others. Different perspectives exist simultaneously. Nevertheless, amidst this multiplicity of images, one image will stand out as the dominant or guiding image of the era. It is this dominant image which becomes the focus of each chapter.

Chapter One presents the image of the West as a cold, barren, desolate, inhospitable wasteland. This image prevailed for two centuries, from 1650 to 1850, and was projected in the reports of explorers and fur traders who were the first to view the region, and in the artistic depictions of the area by Peter Rindisbacher, the first-known painter of the Canadian prairies. Chapter Two examines the romantic image of the West which arose in the mid-nineteenth century. Writers, poets, visitors, and artists, influenced by the ideas of the age of Romanticism, projected in their writings and paintings of the region an image of a pristine wilderness where man was in harmony with the natural world and in communion with God. Co-existent with the romantic image of the West was the image of the region as the fount of national greatness and imperial grandeur, the subject of Chapter Three. Canadian and British nationalists and imperialists envisioned the West as the means to create a great Canadian nation to augment a powerful British Empire. Chapter Four analyzes the utopian image of the West projected in the immigration propaganda, the booster literature, and the artistic and literary depictions of the region in the late nineteenth and early twentieth centuries. The West was presented as "the last best West," the "promised land" where potential settlers were assured of material success and spiritual contentment.

There arose at the same time and especially in the years between the two World Wars, a reaction to this utopian imagery. A realistic image of the West emerged in the accounts of settlers, and in the literature and art of the 1920s and 1930s; it depicted the Canadian prairies as a harsh land that restricted the creative power and freedom of its inhabitants. Chapter Five analyzes this perspective. The final chapter examines the mythic image of the West. In the post-World War II era, the region was seen less as an external entity whose physical landscape shaped people's perception of it, and more as a region of the mind, a cultural landscape shaped by its people and its own mythology—a blending of historical reality and literary creativity.

Each chapter contains a text which explains why the particular image being described arose at that time, discusses its nature, and explains its impact on the historical evolution of the region. I have been conscious of the need to draw attention to the currents of thought and the social context out of which that image emerged so that the reader has a frame of reference by which to understand the image. I have also attempted to illustrate that image by reference to a variety of media through which it was projected to show the predominance of that image. I realize that in an effort to highlight a particular image, I have had to take material out of context and thus make the image appear more prominent than it was at the time. I have also had to overlook other less pronounced images in those works in an effort to insure continuity. A pattern does emerge, however, and I have attempted to discuss that pattern through the text. As well, I have included in the book excerpts from the primary written and visual sources to enable the reader to experience for him or herself how the images of the West were presented and how they changed over time.

1

THE WESTERN WASTELAND
1650–1850

"Barren," "cold," "desolate," and "inhospitable." These words capture the image of the North West (now the Canadian West) in the minds of Western Europeans and North Americans from 1650 to 1850. This negative view of the region appeared in the reports of explorers, fur traders, and missionaries who traversed the area, and in early artistic depictions of the region. So strong was the belief that the North West was a wasteland, ill-suited for settlement and agriculture, that it remained the almost unchallenged domain of the fur trader for over two centuries.

The fur trader entered a territory already occupied by the native people. The natives had lived in the prairie West for at least ten thousand years before the Europeans arrived. A variety of tribes existed that belonged to three linguistic groups: the Algonquian, the Athapaskan, and the Siouan. These Indians did not imagine their land as a region of exploration and exploitation, but rather as their ancestral home and territory granted to them by the Great Spirit. They believed that they lived on a great island of which they were the only inhabitants. Peigan children in southern Alberta, for example, learned the story—carried down from generation to generation by oral tradition—of how Napiwa or "the Old Man," after whom the Oldman River in southern Alberta is named, created the world as a floating island from a grain of sand. They imagined the prairies, with its millions of buffalo roaming freely, as their sacred land to be shared with the plants and animals which, the Indians believed, also possessed spiritual gifts. John Snow, a chief of the Stoney Indians in southern Alberta, describes in *These Mountains are our Sacred Places* (1977) how his people perceived the land:

> In our migrations, as in our vision quests, my people continued to observe the animals, plants, rocks, trees, streams, winds, sun, moon, stars, and all things. Our teaching has always been that everything was created for a purpose by the Great Spirit. We must, therefore, respect all things of creation and learn as much as we can. There are lessons hidden in creation that we must learn in order to live a good life and walk the straight path. Behind these lessons and teachings is the Creator. These things can only be understood through the Great Spirit.[1]

These natives knew the land intimately, and they would be the ones who would guide the Europeans in their early explorations over the prairies, often urging them on with descriptions of what lay ahead.

A Fur Trade Domain

The fur traders who entered the West belonged to one of two great European empires that vied to control the trade with the Indians of the region.[2] In 1670 Charles II, King of England, granted a royal charter to a group of wealthy London merchants to establish the Hudson's Bay Company with the right to "sole Trade and Commerce" over a region known as Rupert's Land (named after Prince Rupert, the king's vigorous and enterprising older cousin), a vast region vaguely defined as all territory whose rivers flowed into Hudson and James Bay. The company located on Hudson Bay, "the Bay of the North," which allowed access to the western interior of the North American continent. It was an imperial trading company, directed by men in London who had no first-hand knowledge of the fur trade but who owned shares and who had the backing of a wealthy and powerful empire. France, with a foothold in the New World since 1608 and an inland empire that surpassed Britain's in territory by 1670, also pushed westward. The French base was at Quebec on the St. Lawrence River, another highway into the heart of the continent. Local French-Canadian traders who had a close association with the native people and intimate knowledge of the trade, operated the French fur trade.

Both empires sent out explorers in search of the "Northwest Passage," a route to the Orient by way of western seas. Although the route could not be found, these explorers reported back of the abundance of furs in the West. Profits from the fur trade soon overrode the concern for the Northwest Passage, and both empires tried to dominate the fur trade in the north western region of the continent. For the next 150 years, European interest in the western interior rested entirely on the fur trade with the native people.

The European explorers and fur traders of the eighteenth century went west with a European view of the world characteristic of "the Age of Enlightenment."[3] They believed that man had the innate ability, through reason, to solve the mysteries of the world by understanding the laws of nature. With confidence and enthusiasm, they explored the distant corners and darkest continents of the world in quest of greater knowledge so as to be able to put the pieces of the world puzzle in place. They saw it as their duty to add the discoveries of the New World to the already impressive body of knowledge from the Old. For theirs was the first age to realize the size of the world and the extent of its oceans and continents. They went forth to conquer nature, to chart new lands and vistas, and to study scientifically and dispassionately previously unknown plants, animals, and peoples. They believed in an orderly natural world that could be broken down into observable elements and understood in minute detail. Their objective was to record their observations for a European audience which had an insatiable appetite to know more.

The North West offered a wonderful natural laboratory. It contained new varieties of plants, exotic animals, and primitive human beings. Here was an unexplored region, a natural world still needing to be understood, a blind spot in the European mind. Explorers, fur traders, and amateur scientists came, in the true Enlightenment tradition, to understand, not to enjoy. To them, the area was devoid of natural beauty and uninviting to the white man.

Henry Kelsey, a lad of twenty who was employed by the Hudson's Bay Company, was probably the first European to see the interior of western Canada.[4] In 1690 he, along with a group of Indian guides, travelled from York Factory on the Bay into the interior, perhaps as far south as present-day The Pas on the South Saskatchewan River, and then, one year later, towards the western plains. As his first report, he playfully submitted a ninety-line poem.[5] Within this verse Kelsey introduced many of the descriptive terms for the region which would reappear in later fur-trading reports. He called the southern grasslands a "plain," used the term "desert" to describe the lonely empty space, and termed the general terrain "barren ground" because of the absence of trees. Throughout he stressed the dangers in this *terra incognita*, this unknown land where no white man had previously been. He conveyed the image of a threatening, desolate wilderness that a European entered at risk to his life.

Kelsey's poem, and his lengthier prose report of the 1691 expedition, were lost to public knowledge until 1926. Nevertheless, they reflected a picture of the North West that prevailed for the next 150 years.

Pierre Gaultier de Varennes, sieur de La Vérendrye, advanced the French presence in the West when in the 1730s he led an expedition, via the familiar St. Lawrence–Great Lake trade route, west to the Lake of the Woods and the Forks of the Saskatchewan River. He was searching for the fabled "mer de l'ouest" or great inland sea that led to the Western Ocean and on to Asia. En route, he reported: "All the savages . . . raise quantities of grain, fruits abound, game is in plenty and is only hunted with bows and arrows; the people there do not know what a canoe is; as there is no wood in all that vast extent of country, for fuel they dry the dung of animals."[6] La Vérendrye failed to find the Western Ocean, but he did succeed in establishing a series of trading posts which strengthened the French position in the West and heightened the rivalry between the English and French fur trading companies in the region.

The French were eliminated from competition when they lost their entire North American empire after the Seven Years War (1756–1763) with Britain. For a short time thereafter the Hudson's Bay Company had undisputed control of the North West, but not for long. By the 1780s British and American traders in Montreal created a new company, the North West Company, made up of veteran French-Canadian voyageurs and traders under English-speaking entrepreneurs and captains. Very quickly this efficient, ambitious, and closely knit Montreal-based company rivalled the Hudson's Bay Company for control of the western fur trade.

This rivalry led to increased exploration of the western interior. Many of the famous men in western exploration—Alexander Mackenzie, Peter Pond, and David Thompson, for example—worked for the North West Company. Peter Pond spent many years in search of the western sea; a year after his retirement, one of his followers, Alexander Mackenzie, who had assisted him in founding Fort Chipewyan on Lake Athabaska in the mid-1780s, took up the challenge.[7] In 1789 Mackenzie, with a party of Métis and French-Canadian voyageurs, made his famous trip down the river that bears his name. Rather than to the Pacific Ocean, the river carried them to the Arctic, a sea "eternally covered with ice." Dejected, he nicknamed his river the "River of Disappointment." He was equally sobering in his judgement on the region of the North West. While he admitted to its fur trade potential, he voiced pessimism about the possibility of settlement. He concluded: "The proportion of it that is fit for cultivation is very small, and is still less in the interior parts; it is also very difficult of access; and whilst any land remains uncultivated to the South of it, there will be no temptation to settle it. Besides, its climate is not in general sufficiently genial to bring the fruits of the earth to maturity."[8]

David Thompson, an energetic and talented surveyor, cartographer, and explorer, and a contemporary of Mackenzie, made a similar indictment of the North West. As an employee of the Hudson's Bay Company he investigated a new route from the Bay to Lake Athabasca. Then he defected to the rival North West Company in 1797. "It was a rare piece of good fortune for the Nor'Westers to gain David Thompson," historian Richard Glover notes, "who, besides being an 'astronomer' was a well-trained clerk and an experienced wilderness traveller."[9] Thompson explored the Saskatchewan country and the northern reaches of the Columbia River. Out of these explorations he produced an amazingly accurate map of Western Canada in 1814, and then, a quarter of a century later, his famed *Narrative*, based on his *Journal* kept during his expedition. In his account, Thompson noted that the North West contained distinct regions, each with its own unique geography, resources, assets, and liabilities. He expressed a love for the region because of, not in spite of, its bleakness, bareness, and isolation. He also extolled the area's virtues, but in terms of fur trade, not settlement. With regard to agricultural potential, he concluded that the territories "appear to be given by Providence to the Red Man for ever as the wilds and sands of Africa are given to the Arabians."[10]

The exploring fur traders described the territory as a wasteland with little potential for settlement and agriculture. As employees of the fur trading companies they instinctively observed the area in terms of that trade. Furthermore, they pursued their exploits in the more northerly regions where fur trading was best. The buffalo hides of the prairies were simply too bulky to transport to the Bay or to Montreal. The most popular route, for example, ran from York Factory up the Nelson River to Norway House and Cumberland House and north to the Churchill River, never leaving the rugged Canadian Shield.

Even those European explorers and travellers who did reach the prairie lands were inclined to a negative image of the North West. Whether they came from Britain or France, they associated agriculture with abundant vegetation, trees, and a moist climate. When they came upon barren grasslands, devoid of trees and lush vegetation, they could only conclude, based on their own experience, that the land was ill-suited for settlement. Daniel Harmon, a Nor'Wester, recorded in his journal that there were two main regions in the western interior – the one plains or prairie, the other parkland. The former he described as "almost entirely destitute of timber and sufficiently dry for any kind of cultivation."[11] The historical geographer Wreford Watson notes: "There developed in the minds of Europeans an equation that went as follows: bareness equals barrenness equals infertility equals uselessness for agriculture."[12]

The "Great American Desert"

American fur traders and explorers projected an equally negative image of the North West. As Americans began exploring the area west of the Mississippi River in the early 1800s, they were struck by the arid landscape. Zebulon Pike, in his exploration of the area along the Arkansas River in 1806–7, referred to it as a "sandy sterile desert." But to Stephen

Long–or, more accurately, to the chronicler of his expedition, Dr. Edwin James–belonged the decisive condemnatory interpretation of the region. On the map that accompanied the report of his 1819–20 expedition to the area west of the Mississippi along the Platte River to the Rocky Mountains was written in bold letters, "Great Desert." The term was applied to a region that extended from the Gulf of Mexico to the Parkland belt, north of the Great Plains. "In regard to this extensive section of country," Edwin James wrote, "we do not hesitate in giving the opinion that it is almost wholly unfit for cultivation and, of course, uninhabitable by a people depending on agriculture for their subsistence."[13] Here, then, was a new negative image of the West as a desert bad-land, as unsuited for settlement as was the northern wilderness.

This image of the southern grassland region of the Canadian prairies as a desert would continue into the 1850s, as is evident in the reports of two scientific expeditions in 1857–the British-sponsored John Palliser expedition and the Canadian-backed Henry Youle Hind and Simon Dawson expedition.[14] Both expeditions expected to find desert-like conditions in the prairie region along the American border. They had read American scientific literature on the American Plains area with its references to the "Great American Desert," and John Palliser had previously explored the Missouri and Yellowstone Rivers area, which was assumed to be a part of the American desert.

Henry Youle Hind was the first to apply the term "Great American Desert" directly to the Canadian prairies. On the map accompanying the *Narrative* of his western expeditions of 1857–58, published in 1860, drawn by John Arrowsmith (also the cartographer for John Palliser's *Report*), Hind applied two sweeping generalizations to the area south of the North Saskatchewan River: "the Great American Desert" to the southern plains, and "a Fertile Belt" to the area immediately north, stretching in an arc from the Lake of the Woods to the Rocky Mountains, passing through the Red and Saskatchewan River countries, and extending into the foothills at the 49th parallel.[15] In the remainder of his *Narrative*, Hind dwelt on the positive qualities of the Fertile Belt for settlement and downplayed the desert area to the south. Thus he has been remembered for his optimistic assessment of the North West for agricultural settlement.

John Palliser, a dashing Irish bachelor, became associated with the negative image of the West as a desert wasteland (although, ironically, he too stressed the existence of a fertile belt north of this region). He pointed out that there was a triangular area in the southern portion of the Hudson's Bay Territory that was an extension of the American desert. Palliser's awareness of the popular view of the "Great American Desert" undoubtedly influenced his thinking. The illusion of an American Desert reached its height in the 1850s, according to the western American historian W. P. Webb—the very time when Palliser was observing the North West.[16] In indicating the presence of a desert, Palliser linked the territory directly to the "desert" area to the south. "The fertile savannahs and valuable woodlands of the Atlantic United States are succeeded . . . on the West by a more or less arid desert, occupying a region on both sides of the Rocky Mountains, which presents a barrier to the continuous growth of settlement between the Mississippi Valley and States on the Pacific coast. This central desert extends . . . into British territory, forming a triangle."[17] The negative image of "Palliser's Triangle," as the area (today south of Red Deer and extending eastward at an angle to southwestern Saskatchewan) became known, still remains one hundred and twenty-five years later.

Thus the Canadian West was viewed prior to the 1860s in negative terms from both a northerly and a southerly perspective. For northern fur traders it was a wilderness full of danger and terror, where the climate was forever cold, the land barren, and the native people inhospitable. For southern travellers it was a desert, lacking trees and water essential for agriculture, and having a monotonous, dreary landscape which was unappealing to the human eye. In both cases, it was considered unsuited for agriculture and best left as a fur trading area under the aegis of the Hudson's Bay Company.

There were exceptions to this negative view of the region. Often they were reports by individuals who opposed the Hudson's Bay Company's monopoly. Arthur Dobbs, an MP and spokesman for British commercial interests who wanted to extend British overseas trade, tried throughout the 1740s and 50s to show, through selective favourable references in reports of fur traders and Company personnel, that the area had a climate and soil suitable for settlement. The full title of Dobbs's book summarized its contents and conveyed his purpose: *An Account of the Countries Adjoining to Hudson's Bay in the North-West Part of America: Containing a Description of Their Soil and Methods of Commerce, and Shewing the Benefits to be made by settling Colonies, and opening a Trade in these parts; whereby the French will be deprived in great Measure of their Traffick in Furs, and the Communication between Canada and Mississippi be cut off. The whole intended to shew the great Possibility of a North-West Passage, so long desired; and which (if discovered) would be of highest Advantage to these Kingdoms.*[18] Dobbs argued that the lands south and southwest of the Bay had agricultural potential comparable to the countries of Europe in similar latitudes.

In 1749 the British government held a parliamentary enquiry into the Hudson's Bay Company and its territory, in which Dobbs and others testified against the fallacious information circulating about the North West as an unsuitable settlement area, but to no avail. The Company's rule remained intact. The popular image of a cold, inhospitable, barren, and infertile region prevailed.

The Red River Settlement: An Oasis in the Wasteland

Some sixty years later, Thomas Douglas, the fifth Earl of Selkirk, held such a positive image of the North West that in 1811 he sponsored an expedition of Scottish crofters to settle in the region of present-day Winnipeg, at the forks of the Red and Assiniboine Rivers. He maintained that there existed in the western interior "a tract of land, consisting of some millions of acres, and in point of soil and climate inferior to none of equal extent in British America."[19] He had no first-hand knowledge of the region — he had not even visited the North West before arranging for his followers to come to the New World; instead, he had based his scheme on his reading of Alexander Mackenzie's *Voyages*, even though Mackenzie had cautioned against settlement. Selkirk became disillusioned with the area once he received word of the innumerable difficulties his settlers encountered establishing a community. Still, the settlement took root, with a sizeable population by mid-century, thus becoming the only significant agricultural settlement in the vast area of Rupert's Land prior to 1850.

Selkirk's settlement aroused controversy from the beginning. It contributed to a long-standing and bitter rivalry between the Hudson's Bay Company and the Métis of the North West Company which peaked in June 1816 when Cuthbert Grant, a Nor'Wester, and a group of Métis, killed twenty Hudson's Bay Company men at Seven Oaks. The "massacre" helped to forge the Métis into a new nation — "the bois-brûle" — and the incident was a prelude to later Métis uprisings under Louis Riel in 1869–70 and again in 1885.

The existence of the Red River colony also raised protests from proponents of settlement in other areas of North America. John Strachan, the Anglican clergyman of York (Toronto) and a powerful figure in Upper Canada, saw the Red River colony as a threat to the settlement aspirations of his own colony; he gave a representative opinion of the Selkirk settlement in 1816 when he characterized it as "one of the most gross impositions that ever was attempted on the British public."[20] Even though he had never visited the North West, Strachan was of the opinion that, in contrast to Upper Canada, the land was useless, the location inappropriate for settlement, and the chances of the settlement surviving minimal.[21]

Other observers were not so negative. They admitted the success of the colony as an agricultural settlement, but saw it as the one exception to the rule; its presence only heightened the contrast to the rest of the North West, which was indeed a wasteland. Thomas Simpson, the nephew of George Simpson, the first governor of Rupert's Land, described the Red River settlement as "a comfortable retreat . . . for such of its retired officers and servants as prefer spending the evening of life, with their native families in this oasis of the desert."[22] This image was reinforced in December of 1836 when Simpson made a trip from the Red River settlement into the interior to Carlton House and experienced terrible winter weather. His account strengthened the image of the land beyond the Red River country as unfit for human survival.

In a book about his journey around the world in 1841–42, Governor George Simpson (1821–1860), the "Little Emperor" of Rupert's Land, gave one of the few optimistic views of the Red River settlement: "The soil of Red River Settlement is a black mould and of considerable depth, which, when first tilled, produces extraordinary crops, as much, on some occasions, as forty returns of wheat; and, even after twenty successive years of cultivation, without the relief of manure or of fallow, or of green crop, it still yields from fifteen to twenty-five bushels an acre."[23] He revised this opinion ten years later at his testimony to the 1857 British parliamentary enquiry into the Hudson's Bay Company, for fear of settlers invading the fur trading country. Now he claimed that he had been over-optimistic in his earlier assessment and that his reference was to "merely a few small alluvial points occupied by the Scotch farmers." The remainder of the North West he considered to be "not well adapted for settlement."[24]

Another observer, Captain Henry Warre, commissioned by the government of the United Canadas to make a military reconnaissance of the Oregon territory in case of war between Britain and the United States, described the Red River colony in 1846 as a successful agricultural settlement, but only to contrast it with the "flat and swampy" country around it. The region offered "little to attract the eye, or tempt the industry, of even the most persevering husbandman."[25]

A Spiritual and Artistic Wasteland

The Red River settlement was seen as an oasis not only in physical terms, as a small agricultural settlement, but in spiritual and moral terms as well.[26] Most of the early missionaries to the North West, heirs of a conservative Christian world view and perpetrators of popular racial and class divisions, saw themselves as working against great odds in trying to Christianize the heathen Indians in this vast wilderness. The Reverend John West, in 1820 the first Protestant missionary in the Red River community, described his efforts in disparaging terms: "Oh! for wisdom, truly Christian faith, integrity and zeal on my labours as a minister, in this heathen and *moral desert*. . . . Thousands are involved in worse than Egyptian darkness around me, wandering in ignorance and perishing through lack of knowledge. When will this wide waste howling wilderness blossom as the rose, and the desert become as a fruitful field!"[27] Father Pierre de Smet, a Jesuit missionary who travelled along the upper Missouri River into present-day Alberta in the mid-1840s, frequently referred to the country as a desolate, empty desert. In his *Life and Travels Among the North American Indians*, de Smet wrote: "We hope that divine Providence has not deferred the epoch when the darkness now over-whelming these immense regions will give place to the beneficial light of the way of salvation these poor and unhappy children of the desert, who, during so many ages, have groaned under the dominion of the devil, and among whom the war-song and the cry of carnage never ceased to resound."[28]

The missionary historian Sarah Tucker, writing in 1850, projected her image of the missionaries in the North West in her book titled *The Rainbow of the North.* "To no mission, perhaps, can this emblem be more truly applied than to that among the North American Indians: no people were ever enveloped in a thicker darkness, and in no spot has the light been reflected in more vivid hues." She described the Red River colony as "an isolated settlement of civilized and half-civilized men in the midst of an immense region of barbarism."[29] A. K. Isbister, the child of a fur trader father and an Indian mother, left the North West in 1842 for a more settled life in London, England. He took up the plight of the natives, who were, he argued, "in a state of utter dependence . . . to pass their lives in the darkest heathenism."[30] He blamed the Hudson's Bay Company rather than the natural environment for this deplorable condition, but his views equally perpetuated the image of the North West as a moral and spiritual wilderness.

Peter Rindisbacher, the only known resident artist to paint the North West in this early period, also conveyed the negative image of a wilderness area.[31] Born in Switzerland, he came with his family to the remote and struggling Red River colony in 1824 at the age of fifteen. Here he painted the everyday life of the Indians and Métis in a stiff neo-classical manner and with care, accuracy, and a realism of expression that was characteristic of painting in the Age of Enlightenment. His paintings of Indians at council and engaged in combat or the buffalo hunt are cold, clear, factual, and scientific—more concerned with detail than with mood, with recording events than with conveying a feeling. They also express images of a hostile environment where conflict and death were common. Given the hardships that the Red River inhabitants faced in the wilderness, it is natural that he should depict the West in stark, harsh terms. His imagery reflected reality as he perceived it.

One painting in particular is representative of his perspective: "The Murder of David Tally [Tully] and Family by the Sissetoon Sioux, a Sioux Tribe (1823)." It depicts a real-life event, the Tullys being attacked while en route from the Red River settlement to the United States. While

Rindisbacher was not present during the attack, he heard the lurid details from survivors upon their return to the Selkirk colony. He then painted the scene as he imagined it, but in acute detail, as though he had been present. The painting projects the image of a hostile western wasteland.

Concerning another of Rindisbacher's paintings, "Buffalo Hunt," an art critic at the time commented: "The landscape and the animals are faithfully depicted; and the wild scene which is daily acted upon our prairies is placed vividly before the eye."[32] While realistic, the image he projected was of a wilderness environment where the struggle for survival was a daily challenge. It was hardly the kind of image that encouraged other settlers to come to the region. Rindisbacher died at the age of 28, a victim of the harsh environment that he depicted.

The image of the North West as a wasteland in the fur traders' reports, the Hind and Palliser expeditions, the accounts of early travellers and missionaries, and in Peter Rindisbacher's paintings, dominated the outlook of many Europeans, Britons, Americans, and Canadians for two centuries. As late as 1849 the British author Robert Montgomery Martin could agree with the description of the Hudson's Bay Company's territory as the "fag end of the world." In *The Hudson's Bay Territories and Vancouver's Island* he neatly summarized a century of opinion on the North West:

> There are, doubtless, several spots, such as the Red River, adapted in some respects for European settlements; but they are like oases in the desert, few and far between—and totally inapplicable for extended colonization; indeed, at a great many of the posts, not only can no corn be grown, but even the potatoe and other crops are cut off by summer frosts, so that the rearing and preservation of a sufficient quantity of human food is an object of the most anxious solicitude throughout the country. By the concession of part of the Oregon country and the Columbia River to the United States in 1846, we gave up a fertile and temperate region, south of the 49th parallel, capable of yielding abundance of food; and the tract now left in the possession of the Hudson's Bay Company will require great care and industry to render even the most promising spots productive.[33]

This characteristically negative image of the North West contributed more than anything else to the Hudson's Bay Company's virtually unchallenged dominance of the region for two centuries. As late as 1849 the Company had successfully fended off another attack on its monopoly by arguing that the region was only suitable for fur trading. Yet Martin was expressing an increasingly minority viewpoint, and the Hudson's Bay Company was becoming less persuasive in its arguments. For there was evidence of a new, positive image of the North West that would end the Company's monopoly and contribute to Canada's acquisition of the territory in 1869.

The Creation of Man (A Peigan Myth)
Claude Mélançon

Long ago, the Spirits above sent the Great Water to flood the world below where men and women used to live. Afterwards Napiwa, the Old Man, created our floating island from a grain of sand in the following manner. When the time came to look for this grain of sand, Napiwa was floating on a raft with Nanoss, the Old Woman, and all the animals. He sent the otter down first. She dived at sunrise and when she surfaced at sunset she was dead. The Old Man examined her paws but didn't find anything, so he told the beaver it was his turn to dive. Two days later, the beaver surfaced lifeless, his paws empty. The loon was next. He stayed under water for three days before he died and he brought back nothing. Napiwa then asked the muskrat to go, and he stayed under for four days. When he floated back up to the surface he, too, was dead. However, one of his front paws was closed. Napiwa opened it, removed the grain of sand hidden inside, and from it made our island.

When he thought our island was big enough, Napiwa sent a young wolf to find out where it ended, but the wolf died of old age before he got there. Nevertheless, the Old Man was satisfied and set out on a journey with the Old Woman.

The two of them were walking beside a river with banks of clay when the Old Woman said to the Old Man,

'Your island is big and beautiful, but something's missing. How about filling it up with some people?'

'That's fine by me,' said the Old Man, 'but I'll have the first word.'

'All right,' said the Old Woman. 'And I'll have the last word.'

'I'll get started then,' announced Napiwa. 'Men will be made of wood and they'll grow like trees.'

'No!' said Nanoss. 'They'll be made of flesh and will reproduce their kind like animals.'

'Let it be so,' said the Old Man. 'But they'll have square faces, with the mouth running up and down and the eyes above, one on top of the other, and an ear on either side of the nose.'

'I don't like that design,' said Nanoss. 'Men will have round faces, with the mouth horizontal, and an eye on either side of the nose. Their ears will be placed on each side of the head. Otherwise, they won't be able to hear their enemies coming without getting a noseful of dirt.'

'Let it be so,' said the Old Man. 'But they'll have four arms and four legs, and ten fingers on each hand.'

'That's far too many,' said Nanoss. 'They won't work any better it they have four arms rather than two, and four legs won't let them walk any more quickly. They'll have two arms, two legs, and four fingers and a thumb on each hand.'

'Let it be so,' said Napiwa. 'But men won't have to eat or wear clothes. They and their wives will spend all their time together playing with their children.'

'No! No!' said Nanoss. 'Men will become bored doing nothing, and their wives will get tired of having them around all the time. Men will hunt all day and won't return to the teepee until sunset. While they're gone, women will gather wood and nuts, pick fruit, and dig up roots. They will also dry meat and tan hides. While they work, they'll think of their men and be glad to see them come home.'

'Let it be so,' said the Old Man. 'But men and women will not die. They will live forever and never part.'

'No,' said Nanoss. 'It's better that they die. Otherwise your island will have too many people, and there won't be enough food for everybody.'

'I don't think it should be so,' replied the Old Man.

'But we agreed,' insisted the Old Woman.

'No, I tell you,' replied the Old Man.

'And I'm telling you "Yes,"' shouted the Old Woman.

'All right! All right!' said Napiwa. 'We'll settle this another way. I'm going to throw this chip of wood into the water. If it floats, men will remain dead for four days and then come back to life.'

He threw the chip of wood into the water, and it floated.

'There, you see,' said Napiwa.

'No,' replied Nanoss, 'we're not going to settle it like that. I'm going to throw a stone into the water. If it floats, men will remain dead for four days and then continue to live. If it sinks, they'll be dead forever.'

She threw the stone in, and it sank immediately.

'There we are,' said Nanoss. 'Now men will feel a little sympathy for one another.'

'Let it be so,' said the Old Man.

Several moons later, Nanoss gave birth to a little girl whom she loved very much. But when the child was old enough to help her mother with the chores, she died. Nanoss regretted having wanted men to remain dead forever. She went to find the Old Man and said to him,

'Can't we go over that problem we disagreed about last time?'

'No,' said the Old Man. 'That problem's settled. What's done is done.'

[pp. 1–2]

A Fur Trade Domain

The Kelsey Papers (1690)

Henry Kelsey his Book being ye Gift of James / Hubbud in the year of our Lord 1693 /

Now Reader Read for I am well assur'd /
Thou dost not know the hardships I endur'd /
In this same desert where Ever y^t I have been /
Nor wilt thou me believe without y^t thou had seen /
The Emynent Dangers that did often me attend /
But still I lived in hopes y^t once it would amend /
And makes me free from hunger & from Cold /
Likewise many other things wch I cannot here unfold /
For many times I have often been oppresst /
With fears & Cares y^t I could not take my rest /
Because I was alone & no friend could find /
And once y^t in my travels I was left behind /
Which struck fear & terror into me /
But still I was resolved this same Country for to see /
Although through many dangers I did pass /
Hoped still to undergo y^m at the Last /
Now Considering y^t it was my dismal fate /
for to repent I thought it now to late /
Trusting still unto my masters Consideration /
Hoping they will Except of this my small Relation /
Which here I have pend & still will Justifie /
Concerning of those Indians & their Country /
If this wont do farewell to all as I may say //

[2]

And for my living i'll seek some other way /
In sixteen hundred & ninety'th year /
I set forth as plainly may appear /
Through Gods assistance for to understand /
The natives language & to see their land /
And for my masters interest I did soon /

Sett from y^e house y^e twealth of June /
Then up y^e River I with heavy heart /
Did take my way & from all English part /
To live amongst y^e$_\wedge$ ^{Natives} of this place /
If god permits me for one two years space /
The Inland Country of Good report hath been /
By Indians but by English yet not seen /
Therefore I on my Journey did not stay /
But making all y^e hast I could upon our way /
Gott on y^e borders of y^e stone Indian Country /
I took possession on y^e tenth Instant July /
And for my masters I speaking for y$^m_.$ all /
This neck of land I deerings point did call /
Distance from hence by Judgement at y^e lest /
From y^e house six hundred miles southwest /
Through Rivers wch run strong with falls /
thirty three Carriages five lakes in all /
The ground begins for to be dry with wood /
Poplo & birch with ash thats very good /
For the Natives of that place w$^{ch}_.$ knows /
No use of Better than their wooden Bows /
According to y^e use & custom of this place /
In September I brought those Natives to a peace /
But I had no sooner from those Natives turnd my back/
Some of the home Indians came upon their track /
And for old grudges & their minds to fill //

[3]

Came up with them Six tents of w$^{ch}_.$ they kill'd /
This ill news kept secrett was from me /
Nor none of those home Indians did I see /
Untill that they their murder all had done /
And the Chief acter was he y^{ts} called y^e Sun /
So far I have spoken concerning of the spoil /
And now will give acco$^t_.$ of that same Country soile /
Which hither part is very thick of wood /
Affords small nutts wth little cherryes very good /
Thus it continues till you leave y^e woods behind /
And then you have beast of severall kind /
The one is a black a Buffillo great /
Another is an outgrown Bear w$^{ch}_.$ is good meat /
His skin to gett I have used all y$^e_.$ m$^{ways}_{\wedge}$eans I can /
He is mans food & he makes food of man /
His hide they would not me it preserve /

But said it was a god & they should Starve /
This plain affords nothing but Beast & grass /
And over it in three days time we past /
getting unto y^e woods on the other side /
It being about forty sixe miles wide /
This wood is poplo ridges with small ponds of water /
there is beavour in abundance but no Otter /
with plains & ridges in the Country throughout /
Their Enemies many whom they cannot rout /
But now of late they hunt their Enemies /
And with our English guns do make y^m flie /
At deerings point after the frost /
I set up their a Certain Cross /
In token of my being their there /
Cut out on it ye date of year /
And Likewise for to veryfie the same /
added to it my master sir Edward deerings name /
So having not more to trouble you wth all I am /
Sir your most obedient & faithfull Servt at Command /
[pp. 1-4]

Journals and Letters of La Vérendrye (ca. 1730s)

They give a great account of that country, saying that it is all very level, without mountains, all fine hard wood with here and there groves of oak; that everywhere there are quantities of fruit trees, and all sorts of wild animals; that the savage tribes are there very numerous, and always wandering, never staying in any fixed place, but carrying their cabins with them continually from one place to another and always camping together to form a village. [pp. 44-45]

I found the water [in the Assiniboine River] very low, as there had been no rain all the summer. The river comes from the west, winds a great deal, is wide, has a strong current and many shallows. There are fine trees along the banks, and behind these a boundless stretch of prairie in which are multitudes of buffalo and deer. [pp. 302-303]

Buffaloes abounded in the prairies, much larger and heavier beasts than those we see in the prairies here, their hides white and of several colours. They showed us some horns cut across the middle which hold nearly three pints, their colour being greenish. There are some in all the lodges which are used as ladles, a proof that they killed a great many of them when the road was open. [pp. 337-38]

The savage tribes of fort La Reine are Assiniboin. Trees grow only on the banks of the rivers [in southern Manitoba] and the prevailing kinds are white oak, elm, ash, some unknown trees, bass and birch. All the rest is prairie, with here and there clumps of oak and wild plum. . . .

It was the Chevalier de la Vérendrye who first discovered it [the Saskatchewan River] and who ascended it as far as the fork [where the North and South Saskatchewan rivers meet], which is the rendezvous every spring of the Cree of the Mountains, Prairies, and Rivers to deliberate as to what they shall do—go and trade with the French or with the English.

It was there that he was in the spring at the meeting of all the Cree, and where he enquired minutely, according to his father's orders, where the source of this great river was. They all replied with one voice that it came from very far, from a height of land where there were very lofty mountains; that they knew of a great lake on the other side of the mountains, the water of which was undrinkable.

The river Poskoyac comes from west one point north, which gives reason to hope for something. [pp. 485, 487]

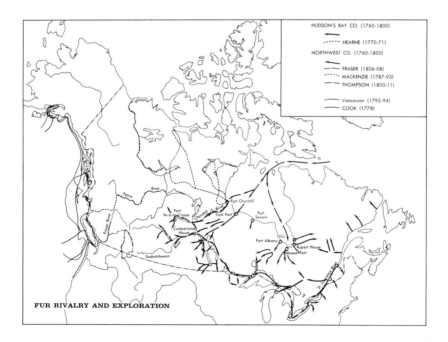

FUR RIVALRY AND EXPLORATION

David Thompson's Narrative of His Explorations in Western America, 1784–1812

At length the Rocky Mountains came in sight like shining white clouds in the horizon, but we doubted what our guide said; but as we proceeded, they rose in height their immense masses of snow appeared above the clouds, and formed an impassable barrier, even to the Eagle. Our guide also told us, that as we approached these mountains of snow we should find the weather become milder, this we could not believe, but it was so, and the month of November was full as mild as the month of October at the trading house we left to the eastward. For the cold of these countries decreases as much by going westward, as by going to the south. About thirty miles from the mountains we crossed the Bow River running in several channels between gravel shoals, near four feet in depth and two hundred yards wide. [p. 95]

These fine plains will, in time to come be the abode of Mankind, probably semi civilized leading a pastoral life tending Cattle and Sheep. The Farmer requires a considerable quantity of wood for buildings, fences and fuel and it is only in chance places, even along the river side, where such can be found. The farmer must place himself on the north side of these plains where he will have abundance of wood, and extend his farm into the plains as far as he pleases, say two miles, all the rest of these plains of 350 miles in length, by about 38 miles in breadth will be pastoral, and inhabited by herdsmen and shepherds dwelling in round leather tents, moving from place to place as circumstances require, and finding in hollows and banks of brooks the little wood they want. There are also many Ponds of medicineal water, the salts of which lie dried on the shore for several feet around them. [p. 96]

Hitherto the Reader has been confined to the sterile Stony Region and the great Valley of the Lakes. My travels will now extend over countries of a very different formation; these are [called] the Great Plains as a general name, and are supposed to be more ancient than the Stony Region and the great Valley of the Lakes.

By a Plain I mean lands bearing grass, but too short for the Scythe; where the grass is long enough for the Scythe, and of which Hay can be made, I name [them] meadows. These Great Plains may be said to commence at the north side of the Gulph of Mexico, and extend northward to the latitude of fifty four degrees; where these plains are bounded by the Forests of the north, which extend unbroken to the arctic Sea. On the east they are bounded by the Mississippe River, and northward of which by the valley of the lakes; and on the west by the Rocky Mountains. The length of these Plains from South to North is 1240 miles; and the breadth from east to west to the foot of the Mountains, from 550 to 800 miles giving an area to the Great Plains of 1,031,500 square miles, in which space the Ozark Hills are included. [pp. 183–84]

From the gulph of Mexico to the Latitude of 44 degrees north, these Great Plains may be said to be barren for great spaces, even of coarse grass, but the cactus grows in abundance on a soil of sand and rolled gravel; even the several Rivers that flow through these plains do not seem to fertilise the grounds adjacent to them; These rivers are too broad in proportion to their depth and in autumn very shallow; the Mountains are comparatively low and therefore sooner exhausted of their winter snows, and travellers often suffer for want of water. But as one advances northward, the soil becomes better, and the Missisourie River through its whole length to it's confluence with the Mississippe carries with it lands of deep soil, on which are many villages of the Natives, who subsist partly by agriculture and partly by hunting. [pp. 186–87]

The River next northward of the Missisourie is the Bow River, so named from a species of Yew Tree on its banks, of which good Bows are made. This is the most southern River of the British Dominions and the South Branch of the Saskatchewan.

The Bow River flows through the most pleasant of the Plains, and is the great resort of the Bison and the Red Deer, and also of the Natives; the soil appears good along it's whole extent, but for the most part is bare of Woods, and those that remain are fast diminishing by fire. The soil of the plains appears to continue increasing in depth, and the same through the Forests. [pp. 188–89]

The whole of this country may be pastoral, but except in a few places, cannot become agricultural. Even the fine Turtle Hill, gently rising, for several miles, with it's Springs and Brooks of fine Water has very little wood fit for the Farmer. The principal is Aspin which soon decays: with small Oaks and Ash. The grass of these plains is so often on fire, by accident or design, and the bark of the Trees so often scorched, that their growth is contracted, or they become dry; and the whole of the great Plains are subject to these fires during the Summer and Autumn before the Snow lies on the ground. These great Plains appear to be given by Providence to the Red Men for ever, as the wilds and sands of Africa are given to the Arabians. [p. 222]

The "Great American Desert"

Narrative of an Expedition to the Source of St. Peter's River, Lake Winnipeek, Lake of the Woods (1823)

In this view it is proper to comprehend not only the extreme northerly frontier of the United States, but to consider it in connexion with the boundary which nature seems to have fixed as the western limit of our population, viz. the Great American Desert. From what has been stated in relation to the country surrounding Lake Superior and extending north-westwardly to Lake Winnepeek, it may be inferred that we shall always remain secure from the inroads of any regular hostile force in that direction. Indeed the nature of the country is such as affords a more formidable barrier to the invasions of an enemy than any *cordon* of posts that art could devise. . . . A large portion of the Great American Desert, a sterile dreary waste, three or four hundred miles in width, stretching along the eastern verge of the Rocky Mountains, from Red River of the South to Athabasca in the north, a distance of more than fourteen hundred miles, may be added as a continuation of the line of our natural defence. Thus a portion of our frontier, embracing an extent of nearly two thousand miles, is so well fortified by nature as to require no artificial structures but such as are appropriate in Indian warfare. No regular military works will of course be required on that extent of frontier, except such as may be required to protect the American fur trade, and counteract the hostile purposes of the Indians. [pp. 238–39]

The Papers of the Palliser Expedition 1857–1860

After leaving the eastern limit of the country that is within the influence of the mountains (which may be considered to commence about 20 miles below where it receives Ispasquehow River), the South Saskatchewan flows in a deep and narrow valley, through a region of arid plains, devoid of timber or pasture of good quality. Even on the alluvial points in the bottom of the valley trees and shrubs only occur in a few isolated patches. The steep and lofty sides of the valley are composed of calcareous marls

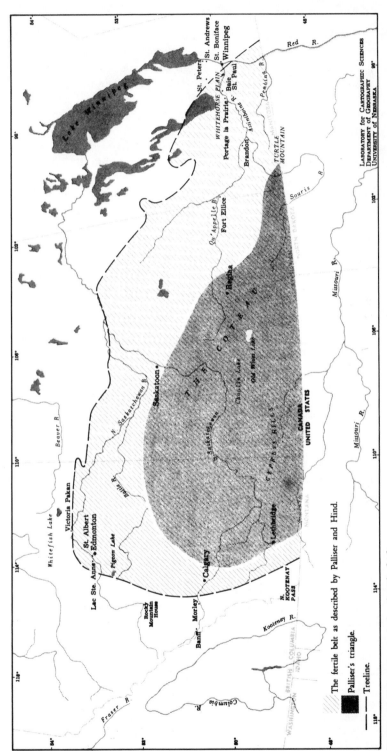

Palliser's Triangle and the fertile belt.

and clays that are baked into a compact mass under the heat of the parching sun. The sage and the cactus abound, and the whole of the scanty vegetation bespeaks an arid climate. The course of its large tributaries, Red Deer River and Belly River, are through the same kind of country, except in the upper part of the former stream, where it flows through rich partially wooded country similar to that on the North Saskatchewan.

Towards the confluence of Red Deer River and the South Saskatchewan, there are extensive sandy wastes. For 60 miles to the east of this point the country was not examined by the Expedition, but at the elbow the same arid description of country was met with, and it seems certain that this prevails throughout the entire distance. Below the elbow the banks of the river and also the adjacent plains begin to improve rapidly as the river follows a north-east course and enters the fertile belt. From the Moose Woods to its confluence with the North Saskatchewan it in no way differs from that river, which indeed is nearly flowing parallel with it, only 30 or 40 miles distant. [p. 18]

The Red River Settlement: An Oasis in the Wasteland

Letter to the Earl of Selkirk on his Settlement at the Red River (1816)
John Strachan

Advertisement

As soon as I heard that the Earl of Selkirk was commencing a Settlement on the Red River, I determined to warn the Public of the deception, and of the great misery which Emigrants must experience in such a distant and inhospitable region. But it was difficult to procure the necessary information; and before it could be obtained, the progress of the American war called my attention to distress nearer home.

It was not till last June that I was able to get a copy of his Lordship's Prospectus, a paper neatly drawn up, but, alas! destitute of truth.—To those who are amazed, after reading my remarks, at the promises and assertions which it contains, I am justified in saying, that promises still more remarkable, and assertions still more extravagant, were made by the Earl of Selkirk himself, at Stromness, in June 1813, to persons whom he was enticing to go out.

Few of these wretched men have any written agreement; an omission, I hope, not wilfully made, to prevent legal redress: for surely punishment ought to be inflicted on Speculators who persuade Families, under false pretences, to leave their native homes.

Of the Settlers who went to the Red River, many died at Church-hill, in Hudson's Bay, from the severity of the climate, and the quality of their food. Others seriously injured their health; and not one of those who have escaped, saw a joyful day, from the time they left Scotland, till they began their journey to Canada. — The following Letter may prevent any more from encountering the miseries of the polar regions; and this is all I am able to effect. But retributive justice is due; and I flatter myself, that among the many great examples of disinterested benevolence so common in Great Britain, one may be found sufficiently powerful to compel Lord Selkirk, and his brother Proprietors, to make ample compensation to the Survivors for the money and effects lost at Church-hill, and the miseries they have endured.

The conditions offered by your Lordship to settlers, in your second attempt at colonization, deserve greater censure than those already noticed. It is, indeed, impossible to behold with complacency a British Peer turning a land speculator, at a moment when his country was in imminent danger, and, instead of flying to her assistance, and disdaining to survive her fall, anticipating that melancholy event, by anxiously preparing an asylum in a distant corner of the earth. [p. 9]

Your projected settlement at the Red River, or third attempt at colonization, appears to me, not only more extravagant than either of the former, but one of the most gross impositions that ever was attempted on the British public, and must be attended with the most baneful consequences to all those unfortunate men, who, deluded by the false promises held out to them, shall leave their homes for such a dreary wilderness. [pp. 10–11]

The Prospectus for the Red River settlement is as follows: —
"A tract of land, consisting of some millions of acres, and in point of soil and climate inferior to none of equal extent in British America, is now to be disposed of; and will be sold extremely cheap, on account of its situation, which is remote from the present settlements. If a tract of the same extent and fertility were offered for sale in Lower Canada, or Nova Scotia, purchasers would be eager to obtain it at one hundred, perhaps two hundred thousand guineas; and, at that price, would make an ample profit, in the course of some years, by retailing it, in small lots, at an advanced price, to actual settlers. The lands in question, no

ways different in advantages, may be purchased for about £10,000 sterling."

In this portion of the Prospectus, I particularly call the reader's attention to the very slight manner of noticing the remoteness of the projected colony. A stranger would naturally suppose, that, as Upper Canada is carefully omitted in comparing the lands of the Red River with the other colonies, they formed part of that extensive province, more especially since they are declared to be equal, in soil and climate, to any in British America. As respects the value of the land, situation is every thing. The most fruitful valley in the world is worth nothing, if surrounded with impassable mountains. The assertion, therefore, that these lands are no ways different in advantages from those of Lower Canada and Nova Scotia, is false, unless their situation be equally favourable.

The proprietors may be ignorant, but you know, my Lord, that situation is the true criterion of the value of lands, and the principal cause of retarding, or accelerating, their settlement. That a similar tract in the maritime colonies would sell at this sum may be freely admitted; for, if we suppose it to consist of four millions of acres, one hundred thousand guineas will be little more than sixpence per acre, and yet the lands on the Red River may not be worth a farthing. The maritime colonies are getting populous. The wants of emigrants can be supplied by their neighbours at a reasonable expence, and the communication is easy and expeditious; but, at the Red River, every thing is the reverse—no population, no comforts, no communication. If, indeed, this projected colony did possess as many advantages as those of Lower Canada, or Nova Scotia, I agree with your Lordship, that the purchase money is exceedingly reasonable, and that the profits of the proprietors would be immense; but, as it possesses no real advantages, it will be found sufficiently dear. [pp. 11–13]

Convinced that your Lordship's intentions of establishing a colony of loyal subjects is perfectly sincere, and that you are too well acquainted with the depravity of the American character to desire any number of that people in your settlement, I am, nevertheless, persuaded, that, so far from raising a colony of British subjects, whose principles and morals shall be free from the contamination of the United States, and prove a bulwark to their encroachments, you are exerting every nerve to tempt British subjects to leave their native homes and friends, to cross the seas, and to risk their lives, who must afterwards, from their situation, become American citizens, or be cut off from all practicable communication with the rest of the world. Perhaps your Lordship is not sufficiently aware of the great difficulty which the projected settlement will have in communicating with Hudson's Bay, or with Canada, and the small distance that intervenes between the source of the Red River, and one of the branches of the Mississippi. These particulars we shall illustrate in the sequel. [pp. 21–22]

It is not easy to discover, in the former part of the Prospectus, any thing to justify the gratuitous assertion with which this paragraph commences. As to Nova Scotia I cannot speak from personal knowledge, but, in Lower and Upper Canada, as good lands remain to be granted, within half a day's journey (in many places within a mile) of navigable streams and lakes, as any that have been given away. To say, therefore, that the lands on the Red River possess important natural advantages over any which now remain unoccupied in Nova Scotia, and the adjacent colonies, is to deceive, unless it can be proved, that a tract of land, far from protection, and surrounded by hostile Indians, is more valuable than richer land, in the midst of wealthy settlements. [p. 24]

"The Red River," says Sir Alex. M'Kenzie, vol. i. page 59, intro, "runs in a Southern direction to near the head-waters of the Mississippi. The country, on either side, is but partially supplied with wood, and consists of plains, covered with Buffalo and Elk, especially on the Western side. On the Eastern side are lakes and rivers, and the whole country is well wooded, level, abounding in Beaver, Bears, Mouse Deer, Fallow Deer, &c. The natives, who are of the Algonquin tribe, are not very numerous, and are considered as the natives of Lake Superior. This country being near the Mississippi, is also inhabited by the Nadowasis, who are the natural enemies of the former, the head of the water being the war line. They are in a continual state of hostility, and, although the Algonquins are equally brave, the others generally out-number them. It is very probable, therefore, that if the latter continue to venture out of the woods, which form their only protection, they will soon be extirpated. There is not, perhaps, a finer country in the world, for the residence of uncivilized man, than that which occupies the space between this river and Lake Superior. It abounds in every thing necessary to the wants and comforts of such a people. Fish, venison, and fowl, with wild rice, are in great plenty; while, at the same time, their subsistence requires that bodily exercise, so necessary to health and vigour."

I quote the whole of this passage, although greater part of the eulogy, with which it concludes, belongs to that part of the country which must fall within the territories of the United States, that I may not be accused of partiality. Sir Alex. praises it only as a fine residence for uncivilized man, and the very circumstances which render it valuable to them detract from its value as a civilized colony. At all events, the soil of the best parts (independent of the bad situation) is not equal to that of millions of acres granting by the Government, in the Canadas, for nothing. [pp. 25–27]

On this route the rivers and lakes begin to break up in the latter end of May; but they are not sufficiently clear of ice to admit of a safe navigation, till the middle of June; nor can a boat or canoe leave York Factory for the Red River, later than the 6th of September. The settler can, therefore, depend only upon eighty-three days in the year for transacting the commercial business of the colony by Hudson's Bay. In the distance between York Factory and Lake Winipie, boats can navigate only one hundred and twelve miles with advantage. From the entrance of the Lakes to the Forks of the Red River, boats are preferable to canoes. Through this whole distance from the sea to the settlement, the crew of a boat or canoe will rarely be able to find five days provisions, and must support themselves with what they have laid in store. During winter, when travelling on the ice and snow, things are still worse. Through all the distance, the country is extremely forbidding, being little more than one vast range of rocks, swamps, and morasses. – Should any misfortune happen to the boat or canoe, the crew must inevitably perish. [p. 33]

The Prospectus proceeds: – "With such advantages the settlers must thrive rapidly, and it will soon become apparent to them that the land is worth a much higher price. At first, however, it cannot be supposed that the common emigrant will understand or become capable of appreciating their advantages. On the contrary, it is to be expected that they will be diffident, and afraid of venturing to a new and (to them) an unknown country: it will therefore be necessary to give some extraordinary encouragement to a few of the first who enter into the plan."

I have failed, my Lord, in communicating my own impressions, if, after reading the preceding remarks on the Prospectus, any disinterested person shall consider the settlers to possess such advantages as the Prospectus promises. The observation, therefore, with which this passage begins, might be considered ironical and excite a smile, were not the subject too serious.

It is too much, my Lord, to bring families from their native homes, many of which were no doubt comfortable, to a wilderness, far from their friends and relatives, where they have to learn new habits, to suffer the greatest privations, and make sacrifices revolting to all their feelings, and after all have no prospect before them but misery and want – and then talk of their advantages!

It is, indeed, well said, that they will not understand or appreciate these advantages: for, had your Lordship visited this country in person, and its avenues of communication, as you ought to have done, before a settlement under your patronage was attempted, you would have found as great difficulty in discovering them as the settlers will do. – In speaking of the soil and climate, I confine myself to the South branch of the Red River, because it is every way more favourable: but the tract of land between it and the North branch, or Assiniboin, is almost one continued plain.—"The soil is sand and gravel, with a slight intermixture of earth, and produces a short grass. Trees are very rare; nor are there on the banks of the river sufficient, except in particular spots, to build houses and supply firewood for the trading establishments, of which there are four principal ones. Both these rivers are navigable for canoes to their source without a fall, though in some parts there are rapids, caused by occasional beds of limestone and gravel; but, in general, they have a sandy bottom."—*(Sir Alexander Mackenzie's Voyage.)* [pp. 47-48]

An Indian, for the most trifling offence, may set fire to their harvests; and as the settlers occupy favourite hunting grounds, they cannot always avoid contention. The loss of a single harvest must be attended with the most dreadful consequences. There are no settlements within reach from which to procure provisions. Should, therefore, such a disaster happen, the settlers would be forced to go to the grass plains to hunt the buffaloe for subsistence. But as the Indians are very tenacious of their rights as sovereigns of the soil, they would be compelled to hunt in great numbers, leaving their helpless families in the meantime exposed for many days to the insults and revenge of their new enemies. Should the surrounding Indians become generally hostile, there is no escape from the Red River even for a populous colony. The navigation is so intricate, and attended with so many difficulties, that a few resolute men could stop and destroy the greatest numbers.

Such is the lamentable situation of your colony, my Lord, that even the frolic of a drunken Indian, in setting fire to the harvest, may prove its ruin;—and it is notorious, that the Savages, when hungry, will kill oxen, cows, and sheep, for a single meal, leaving the remainder of the carcase without regret. Every person, therefore, going to this settlement is a total loss to the nation, for which no compensation directly or indirectly is received. [pp. 53-54]

And now, my Lord, allow me to ask how you could promise so many advantages to settlers on the Red River? No man leaves his native country but with the view of bettering his situation. The difficulties are great when every effort is made in favour of the emigrants. They are particularly exposed, from the very nature of their employment, to the diseases of the country in which they settle, by which many of those advanced in life are sure to be cut off, and some of the youth greatly debilitated. Indeed so many discomforts, disappointments, and painful recollections, crowd upon them, that nothing less than the prospect of an independence, such as he never could obtain in his native land, can possibly support him.

But to speak to your settlers of such an independence would be to trifle with their misery.—Without any market for their produce—any security of title—any expectation of ever becoming comfortable—deprived of the civil advantages possessed by all the British colonies—of the protection of the laws—the consolations of religion, and instruction to their children; they have nothing to compensate these sacrifices and privations but false promises, which they know, the moment after they arrive, can never be realized! [pp. 55–56]

Narrative of the Discoveries on the North Coast of America (1843)
Thomas Simpson

We started next day [January 20, 1837] at the same early hour, and, while in the act of moving out of our bivouac, a troop of prairie wolves came howling around it, as if impatient to seize on anything we might have left. The morning was intolerably cold; and it required our utmost exertions to keep the blood in circulation, and to preserve our faces from freezing. I afterwards ascertained, at Fort Chipewyan, that this was the coldest day of the whole winter there, the thermometer being at -46°. We encamped at the west end of Stony Lake, having travelled twenty-nine miles, through a country consisting of narrow plains, studded with clumps of poplar, and an abundance of underwood, interspersed with little lakes and swamps. A great part of it had been recently overrun by fire; and the only interesting feature it presented was a view, on the left, of the low range of the Beaver Hills, which we could distinguish to be thickly covered with timber. The buffalo frequents this quarter, and we passed several of its old beaten tracks.

On the 22d we made similar progress. In the forenoon we crossed Fishing Lake, six miles wide; then changing our course from west to west-north-west, we struck out into the immense prairies which stretch from thence to the Saskatchewan River. After travelling over the shaggy frozen grass, which bore some recent traces of red-deer, for a few miles, we fell upon a tract of country that the fire had bared to the very soil. The light snowy covering rested on the blackened plain, and our poor dogs once more went on with comparative ease. Far on our right appeared a line of low woods, shooting out from the Nut Hills in an immense curve, the extremity or horn of which we reached at our usual camping hour.

We were now at the commencement of a plain, twenty miles in breadth, which my guide required daylight to cross; we therefore breakfasted, and started at 7 o'clock. The wind blew strongly from the westward; and to face it, where there was not a shrub, or even a blade of grass, to break its force, with a temperature of at least -40°, was a serious undertaking. Muffling up our faces with shawls, pieces of blanket, and leather, in such a manner as to leave only the eyes exposed, we braved the blast. Each eyelash was speedily bedizened with a heavy crop of icicles, and we were obliged, every now and then, to turn our backs to the wind, and thaw off these obstructions with our half-frozen fingers. Early in the afternoon we reached what are called the Cross Woods, where we were glad to make the best lodging we could for the night, there being another wide prairie on the opposite side. Notwithstanding every precaution, two of the men were injured by the cold; one a half-breed from Fort Pelly, who afterwards, at Carlton, lamented his inability to dance in consequence of his frozen heels. Neither bird nor beast was seen during the day; the intense cold having driven all living things, but ourselves, to the shelter of the woods. [pp. 40–42]

What are here called plains, consist of a collection of barren hills and hollows, tossed together in a wild wave-like form, as if some ocean had been suddenly petrified while heaving its huge billows in a tumultuous swell. [p. 45]

Narrative of a Journey Round the World (1841–42)
Sir George Simpson

The wheat produced is plump and heavy; there are also large quantities of grain of all kinds, besides beef, mutton, pork, butter, cheese, and wood in abundance. Agriculture, however, has not been without its misfortunes. In the year 1826, in consequence of the heavy snows and continued severity of the preceding winter, the thaws of the spring flooded the whole country, not only filling the channels of the two rivers, but also covering the adjacent plains to a great depth. Every stream, from mouth to source, was a torrent, and every swamp a lake; till, at last, swamp and stream, as they rose and rose, united to drown nearly all the labours of preceding years. Fence after fence, and house after house, floated away on the bosom of the deluge, while the helpless owners were huddled together on spots which the forbearance alone of the surging sea showed to be higher than the rest; and the receding waters left, and that at a period too late for successful cultivation, little but the site of Red River Settlement.

But the temporary evil, as is generally the case with the devastations of nature, brought with it a permanent benefit. The ruined hovels, (for many of the original settlers had been glad of any shelter) were gradually replaced by dwellings of more convenient structure; and the submerged lands were irrigated and manured into more than their natural fertility.

For the next three seasons, however, frogs were, if possible, more numerous than ever they were in Egypt; and, in a subsequent year, the crops were almost entirely devoured by caterpillars. Previously to the great flood, whole armies of locusts most seriously damaged the crops for three successive years. [pp. 56–57]

About twenty years ago, a large encampment of Gros Ventres and Blackfeet had been formed in this neighbourhood for the purpose of hunting during the summer. Growing tired, however, of so peaceful and ignoble an occupation, the younger warriors of the allied tribes determined to make an incursion into the territories of the Assiniboines. Having gone through all the requisite enchantments, they left behind them only the old men, with the women and children. After a successful campaign, they turned their steps homeward in triumph, loaded with scalps and other spoils; and, on reaching the top of the ridge that overlooked the camp of the infirm and defenceless of their band, they notified their approach in the proudly-swelling tones of their song of victory. Every lodge, however, was as still and silent as the grave; and, at length, singing more loudly, as they advanced, in order to conceal their emotions, they found the full tale of the mangled corpses of their parents and sisters, of their wives and children. In a word, the Assiniboines had been there to take their revenge. [p. 81]

Next afternoon we passed over a space of about four miles in length, where the grass was thoroughly beaten down, apparently the work of hail. Such storms, which are almost always partial in their operation, are often remarkably furious in this country. While travelling from Red River to Canada in the fall of 1837, I was overtaken near Lac la Pluie by a violent tempest of the kind, which, if we had not gained the fort in time, might have proved fatal. As the angular masses of ice rattled on the roof, we entertained fears for the safety of the building; and, in point of fact, the lodges of the Indians were thrown down and their canoes shattered; while their luckless dogs, tumbling about like drunken men, scrambled away howling in quest of shelter. Some of the pieces, measured in presence of Mr. Finlayson, of Red River, and Mr. Hargrave, of York Factory, we found to be fully five inches and a half in circumference.

Throughout this country every thing is in extremes – unparalleled cold and excessive heat; long droughts, balanced by drenching rain and destructive hail. But it is not in climate only that these contrarieties prevail; at some seasons both whites and natives are living, in wasteful abundance, on venison, buffalo, fish, and game of all kinds; while at other times they are reduced to the last degree of hunger, often passing several days without food. [pp. 98–99]

Report from the Select Committee on the Hudson's Bay Company (1857)

Evidence of Sir George Simpson

714. Of course, having administered the affairs of the Hudson's Bay Company during so long a period, you are well acquainted with every part of their territories?—I have travelled through the greater part of the country; I have not visited what are usually known as the Barren Grounds.

715. You are well acquainted with the western portion, as well as the eastern?—Yes; I have not been in Mackenzie's River, but I have been in nearly all the other parts of the country; my usual route in going up the country is from Montreal by Rainy Lake and Lake Winnipeg to Red River; I have crossed the Rocky Mountains at three different points to Oregon.

716. Will you have the goodness to give to the Committee an account of your impressions of the character of the territory of the Hudson's Bay Company in point of soil and climate, particularly with reference to its adaptation for the purposes of cultivation and colonisation?—I do not think that any part of the Hudson's Bay Company's territories is well adapted for settlement; the crops are very uncertain.

717. Do you mean that observation to apply only to Rupert's Land or to the entire of the territory now administered by the Hudson's Bay Company?—I mean it to apply to Rupert's Land.

718. How would you describe the limits of Rupert's Land to the west?—The Rocky Mountains to the west.

719. Would you apply that observation to the district of the Red River?—Yes.

720. And the country immediately behind it?—Yes.

721. Is it not actually settled?—I do not consider it well adapted for settlement.

722. Why so?—On account of the poverty of the soil, except on the banks of the river. The banks of the river are alluvial, and produce very fair crops of wheat; but these crops are frequently destroyed by early frosts; there is no certainty of the crops. We have been under the necessity of importing grain within these last ten years from the United States and from Canada, for the support of the establishment.

723. Have you an equally unfavourable opinion of the country on the Saskatchewan River?—Yes; the climate is more rigorous, and the crops are even less certain on that river; the scarcity of timber also is a great bar; there is little or no wood in the country. The present population of Red River have great difficulty in providing wood for their immediate wants.

724. Is there any part of the territory of Rupert's Land towards Lake

Superior that you think adapted for cultivation?—Immediately upon the right bank of the Rainy Lake River cultivation might be carried on to advantage; but there is merely a slip of land adapted for cultivation; immediately behind are deep morasses which never thaw.

. . . .

1635. *Chairman.* Supposing an arrangement was made by which any portion of the territory now administered by the Hudson's Bay Company, which might be supposed to be fit for the purposes of colonisation, was separated from that administration, such a district of country, for instance, as the Red River, and any land in the neighbourhood of the Red River, or of the frontier of Canada, or land on the extreme west coast in the neighbourhood of Vancouver's Island, would there be any difficulty in the Hudson's Bay Company continuing to conduct their affairs after that separation had taken place?—I think not, because I do not believe there would be any settlement for a great length of time; I do not believe there would be any migration into the country for ages to come.

A Spiritual and Artistic Wasteland

The Substance of a Journey During a Residence at the Red River Colony (1824)
John West

We live in a day when the most distant parts of the earth are opening as the sphere of Missionary labours. The state of the heathen world is becoming better known, and the sympathy of British Christians has been awakened, in zealous endeavours to evangelize and soothe its sorrows. In these encouraging signs of the times, the Author is induced to give the following pages to the public, from having traversed some of the dreary wilds of North America, and felt deeply interested in the religious instruction and amelioration of the condition of the natives. They are wandering, in unnumbered tribes, through vast wilderness, where generation after generation have passed away, in gross ignorance and almost brutal degradation. . . .

July 2nd. An agreeable change has taken place in the scenery around us; the trees are breaking into leaves, and many plants are in blossom, where, but a short time ago, everything bore the aspect of winter. But this almost sudden and pleasing change has brought an unceasing torment: night and day we are perpetually persecuted with the mosquitoes, that swarm around us, and afford no rest but in the annoying respiration of smoky room. They hover in clouds above the domestic cattle, and drive them (almost irritated to madness) to the smoke of fires lighted with tufts of grass for their relief. The trial of this ever busy and tormenting insect is inconceivable, but to those who have endured it. We retire to rest, enveloped in clothes, almost to suffocation, but the musquitoe [*sic*] finds its way under the blankets, piercing with its envenomed trunk, till we often rise in a fever. Nor are we relieved from this painful scourge until the return of a slight frost in September. [pp. 61–63]

The Rainbow in the North: A Short Account of the First Establishment of Christianity in Rupert's Land by the Church Missionary Society (1850)
Sarah Tucker

We shall be better able to appreciate this regularity of attendance at church when we consider the peculiar nature of the climate: sometimes in the summer the thermometer would be from 80° to 100° in the shade, while in the winter it was often 30° or 35° below zero, and occasionally even 40°.

On Sundays, the church being full, the winter cold was not so severely felt during the time of service; but the external air congealing the breath of the people as it rose, when the fire was extinguished the ceiling would be covered with a coat of ice, while the desk pulpit, prayer-book, and Bible shone with silvery particles of frozen vapour. On the week-days in winter when the congregation was smaller, Mr. Cockran describes it as being, not withstanding good fire in the stove, like a 'temple of ice'. [p. 78]

Missionary Intelligence: The North Red River Settlement (1837)
Alfred Brunson, Methodist Superintendent, Upper Mississippi

St. Peters, N.M., July 22, 1837.

Dear Brother:—It is not generally known to either the political or religious world, that there are 25,000 souls connected with this settlement in a civilized and half civilized state. But from an interview with Mr. Peter Haden from that place, I learn that from an actual census, there are 5,000 families, averaging about five persons to a family. Of these, about 1000 families, or the men of them, are employed by the Hudson Bay Fur Company, the remaining 4,000 depend partly on agriculture, and partly on the buffalo for subsistence.

The greatest portion of the inhabitants are French from Canada, and half breeds. There are some English, some Irish, and some Scotch, together with Swiss, Swedes, and some from other northern European nations. The settlement was formed by the Hudson Bay Company, for the purpose of supplying the traders with food. But by mixing blood with the aborigines, they have increased in twenty-five years from a few hundreds to the above number, and have become too numerous for the purpose for which the settlement was formed, so that some families have left it. There are at this place about fifteen families who came from there, and several more at Prairie du Chein, and below it.

When the settlement was first formed, cattle were driven from the states through the vast intervening wilderness, and sold to the settlers at a very high price: — cows for thirty pounds sterling, but now cattle are drove from there to this place and sold for less than a fifth of that price.

There is a Catholic bishop and three priests in the settlement. One of the priests officiates for the white French, one for the half breeds, and one for the Indians. Many of the Indians and half breeds are said to be considerably advanced in civilization; have houses, mills, schools, churches, &c, &c. The half breeds constitute most of the party who roam over the buffalo lands, and are always accompanied by their priest, who makes a speculation out of the hunt. He has his hunters, and also buys game of others, and sells the produce to the traders. He carries with him his *chapel tent* in which he performs mass every Sabbath, receives confessions, and grants absolution. This hunting party often makes war on the Sioux, and are by them considered enemies as well as the Chippewas.

Dr. E. Jones, of the English establishment, has charge of the English Church, and Rev. John Cochran, of the same Church, has charge of Indian missions of that Church. Dr. Jones keeps a fine boarding school for the children of the wealthy half breeds, having 260 girls and 137 boys in it. The whites also have schools for themselves; and Mr. Cochran has four schools and teachers under his direction among the Indians. The Indians connected with this mission have houses, farms, a mill, church, oxen, cows, &c, and live in civilized habits.

The buffalo hunting grounds of the roaming party are within the territory of the United States, west of Red River. They hunt in the summer, and live in the settlement in the winter. They plant a little in the spring before they leave home, and gather the fruits thereof after they return. There were 739 one ox carts accompanied the caravan last summer, besides horses, &c, and it takes the beef, (dried in the sun,) hides, and tallow of ten buffalos to load a cart. These they take home, besides what they consume through the summer; the home load amounting to seven thousand three hundred and ninety buffalo, and the consumption on the plains amounts to considerable, as their whole families accompany them, so that it is presumed that at least 10,000 buffalo are taken on those plains annually. Their skins, upon an average when dressed, are worth five dollars a piece in the States, amounting in the whole to $50,000; and the articles of tallow and dried beef would, if in market, be worth as much more. The hides, however, are now dressed like deer skins and used for clothing. All this trade now goes to Canada.

Many of the inhabitants are said to be wealthy, and all have enough to subsist upon in comfort. The effect of their example on their Indian neighbors, encouraging them to civilization, is visible even in Indians who live seven days' journey from the settlement, as may be seen among those now at this place at the treaty. There is no whiskey in the country to *poison* the people, and were it not for the prevalent sin of lewdness — first introduced by the fur traders — they would be measurably a happy people.

There are salt springs on an east branch of Red River within the States, at which seven or eight hundred bushels of salt is made annually. And between the Red and Missouri rivers, in the buffalo range, are lakes of salt water so strong as to encrust on the shores in the dry seasons, and the water which empties into Red River effects the taste of the water for many miles down its stream. Red River is separated from the St. Peters by a portage of only five miles in low water, but may be passed in high water in canoes, and having large lakes in the neighborhood, a canal could connect the two streams, by making reservoirs of the lakes, to supply the summit level in the dry seasons of the year with water; so that the trade of that country could easily be transported to the Mississippi, if it was settled by the whites, which, from the flood of emigration to the west, we may expect will be the case in a few years, and in which case, most probably, many thousands of those wanderers would settle down with the whites in our territory.

In view of these prospects, it is important that the missionary of the cross pre-occupy the ground; not only to instruct the Indian in the art of living from the soil, so that he can subsist when his hunting grounds are occupied by the whites, and he is pressed into elbow reach of his neighbor, but to guard the morals of the whites, which too often deteriorate in settling a new country.

Peter Rindisbacher, *Indian Taking Scalp* **(n.d.)**
Scalping the victim; images of hostile Indians.

Captain H. Warre, *Fort Ellice on the Assiniboine River* **(1845)**
Providing protection: Indian encampment near Fort Ellice, Rupert's Land.

2

WEST TO EDEN:
THE ROMANTIC WEST
1845–1885

The great ocean itself does not present more infinite variety than does this prairie-ocean of which we speak. In winter, a dazzling surface of purest snow; in early summer, a vast expanse of grass and pale pink roses; in autumn too often a wild sea of raging fire. No ocean of water in the world can vie with its gorgeous sunsets; no solitude can equal the loneliness of a night-shadowed prairie: one feels the stillness, and hears the silence, the wail of the prowling wolf makes the voice of solitude audible, the stars look down through infinite silence upon a silence almost as intense. . . . [T]he prairies had nothing terrible in their aspect, nothing oppressive in their loneliness. One saw here the world as it had taken shape and form from the hands of the Creator.[1]

This paean of praise to the West appeared in William Butler's *The Great Lone Land* (1872). It was a widely-read book whose title entered the lexicon of phrases used to describe the Canadian West for the next fifteen years, only dying out when the completion of the Canadian Pacific Railway in 1885 no longer made the land "lone." Butler was a British major and an intelligence officer in the Red River Expedition of 1870 to put down the Métis uprising; he was commissioned by the Canadian government (which had purchased Rupert's Land from the Hudson's Bay Company) to report on conditions prevailing among the natives in the North West Territories and to recommend how best to establish a Canadian presence in this vast territory. It was his recommendation that led to the formation of the North West Mounted Police in 1873.[2]

In contrast to the pre-1850 image of the West as a hostile, forbidding wasteland, Butler talked about its infinite beauty, its sublime silence, its splendid peacefulness, and its mystical spiritualism. He believed that here in "paradise" could be seen God's wondrous works.

A miraculous transformation in the image of the West occurred in the period from 1845 to 1885. Two factors contributed to this altered perception—romanticism and nationalism. A romantic view of the West arose that was a combination of the influence of European Romanticism and of nostalgia for an unspoiled West that was rapidly disappearing. At the same time a growing nationalism, especially among the inhabitants of Upper Canada who saw their destiny as a people inextricably linked to the North West (see Chapter 3), also transformed the negative image of the West as a wasteland into a positive image of the West as the source of a great Canadian nation and a mighty British Empire. Although these two intellectual currents of thought—romanticism and nationalism—existed at the same time, they were based on opposite images of the West. Romantics imagined the West as a pristine wilderness, untouched by civilization; nationalists envisaged the region as a populated agricultural hinterland of an expanding nation.

The Age of Romanticism

Romanticism was a complex intellectual movement which had its origins in late-eighteenth and notably early nineteenth-century Europe.[3] It took various forms in Britain, and in the United States where it found its best expression in the transcendentalist movement. Romantics reacted against the formality, neo-classicism, and rationalism of the Enlightenment, and emphasized instead sentiment, imagination, and emotions. Romantic writers believed that God could be found through Nature for, as Louis Agassiz, the famous American (Harvard) naturalist, proclaimed, Nature was itself "the thoughts of the Creator." Emotions and imagination rather than reason were the means to penetrate beyond the visible form of nature to its more profound and transcendent truths. William Wordsworth, the famous English romantic poet, stressed the power of emotions over reason in appreciating Nature in his famous poem, *The Tables Turned:*

> One impulse from a vernal wood
> May teach you more of man
> Of mortal evil and of good
> Than all the sages can.
> Enough of science and of art
> Close up these barren leaves

Come forth, and bring with you a heart
That watches and receives.

Man's emotions were in their purest form, the Romantics believed, when he existed in his "natural state," before he had been corrupted, and his senses dulled, by civilization. Man lost his innocence and purity when he became a member of society. To regain his freedom, he needed to return to his natural state. Figuratively that meant regaining a sense of himself as an individual independent of the society of which he was a part. But the belief was interpreted literally as meaning the need to return to the natural world—to the wilderness—where he could live in harmony with Nature and with God, as man had lived before the Fall in the Garden of Eden. This Edenic myth appeared in literature as glowing descriptions of wilderness lands and in art as pastoral settings similar to what the artist imagined the Garden of Eden to have been like. The modern Adam was the individual who lived in harmony with nature, free of the restraints of civilization. To Jean Jacques Rousseau, this was the Indian whom he eulogized as "the noble savage"; to others, it was other primitive people in the world, or the explorer, or the fur trader.

Such an idealized vision of the world presented a more positive perception of the wilderness. A wilderness for a romantic was not a frightening and gloomy wasteland; rather, it was a place of serenity, a source of inspiration, a sanctuary—a primeval cathedral—where man could truly commune with God. The wilderness was virgin territory barely touched by man, untamed, unspoiled, undiscovered.

The Pristine Wilderness

William Butler held just such a romantic image of the wilderness. The image had been formed in his mind before he even set foot in the "great lone land." Butler wrote in his autobiography that "in boyhood I had read the novels of James Fenimore Cooper with an interest never to be known again in reading." In those novels, including *The Pioneer* and *The Last of the Mohicans*, Cooper had eulogized both the Indian as the noble savage and the West as an idyllic wilderness. Travelling in the American West near the Platte River in the autumn of 1867, Butler recorded that he found "the mystic word 'prairie' at last a veritable reality. Since my early boyhood that word has meant to me everything that was possible in the breathing, seeing, and grasping of freedom." With these images in mind, Butler went to the Canadian North West to find the romantic world of Fenimore Cooper. Indeed, in later life, he recalled his visit to the West in a poignant phrase that reversed the usual association of dream and reality. "The reality of the wilderness had become a dream."[4] The closing words of his book captured that "dream": "Midst the smoke and hum of cities, midst the prayer of churches, in streets or *salon*, it needs but little cause to recall again to the wanderer the image of the immense meadows where, far away at the portals of the setting sun, lies the Great Lone Land."[5] Butler was so inspired by his first trip to the North West that he embarked on another; his trip to Lake Athabaska he recorded in equally romantic terms in *The Wild North Land* (1873). Both books captured in their titles alone his image of the North West.

Western Canada became the dream of romantics who saw in the landscape—the rivers, forests, mountains, and plains—the world of Nature and of God. Here was one of the few remaining areas in the world where Nature still remained in its primal state, untainted by civilization. Indeed, the very things that made the West so appealing to Butler and his contemporaries were precisely those features of the region that, ironically, had made it unappealing to an earlier generation: its isolation and its unsettled nature. Butler was very conscious that he would be one of the last to see the West in its "natural state," for civilization was rapidly marching westward with the opening up of the region to settlement and the building of the railway. His own presence in the West was the direct result of Canada's acquisition of Rupert's Land two years earlier and the ensuing uprising among the Métis under Louis Riel in 1869-70 as the Métis' own attempt to stop the advancement of civilization. It was this sense of urgency—this need to capture in print the romantic West for posterity—that heightened Butler's fascination for the West. Soon it, too, would be defaced, conquered, and civilized. Where then would man find a "natural state" where he could see "the world as it had taken shape and form from the hands of the Creator"?

Butler was one of a number of individuals who came to the North West between 1845 and 1885 to enjoy, contemplate, and record its natural beauty, its solitude, and its majesty. They came as well to observe its native inhabitants, or simply to seek adventure, and freedom from civilization. The Victorian world was a world of travellers—the age of the Grand Tour, when travel was viewed as an indispensable part of a young man's education. Many well-to-do youths went off to distant continents like Africa and Asia; others preferred the healthier climate and the challenge of a northern landscape. In either case, travel was an escape from the oppressive monotony of urban industrial life in England or in settled areas of North America, escape to an area known for its exotic plant and animal life, its novelty of lifestyle, its adventure with native people and, perhaps most of all, its freedom from the restraints of civilization.[6]

P. F. Tytler made a trip through the North West as part of his Arctic expedition recorded in *The Northern Coasts of America and the Hudson's Bay Territories* (1853). He was fascinated by the Métis, whom he described as wild gypsies—"demi-savages"—in their brightly coloured costumes, "dashing over the prairies with their black hair streaming; dark eyes flashing; swart faces glittering; loud voices shouting; guns glancing in the sun, and dust flying in clouds from the hoofs of their buffalo runners, as they prance, rear, gallop, and curvette in a species of frenzy."[7] Tytler invited his readers to join him in a buffalo hunt with the Métis, racing across the prairies in pursuit of these animals that were king of the prairies. For his British audience, Tytler's account was the closest they would ever come to wilderness adventure. Such tales sold well to a public imbued with a romantic image of the wilderness.

Even Henry Youle Hind, the pragmatic scientist whose expedition to the West in 1857 had revealed the region's strengths and limitations for settlement, allowed himself to express his emotional enthusiasm for the region in romantic terms. He recorded his first impressions of the prairies: "The vast ocean of level prairie which lies to the west of Red River must be seen in its extraordinary aspects, before it can be rightly valued and understood in reference to its future occupation by an energetic and civilised race, able to improve its vast capabilities and appreciate its marvellous beauties."[8] He went on to reveal the wonders of the region in each season of the year.

The Earl of Southesk was another of these early adventure travellers. In 1859 James Carnegie, sixth Earl of Southesk, embarked on his "Grand Tour" of the North West. A thirty-two-year-old, serious-minded, unhealthy young Scottish aristocrat, Southesk sought adventure "in some part of the world where good sport could be met with among the larger animals, and where, at the same time, I might recruit my health by an active open-air life in a healthy climate." A friend recommended the Hudson's Bay Company territory, and so off he set with glowing images of the region already fixed in his vivid imagination. Not surprisingly, reality did not match his expectations, but that did not dampen his enthusiasm. He endured hardships and physical discomfort, but he willingly saw them as a necessary part of an important lesson in life: the need to challenge oneself to one's fullest potential. "Agonizingly cold yesterday and today, our beards were hung with icicles," he wrote. "During the height of the cold, the thought occurred to me—Why am I enduring this? For pleasure—was the only reply, and the idea seemed so absurd that I laughed myself warm. Then as circulation returned, I remembered that I was taking a lesson in that most valuable of human studies—the art of Endurance: an art the poor learn perforce, and the rich do well to teach themselves—though truly they have their own trials too, in a different fashion." Southesk learned another lesson from nature—that in the agony was the ecstasy. In one passage in *Saskatchewan and the Rocky Mountains* (1875), he recalled after days of weary travel the great joy and the liberating experience he had felt from observing the natural world in its pristine beauty. "What gladness swelled within my heart— oh! never shall I forget it—as I felt the gallant little Morgan bounding and dancing beneath me, scarce able to control himself for joy, while we passed through the pleasant woods on that lovely summer morning, when all nature seemed so fresh and beautiful and sweet. At last, thought I, at last, the prisoner of civilization is free!"[9]

Viscount Milton and Dr. Cheadle represented the adventurous Victorian travellers *par excellence.* William Fitzwilliam, Viscount Milton, was a pale, slight, but impetuous young gentleman of twenty-three with a fighting spirit that matched his tenacity. His companion, William Butler Cheadle, was a robust man of twenty-seven who went along as Milton's personal physician, protector, and tutor. In 1862 they traversed the western Canadian plains, ostensibly in search of a highway from the Atlantic to the Pacific through British territory, but in reality in search of adventure — "for hunting the buffalo and grizzly bear" and "for a glorious life in the far west." In one passage in their account of their journey, *The North-West Passage by Land* (1865), the two men wrote of the land west of Portage La Prairie:

> . . . we entered a fine, undulating country, full of lakes and marshes thronged with wild-fowl, and studded with pretty copses of aspen. . . . The prairies were gay with the flowers of the dark blue gentianella, which grew in great profusion. Each day was like the one before, yet without a wearisome monotony. Sometimes we jogged dreamily along beside the carts, or lay basking in the bright sunshine.[10]

Their book enjoyed great popularity in Britain.

Travel narratives, whether in the form of published journals and diaries, travelogues, or accounts in the illustrated press, had a receptive audience. Victorian readers delighted in sharing vicariously in the experiences of adventures in exotic places. Such accounts satisfied a natural curiosity and offered an escape from the drudgery of everyday life in the factories, on the farms, or even in the drawing room.

The West as God's Sanctum

The transformation of the West from a *terra incognita* to a *paradiso* is evident in the missionary accounts of the period. Juxtaposed in a number of these writings are the two images of wasteland and benevolent wilderness vying for supremacy in the mind of the beholder. To late nineteenth century missionaries, the West still remained a "spiritual wasteland" of heathen Indians and a few struggling isolated religious missions, and a rugged terrain that made communication virtually impossible. But rather than dwell on the negative aspects, as earlier missionaries had done, and thus despair at ever hoping to see the region come within the pale of civilization, these later missionaries stressed the positive features of the West: its spiritual solitude where man could commune with God; its challenge to the Church; its tremendous potential.

There was an evident Victorian optimism in later missionary writings that had been decidedly absent in earlier accounts and that was characteristic of a growing "muscular Christianity," particularly evangelical Protestant Christianity.

George Mountain, Anglican Bishop of Montreal and the son of Jacob Mountain, the first Anglican bishop of Quebec, was inspired during an 1846 visit to the West to record his perceptions in *Songs of the Wilderness.* The dual nature of the landscape, good and evil, forced the poet to come to terms with this wild and empty wasteland.

> All yet is wild: be sure no gardener's knife
> Has trimm'd these shrubs; no sheep have cropp'd the grass:
> No cottage smoke will rise, — no spinning wife
> Peep forth; with milk-pail charged no village lass:
> In stillness all the way and solitude you pass.

Yet in this rugged wilderness he found time to pause and reflect on God's wondrous work of creation, a fulness unknown to civilization.

> And yet, though all be wild, we seem to meet
> Here wandering on, a wilderness more subdued;
> And, in the features of the far retreat,
> Tho' all be waste, a gentler solitude:

> Some rocks there are and fall, but not so rude:
> The pause relieves your mind when off you look
> From objects huge and vastness still renew'd,
> On landscape more confined and quiet nook,
> On willowy streamlet soft, or clear fast-flowing brook.[11]

The Reverend John Ryerson, Bishop Mountain's Methodist contemporary and a brother of the better-known Egerton Ryerson, on a missionary tour of the Hudson's Bay Company territory in the early 1850s presented the same ambivalent attitude towards the West. In a description of a storm on Lake Winnipeg, he juxtaposed within a single sentence the terror and the beauty of the scene: "I never shall forget the terrific grandeur of that dreadful thunder storm." In the end, the romantic image prevailed. He recalled the scene as "too wonderful and sublime to be described but never to be forgotten." "Sublime" was a popular descriptive term in nineteenth-century nature terminology; it meant the presence of God in Nature in a Christian mystical sense.[12]

Reverend Ryerson was equally uplifting in his appraisal of the potential for Christianity in the West. While he spoke of the "waste howling wilderness," he also saw the little missions, such as that at Red River, as evidence of an "advancing" Christianity. More than "oases in the desert"—garrisoned settlements struggling to survive against insurmountable odds — these religious centres were for Ryerson "beacons of light" radiating their Christian message to the heathen people around them. "What an inviting field, 'whitening unto the harvest,' does this region open up to the philanthropist, and the Christian Church, in the thousands of souls waiting to hear God's word." In another passage he described Rupert's Land as "the Saviour's vineyard"—a decidedly romantic image in the Edenic myth tradition; the missionary's labour would one day bear fruit.[13]

By 1881 the Reverend Alexander Sutherland, on a summer tour through western Canada as part of his responsibilities as foreign mission secretary of the Methodist Church in Canada for thirty-six years, could write in the true romantic tradition: "God himself seems nearer in these solitudes than 'in the city full,' for here is nothing to divert the attention or distract the mind; and in the brooding silence the 'still small voice' is heard more clearly than amid the din of human activities or the strife of human tongues."[14]

These Protestant missionaries, although admiring the region's natural beauty and appreciating its godly qualities, contributed, as harbingers of the new order, to the demise of the West. In their ambition to see missions established, their assistance to the government to establish Indian reserves, their desire to see the West populated, and their association of Protestant Christianity with an advancing Anglo-Saxon civilization, they were unconsciously and ironically working to undermine their own romantic image of the West. While they could empathize with the native people and appreciate the "cultural shock" the Indians would experience with the establishment of large-scale white settlement, and while they had found an innate beauty in the natural landscape unknown to their predecessors, nevertheless, they paved the way for the settlement era.[15]

Visions of Natural Beauty

Artists too were imbued with the romantic spirit, and were anxious to capture on canvas the Edenic wilderness.[16] They wanted to depart from the norms of rational analysis of the world, characteristic of the Age of Enlightenment, and instead to marvel at God's beauty through Nature. Paul Kane was the most famous of these nineteenth century romantic painters of the Canadian West.[17] Like other romantics, he realized the need to visit the West and to paint the "noble savage" before the opportunity was lost forever. In the introduction to his *Wanderings of an Artist*, the record of his journey into the North West in the years 1845 to 1848, Kane explained the urgency of his mission:

> On my return to Canada from the continent of Europe, where I had passed nearly four years in studying my profession as a painter, I determined to devote whatever talents and proficiency I possessed to the

painting of a series of pictures illustrative of the North American Indians and scenery. The subject was one in which I felt a deep interest in my boyhood. I had been accustomed to see hundreds of Indians about my native village, then Little York, muddy and dirty, just struggling into existence, now the City of Toronto, bursting forth in all its energy and commercial strength. But the face of the red man is now no longer seen. All traces of his footsteps are fast being obliterated from his once favourite haunts, and those who would see the aborigines of this country in their original state, or seek to study their native manners and customs, must travel far through the pathless forest to find them.[18]

Before Kane left for the West, he was predisposed to find the "noble savage" and an idyllic wilderness. From his studies in Europe he had been exposed to the techniques of the European romantic artists and to the Indian paintings of George Catlin, the famous American artist who had held exhibitions of his paintings in London and Paris. Catlin had painted the Indians in noble stances, wearing their bright costumes, and involved in heroic acts of warfare or buffalo hunting. Kane knew then that he wanted to do as much for the Indian of the North West as Catlin had done for the Indians of the American Plains. He set out in 1845 "with no companion but my portfolio and box of paints, my gun, and a stock of ammunition"—a sure indication of his idyllic image of the West—to make his way by foot, by Indian canoe, and by steamer. At Sault Ste. Marie the Hudson's Bay Company factor convinced him that deeper penetration into the wilderness was impossible without the assistance of a company agent.

He returned to Toronto, elicited the support of George Simpson, Governor of the Company, and in the spring of 1846 embarked on his second trip. This one took him first to Fort Garry where he painted the Métis, "a very hardy race of men, capable of enduring the greatest hardships and fatigue," and then further west via the North Saskatchewan River where he visited Norway House, Fort Carlton, Fort Edmonton, and Jasper House before descending the Columbia River on his way to the Pacific coast. As Kane moved west, his paintings became more romantic. The veil of civilization was stripped from his vision and he was able to see the Indian in his "natural state." As Kane's biographer, J. Russell Harper, notes:

> On the prairies the Indians are no longer pictured wearing clothing with European additions or with government medals about their necks. These men of the plains have not the quiet submissive air of the men of Manitowanig who had been in contact with Europeans for generations and forsaw the end of their free native life as hunters. Instead, his Sioux chieftain, the Assiniboin named Mal-Min or the Blackfoot, Big Snake, are noble beings. Much-Cranium, the Cree from Fort Carlton, is above

all the haughty Indian looking far out over the plains which are his empire. Here is the proud savage, not beaten down by Europeans, the kind of man for whom Catlin had such regard. Kane finally had met the Indians he really wanted to paint.[19]

Kane romanticized not only the Indian but also the landscape. His western scenes, done in soft pastels, depict a tranquil land, giving the observer a sense of looking through a mist or haze. The landscape forms a backdrop where the gentle rolling hills, the stately trees, or the peaceful waters of a lake pose no threat but act only to complement the people in the foreground. The composition is static, as though Kane had isolated this moment in history. Time stops in the peaceful repose of a prairie scene. Harper observes: "Kane's is a romantic and idealized world. He painted the grass of the wildest regions trimmed like an English green sward. Trading boats descending the Saskatchewan River have the dignity of Roman galleys, and buffalo hunts are like wonderful tableaux on some gigantic stage. . . . His personal romantic nature . . . was consistent with the spirit of the age."[20]

Frederick Verner was an admirer of Kane and, according to Harper, "unconsciously patterned his own life on that of the better-known artist," becoming, after Kane's death in 1871, the leading painter of Canadian Indians.[21] Verner was a true romantic, even joining, while at art school in London, the Red Shirt regiment, a legion of foreign volunteers formed to help Giuseppe Garibaldi in the liberation of Italy from papal dominance, before returning three years later to Canada to become a professional painter. Verner's romanticism was tinged with nostalgia for the "Old West." Many of his landscape paintings were done well after the West had been settled.

This native Canadian made only one known trip into the North West Territories, in 1873, but it was sufficient for him to convey his image of the West. That image, like Kane's, was of a calm and tranquil world, an almost secret garden in the wilderness, with Indians and wild animals living in harmony and in a natural state untouched by the white man's influence. It is a primeval wilderness, filled with mystery, enchantment, and beauty. There is a mellow quality to Verner's paintings that sets the observer at rest amidst a mist-rising lake, a sun-drenched prairie, or a lush green woodlot. Here is visualized James Fenimore Cooper's idealized world—"a wild majesty of untouched forests, mountains, and lakes." Verner was well aware that the West of the buffalo had come to a close. In fact, the buffalo had become virtually extinct only a few years after his visit in 1873. Certainly by the time he painted *The Last Buffalo* in 1893 his virgin West, the domain of this monarch of the plains, was pure nostalgia. His romantic West existed more in his mind than in reality.

The Fictitious Romantic West

What Kane and Verner did in the artistic realm, R. M. Ballantyne did in the field of literature. Ballantyne, the most popular romantic writer of the Canadian West, achieved a familiarity among Canadians and Britons comparable to James Fenimore Cooper in the United States.[22] During his lifetime, he wrote some eighty books for boys, a large number set in Hudson's Bay Company territory. Whatever knowledge the Upper Canadians had of this unknown territory in the mid-nineteenth century probably came either from Kane's paintings or, more likely, Ballantyne's popular novels. His image of the West dominated an era in the history of western Canada.

In 1841, at the age of sixteen, Ballantyne became apprenticed to the Hudson's Bay Company; he spent the next six years as a fur trader stationed at various times at Norway House, York Factory, and Fort Garry. Here he gathered first-hand knowledge of the North West that he conveyed in long letters to his mother in Scotland. These letters fell into the hands of a cousin in the printing trade who published them under the auspices of the Hudson's Bay Company. The publisher, William Nelson, then persuaded Ballantyne to write a book for boys based on his adventures in the great lone land. The result was *Snowflakes and Sunbeams, or The Young Fur-Traders* (1863).

Snowflakes and Sunbeams is a fictionalized account of the Kennedy family of Red River. Charles Kennedy, the son of a Hudson's Bay Company servant, dreamed of the day when he would be a fur trader for the Company in some wild and remote region of the North West. The day came, and the ecstatic Charley joined a band of *voyageurs* "one beautiful morning in April"—one of those enchanting and romantic spring mornings that Ballantyne was so adept at describing—to experience the wonders and adventures of the wilderness. In Ballantyne's novels, the fur trader or voyageur was eulogized in the same way that the Indian was in Kane's and Verner's paintings. These "picturesque athletic men" are described as leading a life as free and wild as the land itself. When Charley joined these voyageurs "his spirit boiled within him as he quaffed the first sweet draught of a rover's life—a life in the woods—the wild, free, enchanting woods where all appeared in *his* eyes bright, and sunny, and green, and beautiful!"[23] Like Greek heroes before them, these voyageurs chartered unknown waters and explored new lands.

Ballantyne blended history and fiction even more intimately in *The Pioneers* (1872), a fictionalized account of Alexander Mackenzie's real life explorations of the North West. Depicting Mackenzie in heroic terms, he romanticized the explorer's deeds, making them larger than life while giving an authenticity to them by setting the story in its true setting.

Ballantyne had presented an equally glowing account of the prairies in *The Dog Crusoe and His Master* (1860). All of the Hudson's Bay Territory was "God's country" to this romantic writer. Ballantyne's image of the West as the home of great adventure coloured his own self-image, and he spent the latter days of his life in Scotland, "lecturing about his experiences in Rupert's Land, striding purposefully across the stage, black-bearded and handsome, and dressed in the colourful coat and leggings of a North American trapper."[24]

Another—and more controversial—figure in western Canadian history became the heroic subject of both a romantic poem and a romantic novel. Thomas Scott, the boisterous Protestant Irishman, member of the Orange Lodge, and a vehement anti-Catholic, who was executed by Louis Riel during the Métis uprising of 1869–70, took on mythic proportions among English-speaking Canadians, particularly Ontarians. George Crofton, an Ontarian and one of the first North West Mounted Policemen in the West, was inspired to eulogize Scott—supposedly during a stopover at Scott's grave (although to this day the site of Scott's grave is unknown) while on the Great March west from Fort Dufferin near the Red River settlement to Fort Whoop Up in present-day southern Alberta in 1874. The beginning stanzas capture the mood and spirit of the poem:

> In utter, hopeless, trackless waste,
> In solitude profound,
> By a weird loneliness embraced,
> The Scout's last rest we found.[25]

Accompanying Crofton and the other 150 Mounties on their trek west was Henri Julien, a young French-Canadian artist for the *Canadian Illustrated News*, the Canadian counterpart of the *Illustrated London News*.[26] Julien was as adept with his pen as with his paint brush. His response to the prairies reflected that of Captain William Butler. "This narrow strip of planking [the station platform]," he wrote, "was the dividing line between civilization and the wilderness. Behind us lay the works of man, with their noises; before us stretched out the handiwork of God, with its eternal solitudes. The first sight of the prairie is as impressive as the first sight of the sea. There, at my feet, it spread out, silent, immeasurable, sublime." The comparison of the prairies to the sea was made frequently by romantics and had symbolic significance. Just as the water of the ocean was like a mirror of God's beauty, so too were the prairies a reflection of God's handiwork. Julien also gave a vivid description of the ubiquitous mosquito.

> The mosquito of the prairie must be a distinct species in entomology. We had men among us who had travelled in all parts of the world, and who had been pestered by all manners of insects, but they all agreed that

nowhere had they seen anything to equal the mosquito of the prairie. . . .
As soon as twilight deepens, they make their appearance on the horizon,
in the shape of a cloud, which goes on increasing in density as it
approaches to the encounter. At first, a fair hum is heard in the distance,
then it swells into a roar as it comes nearer. The attack is simply dreadful.
Your eyes, your nose, your ears are invaded. If you open your mouth
to curse at them, they troop into it. They insinuate themselves under your
clothes, down your shirt collar, up your sleeve cuffs, between the buttons
of your shirt bosom. And not one or a dozen, but millions at a time.[27]

J. E. Collins used the historical event of the North West Rebellion
of 1885 as the setting for his romantic novel, *Annette, the Métis Spy*
(1886).[28] Collins, an Ontario writer, had never been west, but he had
been aroused by the emotional fervour surrounding the rebellion,
particularly with the prospect of hanging Louis Riel, the "murderer"
of the Ontario Orangeman Thomas Scott. Collins was so steeped in the
romantic tradition that he felt no compulsion to distinguish between fact
and fiction. In a note to *Annette*, he added: "I present some fiction in
my story, and a large array of fact. I do not feel bound, however, to
state which is the fact, which the fiction." He was equally cavalier on
his treatment of the landscape. In the same note he said:

> The preceding story lays no claim to value or accuracy in its descriptions
> of the North-West Territories. I have never seen that portion of our
> country. . . . I have, therefore, arranged the geography of the Territories
> to suit my own conveniences. I speak of places that no one will be able
> to find upon maps of the present or of the future. Wherever I want a valley
> or a swamp, I put the same; and I have taken the same liberty with respect
> to hills or waterfalls. The birds, and in some instances the plants and
> flowers of the prairies, I have also made to order.[29]

The result of such license was a larger-than-life depiction of a supposedly
true event, the capture and execution of Louis Riel in 1885. Such "tall
tales" are characteristic of western writing, according to the literary critic
Eli Mandel;[30] they were certainly characteristic of romantic writing in
an era when the image was of greater importance than the reality. That
image in *Annette, the Métis Spy* was of a western land of adventure,
intrigue, and righteousness. In the end "moral goodness" triumphed over
"evil" in the vindication of Thomas Scott when, through the courageous
act of his lover, Annette, the guilty Riel is brought to trial and ultimately
to the scaffold.

George Monro Grant, a remarkable Presbyterian minister with a
Victorian sense of adventure and a strong dose of Canadian nationalism,
captured the romantic image of the West on the eve of its demise in the
1880s. Grant had travelled as secretary to Sir Sandford Fleming,
Engineer-in-Chief of the Canadian Pacific Railway Company, on a

gruelling 103-day trip in 1872 to map out the proposed route for the new transcontinental railway that was to link British Columbia to Canada. Grant's account of their journey, *Ocean to Ocean* (1873), is full of positive descriptions of the North West. Upon first laying eyes on the prairies, Grant wrote: "We looked out and beheld a sea of green, sprinkled with yellow, red, lilac, and white. . . . As you cannot know what the ocean is without seeing it, neither can you imagine the prairie."[31]

Ocean to Ocean, however, never reaches the height of romantic writing that his *Picturesque Canada* (1882) did. This latter book was commissioned by the Canadian Pacific Railway Company to celebrate the transcontinental railway and to encourage settlement in the West. In much of the book, Grant talks about the West in terms of settlement potential, but his romantic nature surfaces in descriptive accounts of the beauty of this virgin territory. In one passage he presents the West as a cornucopia of flowers, in another as an unsurpassed wilderness in every season of the year:

> As spring advances, the grasses and plants gather strength. The prairie becomes a sea of green, flecked with particoloured grasses, and an infinite variety of flowering plants. The billowy motion of the taller species as they bend and nod before the breeze is the poetry of motion on a scale so vast that the mind is filled with a sense of the sublime as well as satisfied with the perfect beauty and harmony that extends on all sides to the horizon. The atmosphere, balmy and flower-scented, is also so charged with electricity that the blood courses through the veins under the perpetual influence of a stimulant that brings no lassitude in its train. Summer comes crowded—or rather covered—with roses. The traveller across the prairies walks on roses and sleeps on roses. . . . But the ripe glories of the year are reserved for the season when summer merges into autumn. The tints of the woods in the older provinces are left far behind by the wealth of the prairie's colours. . . . The atmosphere takes on a hazy and smoky look. The sun is red during the day and at its setting. The frosts cease, and the Indian summer of the North-west sets in. Day in and day out, often for weeks, this delicious after-glow, during which existence is a luxury, continues. Then the sun sinks low again. The smoke and the haze clears way. The frost puts an end to farming operations, and the winter fairly commences—winter terrible to the inexperienced for its length and severity, but perhaps the most enjoyable season of the year to Canadians, East and West.[32]

Grant's poetic prose was enriched by the illustrations of artist F. B. Schell. His drawings promoted the garden image, by depicting the prairies as wooded and full of clumps of grasses and flowers. In particular, Schell concentrated on the Mennonite village settlements of Manitoba which, although uncharacteristic in their windmills, herds of cattle, and European-style barns, did, nevertheless, show the romantic beauty and the future potential of the North West.

These writers and artists, as they reflected on the beauty of the western wilderness, were foreshadowing—and in some cases, particularly by the 1870s and 1880s, experiencing—the demise of its pristine beauty with the coming of civilization. Indeed, they were harbingers of that civilization; for ironically their romantic image of the west contributed to its settlement by arousing a desire in others to live in this "paradise." Thomas Rawlings, a spokesman for railway interests in North America, had pointed out as early as 1865 that:

> The splendid landscapes of the Assiniboine that adorn the great picture gallery of nature, cannot be closed for ever. The measureless prairies that stretch in vast waves of beauty from the Lake of the Woods to the base of the Rocky Mountains, redolent and gorgeous with the richest profusion of rose-bushes, blue-bells, woodbine, convolvulus, helianthii, and thousands of nameless and delicate flowers, tell the beholder the wealth of soil that supports them in their entangled and untrained luxuriance of variety and numbers. . . . But all this land has been shut out from the knowledge of the world. A new era is at hand. The people of the Atlantic are wooing the people of the Pacific; they would be united by an iron band. The great North-East invites British Columbia to share her future with her, and to march forward hand in hand with her.[33]

It seemed logical that a railway enthusiast like Rawlings should have predicted the coming of civilization to the West. For it was the Canadian Pacific Railway more than anything else that symbolized, and contributed to, the demise of the romantic West. Not only did its completion in 1885 contribute to a second uprising among the Métis, who were trying to stop the wave of an advancing civilization that would destroy their traditional way of life, but the railway also enabled settlers to pour in in large numbers. By 1885 the buffalo was virtually extinct, the Indians had been shunted onto reserves, and the land had been surveyed and apportioned out for settlement. No longer could there be any illusions of the West as a pristine and untamed wilderness.

The Pristine Wilderness

The Great Lone Land (1872)
William F. Butler

Leaving behind the Medicine Hills, we descended into the plain and held our way until sunset towards the west. It was a calm and beautiful evening; far-away objects stood out sharp and distinct in the pure atmosphere of these elevated regions. For some hours we had lost sight of the mountains, but shortly before sunset the summit of a long ridge was gained, and they burst suddenly into view in greater magnificence than at midday. Telling my men to go on and make the camp at the Medicine River, I rode through some fire-wasted forest to a lofty grass-covered height which the declining sun was bathing in floods of glory. I cannot hope to put into the compass of words the scene which lay rolled beneath from this sunset-lighted eminence; for, as I looked over the immense plain and watched the slow descent of the evening sun upon the frosted crest of these lone mountains, it seemed as if the varied scenes of my long journey had woven themselves into the landscape, filling with the music of memory the earth, the sky, and the mighty panorama of mountains. Here at length lay the barrier to my onward wanderings, here lay the boundary to that 4000 miles of unceasing travel which had carried me by so many varied scenes so far into the lone land; and other thoughts were not wanting. [p. 275]

The Wild North Land (1873)
William F. Butler

What shall we call this land to those who follow us into its depths?

It has prairies, forests, mountains, barren wastes, and rivers; rivers whose single lengths roll through twice a thousand miles of shoreland; prairies over which a rider can steer for months without resting his gaze on aught save the dim verge of the ever-shifting horizon; mountains rent by rivers, ice-topped, glacier-seared, impassable; forests whose sombre pines darken a region half as large as Europe; sterile, treeless wilds whose 400,000 square miles lie spread in awful desolation. How shall it all be called?

In summer, a land of sound, a land echoing with the voices of birds, the ripple of running water, the mournful music of the waving pine-branch; in winter, a land of silence, a land hushed to its inmost depths by the weight of ice, the thick-falling snow, the intense rigour of a merciless cold — its great rivers glimmering in the moonlight, wrapped in their shrouds of ice; its still forests rising weird and spectral against the Aurora-lighted horizon; its notes of bird or brook hushed as if in death; its nights so still that the moving streamers across the northern skies seem to carry to the ear a sense of sound, so motionless around, above, below, lies all other visible nature.

If then we call this region the land of stillness, that name will convey more justly than any other the impress most strongly stamped upon the winter's scene. [pp. 4–5]

He who rides for months through the vast solitudes sees during the hours of his daily travel an unbroken panorama of distance. The seasons come and go; grass grows and flowers die; the fire leaps with tiger bounds along the earth; the snow lies still and quiet over hill and lake; the rivers rise and fall, but the rigid features of the wilderness rest unchanged. Lonely, silent, and impassive; heedless of man, season, or time, the weight of the Infinite seems to brood over it. Once only in the hours of day and night a moment comes when this impassive veil is drawn from its features, and the eye of the wanderer catches a glimpse of the sunken soul of the wilderness; it is the moment which follows the sunset; then a deeper stillness steals over the earth, colours of wondrous hue rise and spread along the western horizon. In a deep sea of emerald and orange of fifty shades, mingled and interwoven together, rose-coloured isles float anchored to great golden threads; while, far away, seemingly beyond and above all, one broad flash of crimson light, the parting sun's last gift, reddens upwards to the zenith. And then, when every moment brings a change, and the night gathers closer to the earth, and some waveless, nameless lake glimmers in uncertain shore-line and in shadow of inverted hilltop; when a light that seems born of another world (so weirdly distant is it from ours) lingers along the western sky, then hanging like a lamp over the tomb of the sun, the Evening Star gleams out upon the darkening wilderness.

It may be only a fancy, a conceit bred from loneliness and long wandering, but at such times the great solitude has seemed to me to open its soul, and that in its depths I read its secrets. [pp. 22–23]

And now let us turn for a moment to that other wild creature which had made its dwelling on the Great Prairie.

Over the grassy ocean of the west there has moved from time immemorial a restless tide. Backwards and forwards, now north, now south — now filling the dark gorges of the Rocky Mountains — now trailing into the valleys of the Rio del Norte—now pouring down the wooded slopes of the Saskatchewan, surged millions on millions of dusky bisons.

What led them in their strange migrations no man could tell, but all at once a mighty impulse seemed to seize the myriad herds, and they moved over the broad realm which gave them birth as the waves of the ocean roll before the storm. Nothing stopped them on their march; great rivers stretched before them with steep, overhanging banks, and beds treacherous with quicksand and shifting bar; huge chasms and earth-rents, the work of subterraneous forces, crossed their line of march, but still the countless thousands swept on. Through day and night the earth trembled beneath their tramp, and the air was filled with the deep bellowing of their unnumbered throats.

Crowds of wolves and flocks of vultures dogged and hovered along their way, for many a huge beast, half sunken in quicksand, caught amidst whirling ice flow, or bruised and maimed at the foot of some steep precipice, marked their line of march, like the wrecks lying spread behind a routed army. Nearly two millions of square miles formed their undivided domain; on three sides a forest boundary encircled it, on the fourth a great mountain range loomed up against the western sky. Through this enormous area countless creeks and rivers meandered through the meadows, where the prairie grass grew thick and rank, and the cotton woods spread their serpentine belts. Out in the vast prairie the Missouri, the Platte, the Sweet Water, the Arkansas, the South Saskatchewan, the Bighorn, the Yellowstone, rolled their volumes towards the east, gathering a thousand affluents as they flowed.

Countless ages passed, tribes warred and wandered, but the life of the wilderness lay deep beneath the waves of time, and the roll of the passing centuries disturbed not its slumber. [pp. 53–54]

Narrative of the Canadian Red River Exploring Expedition of 1857 and of the Assiniboine and Saskatchewan Exploring Expedition of 1858

Henry Youle Hind

The vast ocean of level prairie which lies to the west of Red River must be seen in its extraordinary aspects, before it can be rightly valued and understood in reference to its future occupation by an energetic and civilised race, able to improve its vast capabilities and appreciate its marvellous beauties. It must be seen at sunrise, when the boundless plain suddenly flashes with rose-coloured light, as the first rays of the sun sparkle in the dew on the long rich grass, gently stirred by the unfailing

morning breeze. It must be seen at noon-day, when refraction swells
into the forms of distant hill ranges the ancient beaches and ridges of
Lake Winnipeg, which mark its former extension; when each willow
bush is magnified into a grove, each distant clump of aspens, not seen
before, into wide forests, and the outline of wooded river banks, far
beyond unassisted vision, rise into view. It must be seen at sunset, when,
just as the huge ball of fire is dipping below the horizon, he throws a
flood of red light, indescribably magnificent, upon the illimitable waving
green, the colours blending and separating with the gentle roll of the
long grass in the evening breeze, and seemingly magnified towards the
horizon into the distant heaving swell of a parti-coloured sea. It must
be seen, too, by moonlight, when the summits of the low green grass
waves are tipped with silver, and the stars in the west disappear suddenly
as they touch the earth. Finally, it must be seen at night, when the distant
prairies are in a blaze, thirty, fifty, or seventy miles away; when the fire
reaches clumps of aspen, and the forked tips of the flames, magnified
by refraction, flash and quiver in the horizon, and the reflected lights
from rolling clouds of smoke above tell of the havoc which is raging below.

These are some of the scenes which must be witnessed and felt before
the mind forms a true conception of the Red River prairies in that
unrelieved immensity which belongs to them in common with the ocean,
but which, unlike the ever-changing and unstable sea, seem to promise
a bountiful recompence to millions of our fellow-men. [pp. 134–35]

Humphrey Lloyd Hime, *The Prairie Looking West* (1860)
The Lost Eden: civilization on the march.

Saskatchewan and the Rocky Mountains (1875)
From Qu'Appelle Fort to the Elbow of the Saskatchewan River
Earl of Southesk

This was a prairie country of sand and crisp grass, of level tracts varied with hills and bluffs and undulations, of many little lakes and swamps scattered about here and there. Flowers of the gayest colour enlivened the landscape. The most common were the small tiger-lilies and the roses, and next came blue-bells and white strawberry blossoms. Sometimes acres and acres were covered with intermingled masses of the orange lily and the pendulous blue-bell, the whole of them so short of stem that the glory of the flowers combined with the rich greenness of their leaves, and it seemed as if a vast oriental carpet had been thrown upon the plain.

Towards evening the heat of the weather changed to heavy showers, with flashes of lightning at intervals; we saw that a storm was coming, and made haste to camp in a wild rocky valley that offered itself at no great distance from the track. Three very young wolves appeared when we entered this secluded glen, but I did not care to shoot the poor little creatures. The plains we had been passing through during the day were thickly strewn with buffalo skulls, the relics of former slaughter by Indians or half-breed hunting parties. 'We did not see as many ground-squirrels as usual, but, as usual, saw a pair of small birds chasing a crow.'

July 8th.—The little wolves kept up a chorus all night long, beginning each fresh strain with mewing whines, like a family of peevish kittens, then bursting into tremulous, melancholy howls. The effect was very pleasing; it harmonised so well with the savage loneliness of the scene, that I should have been sorry to miss this wild wolfish music. [p. 70]

The North-West Passage by Land (1867)
Viscount Milton and W. B. Cheadle

After leaving Portage La Prairie, fifty miles beyond Fort Garry, and the western boundary of the settlement, we entered a fine, undulating country, full of lakes and marshes thronged with wild-fowl, and studded with pretty copses of aspen. As we rode along we continually came across the skulls of buffalo, whitened by age and exposure. A few years ago buffalo were plentiful along the road between Red River and Carlton. The prairies were gay with the flowers of the dark blue gentianella, which grew in great profusion.

Each day was like the one before, yet without a wearisome monotony. Sometimes we jogged dreamily along beside the carts, or lay basking in the bright sunshine. When tired of idleness, we cantered ahead, with Rover in attendance, and shot geese and ducks at the lakes, or prairie grouse in the copses. Feathered game was so plentiful that we easily killed enough to feed the whole party, and rarely had occasion to trench on our stock of pemmican. A little before sundown we camped by wood and water, hobbled the horses, and then ate our suppers with appetites such as we had never known before. At night, while smoking our pipes round the camp fire, La Ronde amused us with stories of his hunting adventures, of encounters with the Sioux, or of his journey with Dr. Rae, after which we turned into our blankets and slept soundly till daybreak. [pp. 51–52]

Buffalo running is certainly a most fascinating sport. The wild charge together into the thick of the herd, the pursuit of the animal selected from the band, which a well-trained horse follows and turns as a greyhound courses a hare; the spice of danger in it from the charge of a wounded animal, or a fall from the holes so numerous on the prairies, contrive to render it extremely exciting. [p. 62]

The next day brought us to a lovely little spot, a small prairie of perhaps 200 acres, surrounded by low wooded hills, and on one side a lake winding with many an inlet amongst the hills and into the plain, while here and there a tiny promontory, richly clothed with pines and aspens, stretched out into the water. The beauty of the place had struck the rude voyageurs, its only visitors, except the Indians, and they had named it La Belle Prairie.

As we crossed it, we remarked to one another what a magnificent site for a house one of the promontories would be, and how happy many a poor farmer who tilled unkindly soil at home would feel in possession of the rich land which lay before us. [pp. 71–72]

The West as God's Sanctum

A Summer in Prairie-Land (1881)
Reverend Alexander Sutherland

> "How soft, how beautiful, comes on
> The stilly hour when storms are gone,"

wrote Tom Moore; and any one who witnessed with us a prairie sunset, after leaving St. Paul on the 23rd, must have appreciated the sentiment. The storm of the afternoon had passed by, and the heavy clouds rolled eastward, spanned by a rainbow of wondrous beauty. In the west a thinner stratum lifted from the horizon, exposing a broad band of clear sky, not brightly blue as in the daytime, but with a soft transparent haze, as if seen through a mist of tears. Soon heavier masses of cloud rolled slowly upward, and ranged themselves against the softly-tinted background, their lower edges straight and symmetrical, their upper edges broken and ragged, and constantly changing into new and strange forms. Now they seemed like massive ramparts, crowned with frowning battlements and towers; now like the domes and spires of a great city, with the grand proportions of a vast cathedral towering high above the whole. Then, as the sun sank toward the horizon, from behind the sombre clouds there suddenly issued a mellow flood of golden splendor, and in a moment rampart and battlement, tower and spire, softened into masses of foliage, crowning isles of Eden-like beauty, anchored in a golden sea; while, as if to complete the illusion, fragments of fleecy vapor went floating by, like stately ships sailing amid those happy islands, up to some quiet haven that as yet I could not see. [pp. 4–5]

There is a weird solemnity in the surroundings. Moonlight there is none, and the stars cast only a faint uncertain shimmer on the gliding water. The poplar groves come down to the waters' edge, and hem us in between walls of impenetrable gloom,

> "While, with a sorrowful deep sound,
> The river flows between."

Other sound there is none, save when at intervals, with startling suddeness, the sepulchral note of a night-owl calling to his fellow, or the human-like moan of a beaver, echoes across the stream. We are far from human habitation; and unless some wandering Indian has pitched his tent among the poplars, and, for aught we know, may be peering out of his leafy ambush as we go floating by, we are as completely isolated as if we were out in the middle of the sea. And yet there is something in the very stillness, and in the quiet murmur of the waters that soothes like the touch of a cool, soft hand upon a fevered brow. We are "near to Nature's heart," and the encompassing darkness is like the shadow of a brooding wing, beneath which we sink peacefully to rest. [pp. 135–36]

Visions of Natural Beauty

Wanderings of an Artist among the Indians of North America (1859)
Paul Kane

Towards evening, as we were approaching the place where we were to cross the river, I saw some buffaloes idly grazing in a valley, and as I wished to give a general idea of the beauty of the scenery which lies all along the banks of the Saskatchewan from this point to Edmonton, I sat down to make a sketch, the rest of the party promising to wait for me at the crossing place. It was the commencement of Indian summer; the evening was very fine, and threw that peculiar soft, warm haziness over the landscape, which is supposed to proceed from the burning of the immense prairies. The sleepy buffaloes grazing upon the undulating hills, here and there relieved by clumps of small trees, the unbroken stillness, and the approaching evening, rendered it altogether a scene of most enchanting repose. [p. 80]

Paul Kane, *Assiniboine Hunting Buffalo* **(1850s)**
The romance of the buffalo hunt.

Paul Kane, *Big Snake, a Blackfoot Chief, Recounting his War Exploits* **(1850s)**
Proud Indians of the Prairies.

Paul Kane, *Buffalo at Sunset* **(1850s)**
An idyllic wilderness.

Paul Kane, *Kee-akee-ka-saa-ka-wow,* **"The Man that gives the War Whoop"** **(n.d.)**
The Noble Savage.

Frederick Verner, *Sioux Encampment at Sunset* **(1881)**
In harmony with nature.

Frederick Verner, *Buffalo Grazing under a Moonrise* **(1887)**
The Mighty Buffalo: Monarchs of the Plains

Frederick Verner, *Bison Foraging in Blizzard* **(1909)**
Verner's rugged primeval wilderness.

Frederick Verner, *Indian Warrior Overlooking an Encampment* **(1914)**
A romantic and nostalgic look at the West.

The Fictitious Romantic West

Snowflakes and Sunbeams, or the Young Fur-Trader (1863)
Robert M. Ballantyne

It was a fine sight to see the boats depart for the North. It was a thrilling heart-stirring sight to behold these picturesque athletic men, on receiving the word of command from their guides, spring lightly into the long, heavy boats; to see them let the oars fall into the water with a loud splash; and then, taking their seats, give way with a will, knowing that the eyes of friends and sweethearts and rivals were bent earnestly upon them. It was a splendid sight to see boat after boat shoot out from the landing-place, and cut through the calm bosom of the river, as the men bent their sturdy backs, until the thick oars creaked and groaned on the gunwales, and flashed in the stream, more and more vigorously at each successive stroke, until their friends on the bank, who were anxious to see the last of them, had to run faster and faster in order to keep up with them, as the rowers warmed at their work, and made the water gurgle at the bows—their bright blue and scarlet and white trappings reflected in the dark waters in broken masses of colour, streaked with long lines of shining ripples, as if they floated on a lake of liquid rainbows. And it was a glorious thing to hear the wild, plaintive song, led by one clear, sonorous voice, that rang out, full and strong, in the still air, while, at the close of every two lines, the whole brigade burst into a loud enthusiastic chorus, that rolled far and wide over the smooth waters— telling of their approach to settlers beyond the reach of vision in advance, and floating faintly back, a last farewell, to the listening ears of fathers, mothers, wives, and sisters left behind. And it was interesting to observe how, as the rushing boats sped onwards past the cottages on shore, groups of men and women and children stood before the open doors, and waved adieu; while, ever and anon, a solitary voice rang louder than the others in the chorus; and a pair of dark eyes grew brighter, as a *voyageur* swept past his home, and recognized his little ones screaming farewell and seeking to attract their *sire's* attention by tossing their chubby arms or flourishing round their heads the bright vermilion blades of canoe-paddles. It was interesting, too, to hear the men shout as they ran a small rapid which occurs about the lower part of the settlement, and dashed in full career up to the Lower Fort—which stands about twenty miles down the river from Fort Garry—and then sped onward again with unabated energy, until they passed the Indian settlement, with its scattered wooden buildings and its small church; passed the last cottage on the bank; passed the low swampy land at the river's mouth; and emerged at last, as evening closed, upon the wide, calm, sea-like bosom of Lake Winnipeg. [pp. 95–96]

The spot on which the travellers encamped that evening overlooked one of those scenes in which vast extent, and rich, soft variety of natural objects, were united with much that was grand and savage. It filled the mind with the calm satisfaction that is experienced when one gazes on the wide lawns, studded with noble trees; the spreading fields of waving grain that mingle with stream and copse, rock and dell, vineyard and garden, of the cultivated lands of civilised men; while it produced that exulting throb of freedom which stirs man's heart to its centre, when he casts a first glance over miles and miles of broad lands that are yet unowned, unclaimed; that yet lie in the unmutilated beauty with which the beneficent Creator originally clothed them—far away from the well-known scenes of man's chequered history; entirely devoid of those ancient monuments of man's power and skill, that carry the mind back with feelings of awe to bygone ages; yet stamped with evidences of an antiquity more ancient still, in the wild primeval forests, and the noble trees that have sprouted and spread and towered in their strength for centuries— trees that have fallen at their posts, while others took their place, and rose and fell as they did, like long-lived sentinels, whose duty it was to keep perpetual guard over the vast solitudes of the great American Wilderness. [p. 171]

The Dog Crusoe and His Master
Robert M. Ballantyne

It was a great, a memorable day in the life of Dick Varley, that on which he first beheld the prairie,—the vast boundless prairie. He had heard of it, talked of it, dreamed about it, but he had never,—no, he had never realized it. 'Tis always thus. Our conceptions of things that we have not seen are almost invariably wrong. Dick's eyes glittered, and his heart swelled, and his cheeks flushed, and his breath came thick and quick.

"There it is," he gasped, as the great rolling plain broke suddenly on his enraptured gaze; "that's it—oh!—"

Dick uttered a yell that would have done credit to the fiercest chief of the Pawnees, and, being unable to utter another word, he swung his cap in the air and sprang like an arrow from a bow over the mighty ocean of grass. The sun had just risen to send a flood of golden glory over the scene; the horses were fresh, so the elder hunters, gladdened by the beauty of all around them, and inspired by the irresistible enthusiasm of their young companion, gave the reins to the horses and flew after him. It was a glorious gallop, that first headlong dash over the boundless prairie of the "far west!"

The prairies have often been compared, most justly, to the ocean. There is the same wide circle of space bounded on all sides by the horizon; there is the same swell, or undulation, or succession of long low unbroken waves that marks the ocean when it is calm; they are canopied by the same pure sky, and swept by the same untrammelled breezes. There are islands too—clumps of trees and willow-bushes,—which rise out of this grassy ocean to break and relieve its uniformity; and these vary in size and numbers as do the isles of ocean—being numerous in some places, while in others they are so scarce that the traveller does not meet one in a long day's journey. Thousands of beautiful flowers decked the green sward, and numbers of little birds hopped about among them. [p. 63–64]

Henri Julien, *The Sweet Grass Hills* **(1875)**
Civilization on the march into an untouched wilderness.

Hudson's Bay; or Everyday Life in the Wilds of North America (1848)
Robert M. Ballantyne

Imagine an immense extent of country, many hundred miles broad, and many hundred miles long, covered with dense forests, expanded lakes, broad rivers, and mighty mountains; and all in a state of primeval simplicity—undefaced by the axe of civilized man, and untenanted by aught save a few roving hordes of Red Indians, and myriads of wild animals. Imagine, amid this wilderness, a number of small squares, inclosing half-a-dozen wooden houses, and about a dozen men, and, between each of these establishments, a space of forest varying from fifty to three hundred miles long, and you will have a pretty correct idea of the Hudson's Bay Company's territories, and the number of, and distance between, their forts. The idea, however, may be still more correctly obtained, by imagining populous Great Britain converted into a wilderness and planted in the middle of Rupert's Land; the company would, in that case, build *three* forts in it, one at the Land's-end, one in Wales, and one in the Highlands; so that in Britain there would be but three hamlets, with a population of some thirty men, half-a-dozen women, and a few children! The company's posts extend, with these intervals between, from the Atlantic to the Pacific Ocean, and from within the Arctic Circle to the northern boundaries of the United States. [pp. 28–29]

The night is very dark, as the moon is hid by thick clouds, yet it occasionally breaks out sufficiently to illumine our path to Stemaw's wigwam, and to throw the shadows of the neighbouring trees upon the pale snow, which *crunches* under our feet as we advance, owing to the intense cold. No wind breaks the stillness of the night, or shakes the lumps of snow off the branches of the neighbouring pines or willows; and nothing is heard save the occasional crackling of the trees as the severe frost acts upon their branches. The tent at which we soon arrive is pitched at the foot of an immense tree, which stands in a little hollow where the willows and pines are luxuriant enough to afford a shelter from the north wind. Just in front, a small path leads to the river, of which an extensive view is had through the opening, showing the long fantastic shadows of huge blocks and mounds of ice cast upon the white snow by the flickering moonlight. A huge chasm, filled with fallen trees and mounds of snow, yawns on the left of the tent, and the ruddy sparks of fire which issue from a hole in its top throw this and the surrounding forest into deeper gloom. The effect of this wintry scene upon the mind is melancholy in the extreme — causing it to fly over the bleak and frozen plains, and visit again the warm fireside and happy faces in a far distant home; and yet there is a strange romantic attraction for the wild woods mingled with this feeling that gradually brings the mind back again, and makes us impatient to begin our walk with the Indian. Suddenly the deer-skin robe that covers the aperture of the wigwam is raised, and a bright stream of warm light gushes out, tipping the dark green points of the opposite trees, and mingling strangely with the paler light of the moon — and Stemaw stands erect in the front of his solitary home, to gaze a few moments on the sky and judge of the weather, as he intends to take a long walk before laying his head upon his capote for the night. He is dressed in the usual costume of the Cree Indians: a large leathern coat, very much overlapped in front, and fastened round his waist with a scarlet belt, protects his body from the cold. A small rat-skin cap covers his head, and his legs are cased in the ordinary blue cloth leggins. Large moccasins, with two or three pair of blanket socks, cover his feet, and a pair of fingerless mittens, made of deer-skin, completes his costume. [pp. 58–59]

On Viewing the Grave of the Murdered Scout (ca. 1874)
George F. Crofton

His grave was on the summit of a rocky hill, simply a pile of stones with a rough inscription on a slab of wood erected about 1869 by some trappers; it was in one of the most desolate spots on the prairie.

In utter, hopeless, trackless waste,
In solitude profound,
By a weird loneliness embraced,
The Scout's last rest we found.
A world of stillness so intense,
Save when the moaning blast,
Swept wailing o'er the plains immense,
Like requiems for the past.
So solemn in its vast expanse,
We shudder as we gaze,
O'er Solitudes' domains we prance,
With helpless, blank, amaze.
Have ever here in centuries past,
Conjecture asks in vain,
The busy feet of nations passed,
The sites of cities lain?
Has ever by some mighty throe,

Of Earth's convulsive womb,
A nation's pride been changed to woe,
Her whole extent a tomb.
Has ocean's roar but reigned supreme,
Ever, where now we stand?
But paltry specks on this vast scene,
Indeed, the Great Lone Land?
Sleep on brave Scout in peace sublime,
With awe we leave thy mound,
A daring, reckless life was thine,
A strange dark fate you found.
And yet, how many a wanderer's fate,
Long mourned by a stricken home,
Which fondly hoping, vainly wait,
Is known to God alone.

Annette; The Métis Spy: A Heroine of the N.W. Rebellion (1886)
Edmund Collins

The sun was hanging low in the clear blue over the prairie, as two riders hurried their ponies along a blind trail toward a distant range of purple hills that lay like sleepy watchers along the banks of the Red River.

The beasts must have ridden far, for their flanks were white with foam, and their riders were splashed with froth and mud.

"The day is nearly done, mon ami," said one, stretching out his arm and measuring the height of the sun from the horizon. "How red it is; and mark these blood-stains upon its face! It gives warning to the tyrants who oppress these fair plains; but they cannot read the signs."

There was not a motion anywhere in all the heavens, and the only sound that broke the stillness was the dull trample of the ponies' hoofs upon the sod. On either side was the wide level prairie, covered with thick, tall grass, through which blazed the purple, crimson and garnet blooms, of vetch and wild pease. The tiger lily, too, rose here and there like a sturdy queen of beauty with its great terra cotta petals, specked with umber-brown. Here and there, also, upon the mellow level, stood a clump of poplars or white oaks – prim like virgins without suitors, with their robes drawn close about them; but when over the unmeasured plain the wind blew, they bowed their heads gracefully, as a company of eastern girls when the king commands.

As the two horsemen rode silently around one of these clumps, there suddenly came through the hush the sound of a girl's voice singing. The song was exquisitely worded and touching, and the singer's voice was sweet and limpid as the notes of a bobolink. They marvelled much who the singer might be, and proposed that both should leave the path and join the unknown fair one. Dismounting, they fastened their horses in the shelter of the poplars, and proceeded on foot toward the point whence the singing came. A few minutes walk brought the two beyond a small poplar grove, and there, upon a fallen tree-bole, in the delicious cool of the afternoon, they saw the songstress sitting. She was a maiden of about eighteen years, and her soft, silky, dark hair was over her shoulders. In girlish fancy she had woven for herself a crown of flowers out of marigolds and daisies, and put it upon her head.

She did not hear the footsteps of the men upon the soft prairie, and they did not at once reveal themselves, but stood a little way back listening to her. She had ceased her song, and was gazing beyond intently. On the naked limb of a desolate, thunder-riven tree that stood apart from its lush, green-boughed neighbours, sat a thrush in a most melancholy attitude. Every few seconds he would utter a note of song, sometimes low and sorrowful, then in a louder key, and more plaintive, as if he were calling for some responsive voice from far away over the prairie.

"Dear bird, you have lost your mate, and are crying for her," the girl said, stretching out her little brown hand compassionately toward the crouching songster. "Your companions have gone to the South, and you wait here, trusting that your mate will come back, and not journey to summer lands without you. Is not that so, my poor bird? Ah, would that I could go with you where there are always flowers, and ever can be heard the ripple of little brooks. Here the leaves will soon fall, ah, me! and the daisies wither; and, instead of the delight of summer, we shall have only the cry of hungry wolves, and the bellowing of bitter winds above the lonesome plains. . . ."

She stood up, and raised her arms above her head yearningly. The autumn wind was cooing in her hair, and softly swaying its silken meshes.

"Farewell, my desolate one; may your poor little heart be gladder soon. Could I but be a bird, and you would have me for a companion, your lamenting should not be for long. We should journey, loitering and love-making all the long sweet way, from here to the South, and have no repining."

Turning around, she perceived two men standing close beside her. She became very confused, and clutched for her robe to cover her face, but she had strayed away among the flowers without it. Very deeply she blushed that the strangers should have heard her; and she spake not. [pp. 9–11]

"It is discourteous, perhaps, Mademoiselle, that I should not disclose to you who I am, even though the safety of my present undertaking demands that I should remain unknown."

"If Monsieur has good reasons, or any reasons, for withholding his name, I pray that he will not consider himself under any obligation to reveal it."

"It would be absurd to keep such a secret, Ma petite Brighteye, from the beautiful daughter of a man so prominent in our holy cause as Colonel Marton. You this evening entertain, Mademoiselle, none other than Louis Riel, the Metis chief." [p. 15]

F. B. Schell, *A Prairie Stream* **(1882)**
Beauty in the eyes of the beholder.

3

THE WEST,
THE NATION, AND THE EMPIRE
1845–1885

Nationalism was a powerful force in the nineteenth century. It inspired exploration of unknown regions of the world; it dictated international trade patterns; and it caused wars. Canadians were not immune to the spirit of nationalism, but it was more a by-product of union than an incentive toward it. Before 1867, the four colonies that would unite into Confederation—Nova Scotia, New Brunswick, Quebec, and Ontario— were either isolated from one another or, as in the case of Ontario and Quebec, existed in a state of tension. And each colony had its own history and tradition. They had not done great and unifying things together in the past—such as fighting a revolution—to give them a feeling of nationalism. When they united into a nation in 1867, they did so for practical economic, political, and strategic reasons rather than out of a feeling of nationalism. A common nationalism had still to grow, and it could only grow if there were something to unite Canadians.

The West as the Fount of National and Imperial Greatness

That something for many Canadians—especially English-speaking Canadians—was the West. This vast region held within it, according to national enthusiasts, sufficient natural resources and population potential to make Canada one of the most powerful nations of the world. Charles

Mair, a spokesman for Ontario interests in the North West, pointed out to Canadians in 1875: "The new Dominion should be the wedding of pure tastes, simple life, respect for age and authority, and the true principles of free government on this Continent. It stands, like a youth upon the threshold of his life, clear-eyed, clear-headed, muscular, and strong. Its course is westward. It has traditions and a history of which it may well be proud; but it has a history to make, a national sentiment to embody, and a national idea to carry out."[1] These aspirations could only be achieved in conjunction with the West. Canada needed the West to fulfill the promise of its motto, a nation that would stretch "from sea unto sea." More importantly, it needed the West to achieve its destiny as a great nation, proud to stand amongst other nations that may be greater in power but not in size or potential. The West would be the keystone in the arch of a great Canadian nation.[2]

Many English-speaking Canadians saw a transcontinental nation as only a stepping-stone to something greater — imperial grandeur. They envisioned Canada, and particularly the West, as the last vital link in a continuous chain through British territory that would tie Britain to her Pacific imperial possessions — an "all-red route to the Orient." The Canadian West, therefore, would be the means to ensure the future greatness of the British Empire.

Some English-Canadian imperialists went further, however, to suggest that the Canadian West would even be the centre of a new Britannic Empire. Taking as truth the eighteenth-century British philosopher Bishop George Berkeley's dictum, "Westward the Course of Empire Takes its Way," they saw Anglo-Saxon civilization advancing westward until ultimately its centre would be the Canadian West. Art historian Dawn Glanz explains this nineteenth-century theory of advancing civilization in *How the West Was Drawn* (1978): "From its origins in Mesopotamia, it had moved to Egypt, then to Greece, Rome, Europe, England, and finally across the Atlantic to [North] America."[3] Some Canadian imperialists were convinced that the Canadian West was best able to assume "the mantle of 'the Britain of the West'."[4] This new territory, lacking in tradition, free of archaic values, and unimpeded by a rigid class system, could become an Anglo-Saxon society superior to Britain itself. These Canadians were as much nationalists as they were imperialists, for they saw Canada's association with the Empire as the means to ensure Canadians a "sense of power"; and the West would be the new source of that national and imperial power.[5]

"Nova Britannia" was how Alexander Morris, the second lieutenant governor of Manitoba, envisioned the Canadian West in a book of the same title. "We believe," he wrote in 1859 in a speech composed to persuade Upper Canadians to acquire the West, "that looking at the territory, not from the contracted point of view of a trading company, but from the higher stand-point of Imperial and Colonial interests, we shall come, upon undoubted authority, to the moderate but positive conclusions that there are noble provinces in these territories well adapted for settlement,—provinces which will yet become important members of the New Britannic Empire which is quickly being built-up on these Northern shores."[6]

With these images of national greatness and imperial grandeur in mind, British North Americans would assault the Hudson's Bay Company in the 1850s and 1860s for its monopoly of the North West, purchase Rupert's Land in 1869-70, and incorporate the region into the nation.

The West as an Agricultural and Commercial Hinterland

Significant changes had occurred at mid-century to alter the image that Upper Canadians in the United Canadas (formed by the union of Upper and Lower Canada between 1840 and 1867) had of the North West from that of a wasteland on the fringe of civilization to that of a wealthy land capable of being the heart of a great nation. By the mid-1850s, all the good agricultural land in Upper Canada was under cultivation. Farmers of the future would face the prospect of having to subdivide existing farms into smaller units, or else leave for the American mid-west where good farm land still existed—unless a new area could be found elsewhere in North America. Spokesmen for farming interests in Upper Canada— notably George Brown, editor of the influential Toronto *Globe* and, after 1859, leader of the Reform Party in the United Assembly of the Canadas—believed in the agricultural potential of the North West. Brown had never been west to see for himself, but he projected that image of the region in his frequent editorials on the West in his newspaper throughout the 1850s and 1860s.[7] In his editorial of December 10, 1856, for example, he wrote: "The eagerness with which the Canadian public have taken up the question of extending their sovereign claims over the territories of the Hudson's Bay Company, is sufficient to show that the full time has arrived for acting in the matter. So long as there was a wide extent of country lying between the Company's forts and the Canadian settlements, there was little desire to go far beyond, and to plunge into the wilderness in search of new territory. Now, however, that almost every acre south of Lake Huron is sold, and the head waters of the Ottawa River have been reached by the Government Surveyor, we are looking about for new worlds to conquer." Brown was of the opinion that the North West should be Upper Canada's by "birthright." "The question which presents itself to us in Canada relates to the best method of taking possession of the vast and fertile territory which is our birthright, and which no power on earth can prevent us occupying."

For those Upper Canadians who could not be persuaded to take an interest in the North West for its agricultural potential, Brown held out the prospect of Canadians dominating this vast region as a hinterland for its commercial interests. By 1850, the United Canadas faced a bleak economic future, as "Little Englanders" in Britain convinced that country to abandon its mercantile system of trade, by which she had provided her colonies with manufactured goods in return for raw materials, in favour of free trade. Set adrift, the British North American colonies sought alternatives. One alternative was to work out a trade relationship with the United States similiar to that which they had with Britain. They succeeded in negotiating a Reciprocity Treaty with the United States in 1854. When the Americans refused to re-negotiate the Treaty in 1866, the British North Americans opted for what appeared to be the only alternative – to unite and trade among themselves. This in turn required building an indigenous commercial and industrial base within the country and a hinterland with a sufficient population to buy these manufactured goods once they were produced. The North West became that hinterland in the mind of central Canadian entrepreneurs. As historian Douglas Owram points out in his important study of the ideas of Upper Canadian expansionists, *The Promise of Eden*: "Expansionism did not contain any images of an Arcadian utopia such as ran through the American idea of the frontier. Trade would precede settlement; . . . and the potential for trade was almost invariably put in terms of the benefits that would accrue to the east."[8]

This image of the West as a hinterland of the United Canadas appeared strongest in the minds of Montreal, and especially Toronto, commercial interests in the 1850s and 1860s. George Brown wrote in *The Globe* on August 28, 1856: "Let the merchants of Toronto consider that if their city is ever to be made really great – if it is ever to rise above the rank of a fifth-rate American town – it must be by the development of the great British territory lying to the north and west." In another editorial of January 22, 1863, he reminded his fellow Upper Canadians:

> If Canada acquires this territory it will rise in a few years from a position of a small and weak province to be the greatest colony any country has ever possessed, able to take its place among the empires of the earth. The wealth of 400,000 square miles of territory will flow through our waters and be gathered by our merchants, manufacturers and agriculturalists. Our sons will occupy the chief places of this vast territory, we will form its institutions, supply its rulers, teach its schools, fill its stores, run its mills, navigate its streams. Every article of European manufacture, every pound of tropical produce will pass through our stores. Our seminaries of learning will be filled by its people. Our cities will be the centres of its business and education, its health and refinement. It will afford fields of enterprise for our youth. It is a bright prospect and its realization would be worthy of some sacrifice.

The people of the Ottawa Valley were also being dazzled by the promise of unlimited prosperity if their region could be linked to the great North West by either a canal or a railway system. Philip Vankoughnet, a candidate in the Ottawa Valley for the Legislative Council in 1856, envisioned the "products of China and the East, journeying down the Ottawa valley, and the Gulf of St. Lawrence on their way to Europe."[9]

Lending support to George Brown's arguments for the agricultural potential of the North West was the scientific data of the American climatologist Lorin Blodget. In his well-known book, *Climatology of the United States, and of the Temperate Latitudes of the North American Continent* (1857), he argued that climate was not a function of latitude alone but of geographical features. In this respect, western Canada was the North American equivalent of Poland and could therefore sustain unparalleled agricultural growth: "The commercial and industrial capacity" of the region was "gigantic, and but for the pernicious views entailed by the fur traffic as to the necessity of preserving it as a wilderness, it would long since have been opened to colonization."[10] His popular theory provided part of a growing scientific evidence necessary to justify Canadian expansion into the West.

Two major obstacles stood in the way of Canadians possessing the North West: the Hudson's Bay Company's monopoly, and the American's interest in possessing the territory. Attacks on the Hudson's Bay Company's rule of the area had been leveled as early as the 1750s by critics such as Arthur Dobbs. During the 1840s and 50s, such attacks occurred more frequently. In 1849, for example, James Edward Fitzgerald attacked the British author Robert Montgomery Martin for his denial that the land in the Hudson's Bay Company's possessions was suitable for settlement or that the Company deliberately discouraged progress. Fitzgerald accused the Company of deliberately spreading falsehoods about the North West in an effort to continue its monopoly of the region:

> The Company knows very well that as long as there is a general belief that the interior of the continent of America is of no value, so long they may feel secure in the possession of their privileges; and therefore the idea is circulated, that the whole country north of the 49th parallel of latitude, is a frozen wilderness, where human life can with difficulty be supported, and where the earth will not yield its accustomed fruits: and the same facts are assigned as the necessary and unavoidable cause of those awful and devastating famines, with all their fearful accompaniments of starvation and cannibalism, to which the miserable natives are periodically exposed.
>
> The Company have a direct interest at this moment in keeping up this erroneous idea.

Fitzgerald argued that "there is not a more favourable situation on the face of the earth for the employment of agricultural industry than the locality of the Red River." He agreed that only a small portion of the North West—the prairie district—was fit for settlement, but that that "small portion is a country sufficiently large and fertile to support all the population of Great Britain and all her dependencies."[11]

John McLean, a Hudson's Bay Company employee for twenty-five years, was of the same opinion. What retarded the growth of the Red River colony, he argued in 1849, was not infertile soil or inclement weather but the lack of a sizeable market outside the region for the abundant produce within. "If a sure market were secured to the colonists of Red River, they would speedily become the wealthiest yeomanry in the world." Only the Hudson's Bay Company's continued dominance of the region prevented that from happening. If the region became a Crown colony, McLean pointed out, then "Assineboine would become a great and flourishing colony—the centre of civilization and Christianity to the surrounding tribes."[12]

Previously, such attacks would have had little effect, as they went against the prevailing image of the West as a wasteland. By the 1850s, however, Fitzgerald and McLean expressed opinions that were becoming common-place. These attacks, with their positive image of the North West for agricultural settlement and commerce, along with other pressures, caused the British House of Commons to establish a Select Committee in 1857 to study the Hudson's Bay Company's affairs, with the ultimate issue being whether to renew its trading license in Rupert's Land or to revoke it.

Chief Justice Draper was the representative for the United Canadas at the hearings, although he admitted that he knew little about the region. He relied on William Dawson and Alfred Roche, two Canadian enthusiasts of the West and employees of the Crown Land Department, for much of his information. Roche was so committed to Canadian acquisition of the North West that he presented his own testimony before the Committee. He made it clear that in his opinion no obstacle to agricultural settlement existed.

In the end, the government of the United Canadas lay claim through the Select Committee to its right to annex sections of the North West, but it did so without substantial knowledge of the region. In fact, what emerged from the hearings was the realization that the North West was indeed a *terra incognita*. Both the British government and the government of the United Canadas decided, therefore, to sponsor separate expeditions to the West to acquire objective, scientific, detailed information on the region's soil, climate, and natural resources.

The Image of a "Fertile Belt"

Henry Youle Hind, a self-assured professor of chemistry and geology at Trinity College, Toronto, and Simon J. Dawson, a surveyor, headed the Canadian expedition. Their mandate was to examine the North West in light of its agricultural potential; thus, they went already predisposed to look at the region other than for its traditional fur-trading activity. Not surprisingly, they found what they were looking for—a "Fertile Belt" of rich agricultural land forming an arc from the Red River colony to the foothills of the Rockies. Hind also found a "desert" south of this arc, but used the "desert" region (which he claimed existed mainly in the United States) so as to stress the positive image of the remainder of the west as an agricultural paradise. On the map accompanying his *Report*, this "Fertile Belt" was accentuated in yellow against the white of the map; in the text, he declared its presence in bold capitals: "IT IS A PHYSICAL REALITY OF THE HIGHEST IMPORTANCE TO THE INTERESTS OF BRITISH NORTH AMERICA THAT THE CONTINUOUS BELT CAN BE SETTLED AND CULTIVATED FROM A FEW MILES WEST OF THE LAKE OF THE WOODS TO THE PASSES OF THE ROCKY MOUNTAINS, AND ANY LINE OF COMMU-NICATION, WHETHER BY WAGGON ROAD OR RAILROAD, PASSING THROUGH IT, WILL EVENTUALLY ENJOY THE GREAT ADVANTAGE OF BEING FED BY AN AGRICULTURAL POPULATION FROM ONE EXTREMITY TO ANOTHER."[13]

It is unnecessary to point out that the "Fertile Belt" existed before Hind "discovered" it. The West had not changed physically over time; only the image had, from that of a "wasteland" to that of an "agricultural utopia." Existing sources yielded new and now optimistic information on the region. Hind himself realized the importance of his expedition in making the North West "no longer a terra incognita." His scientific findings had provided the necessary "proof" of the West's physical and economic potential for national greatness. He found what he had been conditioned by the image-makers to find; he had discovered a "new West."

An Advancing Civilization

Humphrey Lloyd Hime, the first photographer of western Canada, accompanied Hind on his expedition.[14] Photography added an authenticity to visual images of the West that contrasted with the more subjective depiction of artists who often painted according to the whims of artistic licence. But photographers also reflect the prevailing mythology of their society. Their preconceived notions dictated what they chose, and chose not, to photograph, as much as such preconceptions affected what artists chose to paint. Edward Cavell notes in the introduction to *Journeys to the Far West*, a collection of historical photographs: "Cast in the same imperial mould, the photographers tended to substantiate the observations and attitudes of the writers."[15] Early photographers, like Hime, chose to record only the triumphs of the white man in bringing "civilization" to the West. Unlike the romantic painters Kane and Verner, who were at the same time depicting the Indians of the prairies as "noble savages," a proud, independent, and strong people, Hime photographed the western Indian—when he photographed the native people at all—in quaint poses, passively and willingly accepting the white man. He preferred to photograph scenes of settlement—evidence of the "advancing" West, prepared and welcoming for thousands of potential immigrants. Later photographers, such as Benjamin Baltzly of the Geological Survey of Canada in 1871, and Charles George Horetzky who had been the official photographer for the Fleming-Grant expedition and a member of the Canadian Pacific Railway Surveys between 1871-79, did the same. Their photographs reflected the prevailing image of the West.[16]

The artist William G. R. Hind, brother of Henry Youle Hind, also contributed to the image of the West as the fount of British civilization.[17] He was one of a group of forty-four "Overlanders" who left Toronto in 1862 for the Cariboo goldfields of British Columbia by the old fur traders' route across the prairies and the mountains. They were the largest single group ever to cross the prairies through British territory before the building of the railway. Hind recorded the trip through a series of paintings which gave accurate and detailed descriptions of what he saw. Hind also painted scenes of the Red River colony in 1869, one of the few precise visual sources of Métis society at the time of the Canadian takeover. In contrast to Kane's romantic image of the West, Hind emphasized, through pre-Raphaelite techniques, a punctilious depiction of the West. He wanted to paint in scientific precision, more as a recorder than an interpreter of nature.

American threats to annex the North West were the other obstacle, besides the monopoly of the Hudson's Bay Company, to Canadian possession. That the Americans had their own expansionist ambitions in the West was common knowledge in the Canadas of the 1850s. James Polk had campaigned for the American presidency in 1844 on the promise of "54/40 or fight"—total control of the Oregon territory or war with Britain. As American settlers pushed westward into the valleys of the Mississippi, Ohio, and Missouri Rivers in the 1850s, they turned a longing eye northward to Rupert's Land. In 1860 James W. Taylor made an excursion into the southern region of the Hudson's Bay Company territory on behalf of the Minnesota State government to judge its potential for American settlers and to acquire knowledge about the receptiveness of Red River settlers to American control of their area. Taylor agreed with a New York Chamber of Commerce report that the Red River Valley was equal in fertility to the St. Lawrence and Mississippi Valleys. "In other words, it is admirably fitted to become the seat of a numerous, hardy, and prosperous community."[18]

Minnesota expansionists were forever trying to convince the American government to advance into British territory and incorporate the region into the American West as part of the nation's "Manifest Destiny"—a belief that the United States was destined by God to control the entire North American continent.[19] As late as 1875, by which time Canada had already purchased Rupert's Land, the exuberant Charles Mair warned of American annexationist ambitions: "Many features of recent American diplomacy and legislation point to an eager desire to encroach upon our rights, and to cramp and confine our trade. The purchase of Alaska [in 1867], as an act of national policy, can only be explained in one way, and the journals of the Western States are almost a unit in insolent opinion as to the future of our North-west Territories."[20]

To secure Canadian control over the West and to integrate this hinterland region into the national edifice required a railway to the Pacific. Without a rail line, the West was lost—isolated from the rest of British North America by a thousand miles of Precambrian Shield; without the West, British North America could never rise to national greatness. As one observer put it, Canadians had the choice, "whether this country shall ultimately become a Petty State, or one of the Great Powers of the earth."[21] The West would decide that choice, and the railroad would be the means of choosing.

Visions of a transcontinental railroad through British North American territory prevailed as early as the appearance of railroads themselves. The railroad symbolized progress, national greatness and, ultimately, Anglo-Saxon civilization. It was technological improvement moving west. Thomas Keefer, an engineer and the author of the *Philosophy of Railroads* (1849), expressed a truism of the times when he wrote: "as a people we may as well . . . attempt to live without books or newspapers, as without Railroads."[22] Railroads were seen as the panacea to a nation's ills. Although railroads in the established colonies ran the governments into considerable debt, the belief prevailed that railroads meant prosperity. In this euphoric atmosphere, British North Americans envisioned a "band of steel" running across the northern half of North America "from ocean to ocean." In fact, F. A. Wilson and A. B. Richards, two railway enthusiasts who wrote *Britain Redeemed and Canada Preserved* (1850), proposed a railroad that would run in a straight line from the Pacific to a point east of Lake Superior and then on an angle to the St. Lawrence, irrespective of the fact that their proposed route missed every established community in Canada West! As they noted, "pictures of certain prosperity and grandeur and enterprise crowd upon the mind with the prospect of a wilderness peopled—a remote ocean converted to an immediate and familiar high-road."[23]

Two arguments supported the vision: railroads were the vehicles of national greatness; they were also the source of imperial grandeur by providing "an all-red-route to the Orient" and the riches of China, Japan, and India. Major Robert Carmichael-Smyth, a forty-nine-year-old British engineer and career soldier since the age of sixteen, pointed out in 1849 in a public letter to the Rt. Honourable Earl Grey, Governor of the Canadas, that a railroad through British North America "would enable the merchants of Great Britain and of Europe to communicate in less than a month with one of the most important points in the Pacific, to say nothing of the direct communication to Japan and China, and the whole route be under the Imperial Government of Great Britain."[24] Millington Henry Synge, an Irish subaltern in the Royal Engineers and a relative of John Millington Synge, the Irish playwright, was of the same opinion, and added that a railroad to the North West would integrate the region with the other British North American colonies and ultimately with Britain, and thus stem the disintegration of the Empire.[25] He proposed a series of canals through the Rockies—"steps of still water" as he described it in his more imaginative moments, the idea no doubt a result of the fact that he was stationed at Bytown on the Rideau Canal. Thomas Rawlings, a British railroad enthusiast writing in 1865, compared the building of a transcontinental railroad to the search for a Northwest Passage to the Orient. Both would enhance the importance of British North America in Britain's eyes.

The need for a railroad became the chief incentive for Confederation. To undertake such a gargantuan task—a railroad that, when completed, would be the longest in the world—required major financing and a strong, united effort on the part of the existing colonies; this meant a united nation. Thus, expansionism and nationalism became intertwined. Canadians, in other words, had their own version of "Manifest Destiny." For one thing, British financial interests were reluctant to invest in such a major undertaking unless a single strong government existed in British North America to handle the project. For another, all the resources of the existing colonies were needed to accomplish such a task. These were strong incentives for Confederation.

Looked at from this perspective, the evolution of Canada as a nation takes on a different sequence than the traditional one. Traditionally, the chronology runs as follows: Confederation in 1867; acquisition of the West in 1869–70; then the building of a transcontinental railway between 1871 and 1885 to tie the nation together. In this scenario, the key event is Confederation, from which the other events follow. From the new perspective, the first stage in Canada's evolution to nationhood was an interest in the West as a means of achieving national and imperial greatness. When British North Americans became convinced of the West's potential, then came an interest in building a railway to link East and West. This major undertaking required a united nation, hence Confederation. Here the significant initial event in Canadian nation building was an interest in the acquiring of the West. That interest in turn resulted from a new and more positive image of the West that emerged in the romantic and nationalistic milieu of the 1850s and 60s.

Thus, when a new group of British railway and general investment promoters, with Edward Watkins as their chief negotiator, came forward in 1863 to purchase a controlling interest in the Hudson's Bay Company for the purpose of acquiring the North West and building a railway across it, they emphasized in their prospectus the great agricultural potential of the area for settlement. "The soil of this portion of the territory is fertile, producing in abundance wheat and other cereal crops, and is capable of sustaining a numerous population."[26] The scheme fell through, but not without convincing the British and British North American politicians of the great national and imperial potential of the West if freed from the Hudson's Bay Company.

The West as the Linchpin of the Nation

Once Rupert's Land was incorporated into Canada as the Province of Manitoba and the North West Territories in 1870, the focus shifted away from the West as a hinterland of central Canada to the West as the fountainhead of national greatness and imperial grandeur. Enthusiasts wanted to prove that this region was indeed as great as the romantic and expansionist writers had claimed. By showing its innate strengths, it was seen less as an appendage and more as the linchpin of the nation and the empire. The popular song "Manitoba" projected that image by describing the new province as "the bond that binds our great Dominion, East to West from foam to foam." John Cameron expressed in poetry his view of the importance of the West for Canada's self-image:

> O'er our rich acres of vast prairie,
> Our hopes as boundless, and our souls as free,
> Far as the heart can wish, the fancy roam,
> Survey our empire, and behold our home.[27]

The Reverend George Monro Grant, on his 1872 tour with Sandford Fleming, was struck at the national spirit and optimism that pervaded the West. He had gone on the tour already an ardent enthusiast of Confederation and a transcontinental nation. He wanted to believe in the West's potential for settlement as a means to fulfill his aspiration for Confederation. He had, in fact, collected three thousand dollars in 1868 to help the Red River settlers during the devastating grasshopper plague of that year. As Mary Quayle Innis points out in her vignette of Grant in *Travellers West* (1973), "The railroad motivated the journey; settlement was continuously in his thoughts. He looked everywhere for possible farming land and likely town sites, attacking the west with the energy and vigour which marked his whole life."[28] What he saw only reaffirmed his predisposition to see the West's potential. Near the end of his life he confessed: "This journey resolved the uneasy doubt in my mind as to whether or not Canada had a future; for from the day we left Collingwood till we reached Victoria, the great possibilities of our great North-West impressed us." He had predicted at the time of the trip: "This Great West will, in the future, probably manifest this spirit more than even the Eastern Provinces, and so be the very backbone of the new Dominion."[29] Everywhere Grant looked in the West, he saw visions of material wealth as the basis of national greatness. *Ocean to Ocean* was his contribution to domesticating the West; he described the land in terms of settlement potential more than in terms of innate beauty.

The West through Nationalist Eyes

A group of national artists—among them Lucius O'Brien, John Fraser, F. M. Bell-Smith, J. C. Forbes, and William Brymner—arose in the 1880s to link the West to the nation artistically.[30] Many of these artists, members of the recently established Royal Canadian Academy, obtained free rail passes from William Cornelius Van Horne, CPR General Manager, in exchange for their painting scenes along the rail lines. The vast landscape and the rugged mountains became symbolic of national grandeur. As Edward Cavell and Dennis Reid note in *When Winter Was King*, "There was more than a small amount of Victorian boosterism in their vision; and the railway entrepreneurs who saw in their images of a vast, dynamic land the symbols of all they wished to accomplish with their business efforts, patronized them heavily."[31] The "ribbon of steel" became the practical and symbolic means to fuse the two, by providing the physical means to bind the nation together. The trilogy of the West, the railroad and the nation became one in the minds of early Canadian promotional artists and, through their paintings, in the minds of ordinary Canadians. Lucius O'Brien, one of the better-known artists, made the link explicit:

> If literature and politics have so far failed to awaken in Canadians any lively national spirit, surely the pictures of all that glorious land, a veritable promised land, that is ours, must send the blood tingling through our veins with wild enthusiasm and wilder hopes.[32]

The West became the inspiration for their national vision.

Governors-General also led promotional tours to link the West to the nation. These vice-regal visits were highly publicized, and their optimistic speeches about the West widely reported; their views took on importance because of their status. In 1877 Lord Dufferin toured Manitoba, and gave his impressions in a much publicized speech at Winnipeg. Manitoba he described as "the key-stone of that mighty arch of sister provinces which spans the continent from the Atlantic to the Pacific . . . whose illimitable dimensions alike confound the arithmetic of the surveyor and the verification of the explorer."[33]

Four years later, an even more well-advertised tour by the young and attractive Marquis of Lorne, the new Governor-General and son-in-law to Queen Victoria, focused national attention on the West. He travelled to Portage la Prairie by train, then the "end of the steel," and from there westward by horse-drawn vehicles. A North West Mounted Police detachment accompanied him as a symbol of Canadian authority as well as Poundmaker, the Cree chieftain, for the Battleford-Edmonton leg of the tour—a sad and ironic commentary on the subjectivity of the Western Indians. Lorne pointed out: "Unknown a few years ago except for some differences which had arisen amongst its people, we see Winnipeg now with a population unanimously joining in happy concord, and rapidly lifting it to the front rank amongst the commercial centres of the continent. We may look in vain elsewhere for a situation . . . whose natural advantages promise so great a future as that which seems ensured to Manitoba and to Winnipeg, the Heart city of our Dominion." He recorded his most vivid impressions in verse:

Away to the West! Westward ho! Westward ho!
Where over the prairies the summer winds blow.

The West for you boys! where God has made room
For field and for city, for plough and for loom.
The West for you girls! for our Canada deems
Love's home better luck than a gold-seeker's dreams.
Away! and your children shall bless you, for they
Shall rule o'er land fairer than Cathay.[34]

Accompanying the Marquis of Lorne's entourage was Sydney Prior Hall, special artist for the illustrated journal, the *Graphic*, and an acquaintance of the governor-general.[35] He had accompanied royalty on earlier tours. His mission was to arouse British interest in the North West as a place of settlement and as a means to link this area to Britain for effective imperial trade. His numerous drawings along the way depicted a rich land waiting to be settled, and an Indian population already brought under submission to British rule. In fact, one of Hall's greatest paintings was of the historic meeting of the Marquis of Lorne with Crowfoot, chief of the Blackfoot Indians, Crowfoot's fellow chiefs, and Bullhead, chief of the Sarcee Indians. The painting captured on canvas the national and imperial control of the West—once the home of the native people.

Alexander Begg, a migrant from Upper Canada and long-time resident writer of the North West, summed up the national and imperial accomplishments in the region in a paper delivered in 1886, on the eve of the completion of the transcontinental railroad:

Previous to 1870 the country had been regarded as a land fit only for the hunter and trapper; and the fur traders knowing that the advent of civilisation meant the destruction of the fur trade, spared no pains to circulate the idea that it was a cold, inhospitable, and barren country. This, combined with the imperfect means of communication, was undoubtedly the cause of its remaining isolated and sparsely populated for so many years. . . . Its productiveness and adaptability to settlement only began to dawn upon the minds of people after it became a recognized portion of the Dominion. . . . [A]ll at once the Dominion of Canada found that in the Great North-West they had secured an estate of inestimable value, the development of which would bring about an expansion of the resources of the whole Dominion such as had never been dreamt of by even the most sanguine, when Confederation was first contemplated. . . .

He went on to add:

The character of our great national work is Imperial as much as Canadian. . . . My humble work on this side of the Atlantic is to assist in placing a guard of British subjects — of honest, sturdy settlers along that line, who will protect it from end to end by the happy arts of peace, and keep the way open for England should she ever find it necessary to use it in defending her rich possessions in the East, or to preserve the integrity of the Empire as a whole, and of this humble work, my lord, ladies, and gentlemen, I am proud.[36]

Thus, with Canada's acquisition of the West and the integration through a transcontinental railroad of the region into the nation and into the empire as the promising jewel, the stage was set for a new image of the West in the settlement period. Building on the romantic image of an Edenic West and the expansionist image of the West as the embodiment of national greatness and imperial grandeur, enthusiasts now created the image of the utopian West — the "promised land," "the last best West" where the possibility still existed for immigrants to create a perfect society.

The West as the Fount of National and Imperial Greatness

The New Canada: Its Resources and Productions (1875)
Charles Mair

I have now sketched, perhaps with more rapidity than exactness, the leading features of a territory which, according to our management of it, will either make of us a great and powerful nation, or extinguish our political existence altogether.

Do we faint at the portals of a realm so vast; or does the contemplation and possession of so much material grandeur lift our minds to the plane of more strenuous efforts and higher duties than have enriched our history in the past? Shall it be our gracious privilege to pioneer its wondrous slopes, to erect mighty provinces, and honeycomb them with enterprise, and invite the yeomanry of Europe to come and share with us our fertile soil, and our political estate? Or shall it be the privilege of an obdurate and jealous nationality to seal it with a mucilage of iron until the swift extension of American settlement, and the intrusive fingers of American ambition, grasp it from our keeping for ever? [pp. 160–61]

There was a time when there was no fixed principle or national feeling in Canada; when men were Englishmen, Scotchmen, Irishmen, or Frenchmen, and when to be a Canadian was almost to hang the head. But that time has passed away. Young Canada has come to the front, and we are now a nation, with a nation's duties to perform, privileges to maintain, and honour to protect. That national sentiment which has yet to defend the "meteor flag" from the Atlantic to the Pacific, is opening amongst us like a flower. All true men will carefully water the plant; all wise men will assiduously nourish its growth. Its vegetation has, indeed, been slow. Individual nationalities have militated against it. Local jealousies and heartburnings here, and mediaeval politics there, have trammelled its growth and screened it from the light. But its power and cohesiveness are being felt at last, and already is it binding the scattered communities of British America together in the bonds of a common cause, a common language, and a common destiny. . . .

This, then, is the light which we must cause to shine before men and before nations; the abstract of our national life and ideas; the concrete feeling and inspiration of the country, which Canadians must project into the fertile immensity of the west. It is not they only, but they first, who should carry to the Saskatchewan and the Athabasca our language and our laws, establish our Provinces, and lay the groundwork of that national feeling without which we can never become eminent as a nation.

And what a noble heritage is before them! An atmosphere of crystal, a climate suited above all others to develop the broad shoulder, the tense muscle, and the clear brain, and which will build up the most herculean and robust nation upon earth. Mighty rivers whose turbid streams drain half a continent, and bury themselves in the Northern Ocean. Measures of coal and iron, the sources of England's material greatness, and which will make any nation great which can use them aright, almost locked together. Above all, the hope of the despairing poor of the world, a boundless ocean of land, diversified by rolling hills, by lakes and woods, or swelling into illimitable plain. The haunt of the Indian, the bison, and the antelope, waiting with majestic patience for the flocks and the fields, the schools, the churches, the Christian faith and love of freedom of the coming men. [pp. 163–64]

Nova Britannia (1859)
Alexander Morris

Above us, again, is that vast expanse claimed by the Hudson's Bay adventurers, which will yet, and possibly soon, be inhabited by a large population, comprising as it does, 3,060,000 square miles.

This great country cannot much longer remain unoccupied; and if we do not proceed to settle it the Americans will appropriate it, as they did Oregon. Without entering into the question of the alleged vices in the charter by which that powerful company holds its possessions, and the mode of adjudicating thereon, there are certain practical measures which should be at once adopted. A means of communication by road and water, for summer and winter use, should be opened between Lake Superior and the Red River settlement; and that settlement should be placed under the jurisdiction of Canada, with power to this Province to colonize the territory. This power should at once be given, and will doubtless be conceded on application. This obtained, and a settlement of 7,000 souls added to our population as a centre of operations, steps can be taken for obtaining more accurate information as to the nature of the immense tract of territory, of which a large part once belonged to the Hundred Partners of Old France, and which, though believed to be the property of Canada, is now held by the Hudson's Bay Company. The great valley of the Saskatchewan should form the subject of immediate attention. Enough is known to satisfy us that in the territory commonly known as the Hudson's Bay Territory there is a vast region well adapted for becoming the residence of a large population. Once the Red River settlement is opened to our commerce, a wide field extends before our enterprise; and those who recollect or have otherwise become familiar with the struggles, forty years ago, of the settlers in Western Canada, and the painful, toilsome warfare with which they conquered that rising portion of the Province from the wilderness, will regard the task of colonization as a comparatively light one.

The press has for some time been teeming with articles on the subject of this Territory, and has done good service thereby; and, though there is not opportunity here to enter upon the subject at length, yet, while not going so far as those who would paint all that Teritory—some of it bleak and inhospitable enough—as a Paradise, I hesitate not to assert there are many millions of acres richly arable, and possessed of a climate milder than our own. [pp. 25–26]

Imperial as well as colonial interests urgently demand the opening up of that vast stretch of rich agricultural territory of which the Red River "holds the key." Apart from the arable areas on the highway between Canada and the Red River, that settlement forms a nucleus round which will gather a dense population scattered over those vast prairies, covered with the rankest luxuriance of vegetation, and holding out to settlers rich inducements to go in and possess the land. Should such a "Paradise of fertility" as this remain longer locked up? Will the gathering of a few peltries compensate for the withdrawal of such a region from the industry of our race? Assuredly not. The knell of arbitrary rule has been rung. [pp. 29–30]

But time does not permit the dwelling longer on this relic of antiquity. It will suffice to express my confident belief that Canada has only to express in firm but respectful tones her demands as to that vast territory, and these will be cheerfully acceded to by Great Britain. Those demands should be ripely considered, and so matured as to evince, not a mere grasping thirst of territorial aggrandizement, but a large-spirited and comprehensive appreciation of the requirements of the country, and a proper sense of the responsibilities to be assumed in regard to the well-being of the native and other inhabitants, and the due development of the resources of the territory. In such a spirit our statesmen will I trust be found acting. The position of our Province, too, is to be weighed. To a large portion of the territory we have an indubitable legal claim; to another portion the Crown of Britain would be entitled; but all that is adapted for settlement should be placed under the jurisdiction of representative government, and any further extension of the rights of the Company to trade in the more northerly regions should be subjected to the approval or control of colonial authorities. The subject is not without its difficulties; but, I doubt not, these can all be satisfactorily overcome, and the interests of the whole Empire imperiously demand their prompt and satisfactory adjustment. [p. 32]

Our Northern rising nationality has an ample field before it—a brilliant future in the distance. To occupy that field—to attain to that future in all its grandeur—the people of British North America must take high views of their plain and manifest responsibilities. They must evince an adequate appreciation of their duties, and must possess a thorough knowledge of the advantages which they possess, and of the vast resources which Providence has placed at their disposal, in order that they may advance steadily toward that high position among the nations which they may yet attain—in order that they may enter upon the full fruition of that rich inheritance of civil and religious liberty, and of high social and political privileges, which is their birthright as an offshoot of the three united nations who compose the British people.

It is, then, under the influence of such trains of thought, and with such objects in view, that I ask you to-night to travel with me up the Ottawa Valley, and over the trail of the enterprising adventurers of the old Canadian North-West Company, and, taking our stand there, judge for ourselves, like the Israelitish spies, of the character of that section of a future great empire, which has for a century past been claimed as the domain of a company of merchants—the vast preserve which has been so carefully guarded from the encroachments of modern civilization, and which is popularly known as the HUDSON'S BAY TERRITORIES. [p. 53]

The West as an Agricultural and Commercial Hinterland

The Great North West (1856)
Toronto *Globe*

The question which presents itself to us in Canada relates to the best method of taking possession of the vast and fertile territory which is our birthright, and which no power on earth can prevent us occupying. In the adoption of our course of action, attempts will no doubt be made to influence us for the benefit of the monopoly. Members of the government and its organists in the press, who were a few days ago very warm in their support of this scheme, have changed their tone wonderfully within that time. The wily and wealthy Company which maintains military control over a great territory, and subordination amid thousands of employees, will not suffer anything to be done in Canada prejudicial to their interests, if money or influence can affect the decisions of Ministers or members of the press. From the [Toronto] *Leader*, we learn that the monopolists are willing to give up a slice of territory for a consideration, but hope to retain their exclusive right of trading throughout the remaining portions. We are not informed how much they are willing to give, but that is of little importance. It is the duty of the Canadian public to have it established at once, that no part of this continent is to be considered closed to their enterprise, and that if they can establish a profitable trading connection with the Mackenzie River, or the Fraser River, or the Moose River, they are at liberty to do so. The *Leader* says that the Company exercises a control over the territory which the Province could not do; but we entirely dissent from the statement. We are quite as well able to preserve the peace of our borders against hostile Indians as the United States; and it will be strange, indeed, if the Aborigines were not better satisfied with our rule than that of the Company. . . .

Lake Superior and the Northern Country (1850)
Toronto *Globe*

Our present purpose is not, however, with the validity of the Hudson Bay Company's claim to the country north of the Canadian line, — but to call attention to the value of that region, and the vast commercial importance to the country and especially to this section, which must ere long, attach to it. The too-general impression entertained is, that the territory in question is a frozen wilderness, incapable of cultivation, and utterly unfit for European colonization. This impression was undoubtedly set afloat, and has been maintained by the Company for its own very evident purposes; so long as that opinion could be kept up, their charter was not likely to be disturbed. But light has been breaking in on the subject, in spite of their efforts to keep it out. Europeans unconnected with the Company, and servants of the Company with whom ruptures have occurred, have, from time to time, been dropping information on the capabilities of the soil, and we believe it is now established to the satisfaction of all who have studied the subject, that there is an immense tract of most valuable land immediately north of Upper Canada, which will, ere long yield a rich return to the hardy pioneer of the forest.

The North West (1863)
Toronto *Globe*

Nature seems to have marked out the vast and fertile valleys of North-West British North America, from their extent and the character of their climate and soil, to be the chief food-producing region on this continent. They appear to be more suited for this purpose than even the Western States, lying farther south, whose wheat-productiveness, some writers tell us, is already showing signs of exhaustion. That such a region should remain a wilderness in the hands of a fur-hunting company, is an outrage against common sense and the interests of humanity.

The Image of a "Fertile Belt"

Climatology of the United States, and of the Temperate Latitudes of the North American Continent (1857)
Lorin Blodget

The assertion may at first appear unwarranted, but it is demonstrable that an area, not inferior in size to the whole United States east of the Mississippi, now almost wholly unoccupied, lies west of the 98th meridian and above the 43d parallel, which is perfectly adapted to the fullest occupation by cultivated nations. The west and north of Europe are there reproduced, with the exceptions caused by vertical configuration only; and important as this feature of configuration is in giving us a lofty mountain boundary on the west, we may charge much of disadvantage to that account and still leave all that is here claimed—an immense and yet unmeasured capacity for occupation and expansion. By reference to the illustration of the distribution of heat we see that the cold at the north of the great lakes does not represent the same latitude farther west, and that beyond them the thermal lines rise as high in latitude, in most cases, as at the west of Europe. . . .

The parallel in regard to the advancement of American States here may be drawn with the period of the earliest trans-Alpine Roman expansion, when Gaul, Scandinavia, and Britain were regarded as inhospitable regions, fit only for barbarian occupation. The enlightened nations then occupied the latitudes near the Mediterranean, and the richer northern and western countries were unopened and unknown. Climate is indisputably the decisive condition, and when we find the isothermal of 60° for the summer rising on the interior American plains to the 61st parallel, or fully as high as its average position for Europe, it is impossible to doubt the existence of favorable climates over vast areas now unoccupied. This favorable comparison may be traced for the winter also, and in the averages for the year. [p. 530]

An Examination of the Charter and Proceedings of the Hudson's Bay Company (1849)
James Edward Fitzgerald

The Company know very well that as long as there is a general belief that the interior of the continent of America is of no value, so long they may feel secure in the possession of their privileges; and therefore the idea is circulated, that the whole country north of the 49th parallel of latitude, is a frozen wilderness, where human life can with difficulty be supported, and where the earth will not yield its accustomed fruits: and the same facts are assigned as the necessary and unavoidable cause of those awful and devastating famines, with all their fearful accompaniments of starvation and cannibalism, to which the miserable natives are periodically exposed.

The Company have a direct interest at this moment in keeping up this erroneous idea.

There is a good example of how the facts of the case may be distorted, for interested motives, in the representations made at first about the country in which the Red River settlement is situated. The North-West Company saw at once that the settlement was directed against, and would be fatal to, their trade; and so we have, in their efforts to cry it down, frequent assertions of the impossibility of founding a settlement in so remote and desolate a country. Yet experience has shewn that there is not a more favourable situation on the face of the earth for the employment of agricultural industry than the locality of the Red River. As far as the produce of the soil is concerned, the settlers revel in abundance. [p. 114]

Now it may be quite true that only a small portion of the Hudson's Bay Company's territories is fit for colonization, and indeed for anything except the chase; but it may be, and *is* true, that that small portion is a country sufficiently large and fertile to support all the population of Great Britain and all her dependencies. [p. 120]

The part of the possessions of the Hudson's Bay Company which is habitable and applicable for settlement, is the Prairie district—a broad belt stretching from Lake Superior, in a north-westerly direction, to the

Rocky Mountains. It is a country of varied features: immense plains, hills, lakes, and woods, are chequered over its surface, abounding with every animal and fish which contribute to the support of man in his savage state, and which, therefore, render the advancement of civilized man into the wilderness a matter comparatively neither of difficulty nor of expense. [p. 289]

Report from the Select Committee on the Hudson's Bay Company (1857)

4548. *Chairman.*] The Committee wish that paper to be put in? (*The Witness delivered in the same.*)—I have a copy of a petition from the Red River, which has been presented to the Parliament in Canada.

4549. Mr. *Christy.*] What is the nature of the petition which you have from the Red River?—It is stating certain grievances, and asking to be annexed to the Canadian territory.

4550. I should rather have asked you to whom it is addressed?—It is addressed to the Parliament of Canada; one petition to the Upper House, and one to the Lower House, in the usual form.

4551. What is the date of it?—In April of this year.

4552. By whom is it signed?—I have not the signatures here; but it is signed by, I believe, about 600.

4553. Persons resident at Red River?—Persons resident at Red River.

4554. *Chairman.*] All males?—Yes.

4555. Mr. *Christy.*] Just describe to the Committee what the nature of the petition is?—It states certain grievances; it gives a history of the settlement. The petitioners say that they have invested large sums of money in payment for land to the Hudson's Bay Company, and that they cannot get any deeds for the same; that is one complaint. They say that the Company's agents have endeavoured to force deeds upon them to which they object, which would subject them to become slaves to that body. Then they believe the charter of the Company not to be legal, and so forth. They say that on their annual journeys into Minnesota they have been pursued like felons by armed constables; that they have been searched, and their property taken from them and confiscated.

4556. Do they speak generally with regard to their property, or describe what particular property has been taken from them?—"They searched our property, even by breaking open our trunks, and all furs found were confiscated." Furs they speak of. Then they complain that "the valuable commercial productions of the country are exported for the exclusive benefit of a company of traders, who are strangers to ourselves and to our country." They also complain of being obliged to import everything through the Company, and then they speak of the rule of the Company paralysing the whole of their energies, and therefore they wish to be attached to Canada. They say that they have appealed to the Imperial authorities without effect, and therefore they petition the Parliament of Canada. [p. 254]

An Advancing Civilization

Humphrey Lloyd Hime, *Encampment on the Red River* **(1858)**
Into the silent land.

Corps of Royal Engineers, *Survey Camp on North Antler River* **(1873)**
Surveying the West; mapping out the great lone land.

W. G. R. Hind, *Oxen with Red River Cart* **(ca. 1870)**
Settlement moving apace.

W. G. R. Hind, *Roadside Scene with Three Houses* **(ca. 1870)**
Fencing-in the wilderness.

Northwest British America and Its Relations to the State of Minnesota (1860)
James W. Taylor

A report to the New York Chamber of Commerce very distinctly corrected the erroneous impression, that the valleys of the Mississippi and St. Lawrence rivers exhausted the northern and central areas which are available for agriculture. 'There is in the heart of North America,' said the report, 'a distinct subdivision, of which Lake Winnipeg may be regarded as the center. This subdivision, like the valley of the Mississippi, is distinguished for the fertility of its soil, and for the extent and gentle slope of its great plains, watered by rivers of great length, and admirably adapted for steam navigation. It has a climate not exceeding in severity that of many portions of Canada and the Eastern States. It will, in all respects, compare favourably with some of the most densely peopled portions of the continent of Europe. In other words, it is admirably fitted to become the seat of a numerous, hardy, and prosperous community. It has an area equal to eight or ten first class American States. Its great river, the Saskatchewan, carries a navigable water line to the very base of the Rocky Mountains. It is not at all improbable that the valley of this river may yet offer the best route for a railroad to the Pacific. The navigable waters of this great subdivision interlock with those of the Mississippi. The Red River of the North, in connection with Lake Winnipeg, into which it falls, forms a navigable water line, extending directly north and south nearly eight hundred miles. The Red River is one of the best adapted to the use of steam in the world, and waters one of the finest regions on the continent. Between the highest point at which it is navigable, and St. Paul, on the Mississippi, a railroad is in process of construction; and when this road is completed, another grand division of the continent, comprising half a million square miles, will be open to settlement.' [p. 12]

Letter to the Right Honourable Earl Grey, on the Subject of Transportation and Emigration as Connected with an Imperial Railway Communication between the Atlantic and Pacific (1850)
R. Carmichael-Smyth

Humbly do I conceive that Providence has retained for our use, and pointed out to us the field, whereon the generous and enlightened sons of England may work out the noble destiny that awaits them, and become as far-famed and victorious in the productive works of peace, as they ever have been in the destructive splendour of war.

Let but the people of the British Empire will it; – and in a few years, when the Royal Standard shall be hoisted at Halifax, and the royal salute fired in honour of her Majesty's Natal Day – then shall be heard the continuous roar of British artillery, and the inspiring sound of British cheers, from ocean to ocean, – from the Atlantic to the Pacific; and the wire of the electric telegraph will point to the astounding news, – that the morning gun, which in Nova Scotia announced the approach of a day so welcome to all English hearts, had been responded to at sunset, from the rock of Alexander Mackenzie, in New Caledonia. Who then will talk of annexation, and what enemy will approach the frontier with hostile intentions, when the first gun fired would be answered by an instantaneous peal of British artillery across the Continent of North America? [p. iv]

Great Britain One Empire (1852)
Millington Henry Synge

It might at first sight be supposed, and would doubtless be very generally assumed, that because British America is the scene on which the great proposed communication must be carried into effect, it must therefore be of local, rather than of imperial national importance; and it may be well briefly to vindicate the general and equal value of the proposal, in its bearings on every portion of the empire. The general benefit is, indeed, implied, if it can be proved to be the best way of approach to countries washed by the Pacific; but it can be exemplified in greater comparative detail.

It is the shortest route to China, Japan, Australia, and New Zealand, and to all the countries contiguous to them: to India it affords the only invulnerable approach, and to all it opens the most comprehensive, salubrious, and profitable one. Now none of these considerations affect British America directly, and the indirect influences of commerce operate equally upon all. Neither do they relate pre-eminently to the interests of the peopled portion of British America; the local effect of the proposed route, in this respect, would be essentially imperial, by giving a British and national direction to the trade and commerce of the existing British provinces, instead of allowing it to deflect daily more and more towards the United States. Humanly speaking, it would prevent the disruption of the colonial empire in this direction, and thereby perhaps obviate the dangers of its total dissolution.

These are considerations eminently imperial; that is, of importance to the whole empire, and *based* upon its interests. Again; the new empire, and the new local commerce that would be called into existence by means of the construction of the route, would be upon territory west of Upper Canada, upon territory now wholly, utterly, wretchedly, and sinfully waste and wasted. The existing countries east and west of that gigantic but reclaimable desert, would equally be gainers; the countries of the Pacific specially so; since to them a new seaboard, with very numerous and admirable harbours, would be opened. To the east, an inland country only, with only an inland (though an unrivalled inland) navigation, would be added. Lastly, it is scarcely a question that admits of an alternative. The country which *occupies* the American seaboard of the Pacific, will and must command the commerce and supremacy of the Pacific and the East. Our nominal sovereignty of the remnant of our North-American possessions, especially of our portion of the Pacific seaboard, may very safely be left undisturbed by the United States, so long as we ourselves bury it in the darkness of the tomb. Indeed, the continued neglect of the British Pacific seaboard, contemporaneously with the unparalleled development of that of the United States, would be the 'symptom and cause' that British supremacy had virtually passed away even from British India. Those who may develop the western coasts of America will be the merchants and masters of the East. All these are points of imperial importance, not of local partiality. [pp. 55–57]

Little remains to be added. The route has been shown to be the shortest, quickest, and best situated, the most healthy and the most comprehensive, that can be found between the hemispheres.

It is also inviolable, and therefore of the utmost national importance. It would connect the most distant and most densely-populated regions of the globe, and knit together all the various parts of the British empire in a complete and indissoluble union by identity of interests. It would be the means of peopling British America, and render it for the first time of practical value in some measure commensurate with its intrinsic worth. That vast territory would be rescued from the condition of a wilderness scarcely trodden by civilized man, and be transformed into an empire teeming with activity and life. A commerce would be called into existence, which even the quickest tracings of mental activity cannot easily follow. Its only limits would be those of the zeal and energy brought to bear on its development. The aspects of the whole colonial policy and practice of Great Britain would be placed upon the firm basis of imperial unity, and the maritime supremacy of the empire, under the effects of influences such as these, would not only be secured, but immeasurably elevated. [pp. 118-19]

The Confederation of the British North American Provinces (1865)
Thomas Rawlings

Topographical engineers, scientific explorers, and itineraries, have explored the American Continent from end to end, and the conclusion arrived at is that the most feasible route to the Pacific is through the Fertile Belt of the Hudson's Bay Territory, and over the Rocky Mountains north of the boundary-line; and as it is the purpose of the proposed confederation of the British Territories to complete, at an early period, the intercolonial line, uniting Nova Scotia to the Canadas, with the splendid system of railway which constitutes the Grand Trunk Railway and its connexions, we shall have already completed one-half of the passage across the American Continent, and opened a through line which, at all seasons of the year, will draw the products of the West through British Territory to the sea; starting from La Crosse to St. Paul, Minnesota; from Fond du Lac, at the head of Lake Superior; and from St. Paul we have a system of railways, which are partly built and which are now under contract and construction, to Pembina, on the boundary-line and on the Red River Settlement. This will open the whole of 80,000 square miles of rich prairie land in Hudson's Bay Territory to the emigrant. But from Pembina the great Fertile Belt offers every facility to build the Pacific Railroad; the lands themselves will eventually pay for it. For the present we have a waggon-road passing over these prairies, and across the Saskatchewan Valley to the foot of the Rocky Mountains. Carry out the project of a railroad to the Pacific Ocean, at whatever cost to the British Government or people, and the future of that country will present a panorama of magnificence unexampled in history, and before which the splendour of Roman wealth, in the days of Augustus, will sink into insignificance. The silks, teas, and opium of China will swiftly speed over the Rocky Mountains to the warehouses of Europe; the spices and Oriental luxuries of India will be transported over lands where the red race but an age since had trapped the beaver and the ermine; the re-awakened commerce of Japan would find a way across the prairie land of Hudson's Bay Territory; the gold of California, or British Columbia, and the Saskatchewan Valley, would find a safe passage by the great lakes to the Atlantic; the wool of California would find a more direct route to England; and the homeward and the outward bound would cross the Atlantic on their way to India, China, Australia, California, British Columbia, British North America, and the United States, in social companionship. What scenes would be witnessed on their route! What a continent to journey over! What mountains—what lakes—what rivers—what mighty cataracts—what lovely prairies—what splendid forests—and what a world of knowledge would daguerreotype itself upon the brain! [pp. 6–7]

Prospectus issued for the sale of new capital stock of the Hudson's Bay Company (1863)

The Company's territory embraces an estimated area of more than 1,400,000 square miles, or eight hundred and ninety-six millions of acres, of which a large area, on the Southern frontier, is well adapted for European colonization. The soil of this portion of the territory is fertile, producing in abundance wheat and other cereal crops, and is capable of sustaining a numerous population. It contains 1,400 miles of navigable lakes and rivers, running for the greater part east and west, which constitute an important feature in plans for establishing the means of communication between the Atlantic and Pacific Oceans, across the continent of British North America, as well as for immediate settlement in the intervening country. The territory is, moreover, rich in mineral wealth, including coal, lead, and iron.

. . . .

The trading operations of the Company are chiefly carried on in the fur-bearing and northern portion of the territory, where the climate is too severe for European colonization. These trading operations will be actively continued, and as far as possible extended, whilst the management will be judiciously economized.

Consistently with these objects, the outlying estates and valuable farms will be realized where the land is not required for the use of the Company. The southern district will be opened to European colonization, under a liberal and systematic scheme of land settlement. Possessing a staff of factors and officers who are distributed in small centres of civilization over the territory, the Company can, without creating new and costly establishments, inaugurate the new policy of colonization, and at the same time dispose of mining grants. [pp. 17–18]

The West as the Linchpin of the Nation

Manitoba

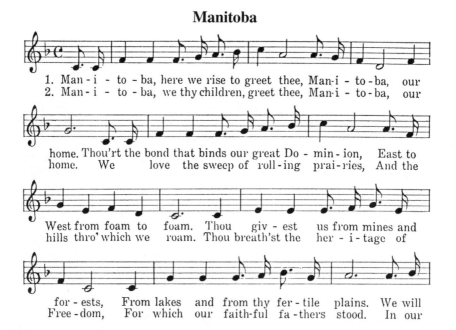

1. Man - i - to - ba, here we rise to greet thee, Man-i - to-ba, our
2. Man - i - to - ba, we thy children, greet thee, Man-i - to-ba, our

home. Thou'rt the bond that binds our great Do - min - ion,   East to
home.   We   love   the sweep of roll-ing   prai-ries,   And the

West from foam to   foam.   Thou   giv - est   us from mines and
hills thro' which we   roam. Thou breath'st the   her - i - tage of

for - ests,   From lakes   and from thy fer - tile   plains. We will
Free - dom,   For which   our faith-ful fa - thers stood.   In our

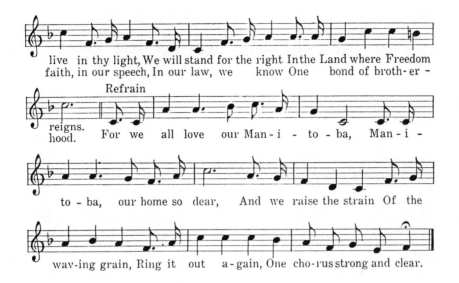

live   in thy light, We will stand for the right In the Land where Freedom
faith, in our speech, In our law, we   know One   bond of broth-er -

Refrain

reigns.
hood.   For   we   all love   our Man - i - to - ba,   Man - i -

to - ba,   our home so   dear,   And we raise the strain Of the

wav-ing grain, Ring it   out   a - gain, One cho-rus strong and clear.

Ocean to Ocean (1873)
George M. Grant

This Great West will, in the future, probably manifest this spirit more than even the Eastern Provinces, and so be the very backbone of the Dominion; just as the prairie States of the neighbouring republic are the most strongly imbued with patriotic sentiments. The sight, the possession of these boundless seas of rich land stirs in one that feeling of—shall we call it bumptiousness—that Western men have been accused of displaying. It is easy to ridicule and caricature the self sufficiency, but the fact is, a man out West feels like a young giant, who cannot help indulging a little tall talk, and in displays of his big limbs. [p. 97]

The West through Nationalist Eyes

Lucius O'Brien, *Oat Harvest* **(1896)**
National artists "selling" the western landscape.

Sydney Prior Hall, *Lord Lorne Interviewing a Settler on the Prairies* **(1881)**
Vice-regal visitors: agents of imperial authority in the West.

Sydney Prior Hall, *The Beginnings of Calgary, Alberta* **(1881)**
Prairie towns: bastions of civilization in the great lone land.

Sydney Prior Hall, *The Prairie* **(1881)**
A land awaiting the plough.

4

THE PROMISED LAND:
THE UTOPIAN WEST
1880-1920

All the fabled mutations of wand and enchantment sink into insignificance before the change which this free world works in the serf of Europe. Toil, combined with freedom and equality—and you have a more marvellous as well as nobler force than the fabled secret of the philosopher's stone. What they are weaving here [in the Canadian West] for humanity Time will show; "there's magic in the web of it"; something better anyway than the tear-drenched, blood-stained tapestry of the old world's past.[1]

To Nicholas Flood Davin, editor and owner of the *Regina Leader*, the first (1883) newspaper issued in Assiniboia, and a pamphleteer for the Canadian Pacific Railway Company, the Canadian West was the utopia for which men had searched for centuries. Here on the golden prairies with its invigorating climate, ordinary men were transformed into superior beings. This image of a new and better society—the promised land, a garden of abundance in which all material wants would be provided and where moral and civic virtues would be perfected—infused the immigration literature that lured thousands of immigrants to the prairies, inspired numerous utopian settlement schemes, and dominated the early literary and artistic depictions of the West.

The image of the West as a utopian settlement region appeared shortly after Canada acquired the territory in 1869-70, and especially during the expansionist era at the turn of the century, which continued up to

World War I. It stood in contrast to the romantic view of the West as pristine wilderness. The challenge now was to turn this virgin territory into a subdued and bountiful land, a new society where people could prosper. Robert Stead, the western Canadian poet and novelist, captured the changed imagery of the West from unspoiled wilderness to utopian settlement in his poem "The Plough":

> [A]ll the land lay desolate and bare,
> Its wealth of plain, its forest riches rare
> Unguessed by those who saw it through their tears,
> And Nature — miser of a thousand years —
> Most jealously her treasure-trove concealed
> Which only at your coming she revealed;
> But all lay silent, useless, and unused
> And useless it because it was unused.
>
> You came. Straightway the silent plain
> Grew mellow with the glow of golden grain;
> The axes in the solitary wood
> Rang out where stately oak and maple stood;
> The land became alive with busy din,
> And as the many settled, more came in;
> The Earth gave up her hoard, and in a stream
> The gold poured forth behind your busy beam![2]

Robert Stead only mused about the West's potential for settlement; Clifford Sifton, Minister of the Interior for the new Liberal government that took power under Wilfrid Laurier in 1896, turned the dream into reality. He initiated the most extensive immigration propaganda campaign in Canadian history, a campaign that would ultimately turn the West from a near-vacant land with fewer than 300,000 people in 1896 to a region with a population of over one and a half million by 1914. A western Canadian businessman, he had faith in the West's potential if it were populated by the right people — hardworking, determined, and committed farmers. He set out to attract these immigrants from the United States, Britain, and from western and eastern Europe. His plan coincided with a time of world prosperity which ensured its success. Within a single generation, the West became a "home for millions."

Sifton used a variety of techniques to attract immigrants. He offered free tours to western Canada for American reporters in hopes that they would write glowing accounts of the Canadian West in their newspapers; he hired agents to make speeches in foreign lands extolling the virtues of the prairie West. He set up a clandestine North Atlantic Trading Company that paid bonuses to steamship agents who brought immigrants from western European countries that had restrictions on emigration.

But his most effective promotional scheme was the publication of immigration pamphlets that presented glowing visual and literary images of the Canadian West. In 1896 the Immigration Department sent out sixty-five thousand pamphlets; by 1900 the number had reached one million. These pamphlets did not necessarily reflect the views of the authors, since they were being paid to present them, but their writings decidedly fostered utopian images in others.[3]

Agrarian Paradise

Pamphleteers extolled the virtues of the West often in superlative terms, implying that with such abundant assets at his disposal, a settler had every reason to succeed. The West was "the land of opportunity" where every hard-working and committed immigrant would be able to survive and, indeed, was almost assured of success. Nowhere did the pamphlets acknowledge that some failed to make a go of it, or that others regretted coming and wanted to return home. Anyone, they claimed, stood to gain if he was willing to apply himself. Europeans already struggling to eke out a living could not help but be attracted by an official government or Canadian Pacific Railway pamphlet that offered assurance of success for one's toil in this promised land. "It is no Utopian dream," one pamphleteer wrote, "to look foward and see these endless plains thickly populated with millions to whom Western Canada has given happy homes, larger opportunities in life, and the assurance of a prosperous future."[4] Readers wanted to believe what they read, and so read their dreams into the pamphlet. As one author notes: "Imagine what the words 'The West' suggested to the desk-tethered clerk, the factory-weary British workman, the mortgage-burdened Ontario farmer, or the landless Galician peasant? It offered a new chance, a new life, a new freedom."[5] To every immigrant the West was the promised land. Their motives for migration might differ—persecution, slum conditions, poverty, lack of opportunity for themselves, better opportunities for their children, even adventure— but all had a common image of the West as a place where they could succeed. In this sense, the West was a utopia.

The pamphlets followed a standard format. An introductory section describing the West as a land of opportunity was followed by sections on climate, soil, crops, the means to locate a homestead, advice on how to get started, transportation facilities, and social and cultural facilities. Such matter-of-fact information was embellished. Pamphlets described the climate, for example, in terms of its positive effect on farming and on people's physical well-being. Sifton wanted to ban the daily publication of Manitoba's temperature and to dissociate the West from Rupert's Land, which conjured up images of furs, frost, and snow. In their publications, he and his pamphleteers eliminated certain negative words like "snow" and "cold" and used instead such positive terms as "bracing" and "invigorating." George Livingstone Dodds, a Saskatchewan pamphleteer, described Western Canada in one of his poems as "Lady Bountiful not the Lady of Snows," a clear rejection of Rudyard Kipling's description of the region.[6] Kipling had used the expression in a poem about Canada of the same title, first published in *The London Times* of 1897. It was immediately denounced as an unkind criticism of Canada, and in particular western Canada, and as an impediment to tourism and immigration.

Others dwelt on the positive effect of climate on character. In an age of racial theories, it was believed that climate had a profound effect in moulding character. In particular, the belief prevailed that a cold climate created fecundity and virility, and that these traits in turn produced qualities that made northern people superior. As Canadian intellectual historian Carl Berger explains: "The result of life in the northern latitudes was the creation and sustenance of self-reliance, strength, hardness — in short, all the attributes of a dominant race."[7] Since the Canadian West was in the northern latitudes and northerly climes, the image was of a hearty, healthy, wholesome West. Thomas Spence, "the father of Western immigration pamphlets," boldly and naively proclaimed that "climate gives quality to the blood, strength to the muscles, power to the brain. Indolence is characteristic of people living in the tropics, and energy of those in temperate zones."[8] Living in the *North* West was an asset, not a liability. Another pamphleteer proclaimed that "the climate of Western Canada does more than make wheat — it breeds a hardy race."[9] Charles Mair, the effervescent poet of the West, was more imaginative in describing how climate affected character:

> A peculiar feature of the climate [of the North West] is its lightness and sparkle. There is a dryness and a relish in its pure ether akin to those rare vintages which quicken the circulation without impairing the system. The atmosphere is highly purified, joyous and clear, and charged with ozone — that element which is mysteriously associated with soundness of mind and body and at war with their morbid phenomena.
>
> Surrounded by this invisible influence, one lives a fuller and healthier life than in the denser atmosphere of the east. The cares of manhood press less heavily on the brain, and the severest toil of exposure finds increased capacity to endure it.[10]

One pamphlet contained a letter by Fred Hopping of Forshee, Alberta, who related how he had left Chicago in sickly health from overwork in poorly ventilated shops to come to the Canadian North West in search of "health or wealth." "I was thin and pale, had a cough," he wrote, "and suffered from rheumatism, so that my mother gave up hopes of seeing me again. . . . I arrived at Lacombe, Alberta, April 5th. . . . Breathing plenty of fresh air and wrestling with my old cow soon improved my health. When winter came I found it to be the most pleasant part of the year, as the dry, cold air was bracing and entirely different from the damp, chilly wind I was used to. In 1895 it was two degrees below zero in Alabama, and I suffered more from cold in the Sunny South than I ever did in Alberta."[11]

Ebullient descriptions of the land matched those of the climate. The image of the prairies as ideal farm land—"the last best West"—was popular in immigration literature. A delegation visiting the West recorded their impressions in one of the pamphlets: "Altogether the whole district is very encouraging and hopeful to us. It is a nice prairie, covered with beautiful grass, and dotted here and there with little poplar forests which gives the whole a very romantic appearance. The settlers whom we visited look forward to a very happy and contented future."[12]

Consistently, the emphasis was on the rural, agricultural West. "Only farmers need apply" was the slogan of the Department of the Interior. Sifton made it emphatically clear to his agents: "We do not want anything but agricultural labourers and farmers and people who are coming for the purpose of engaging in agriculture, whether as farmers or farm labourers." Towns and cities were referred to only in terms of their benefit to farming. It was the myth that a man with his wife and children could enjoy a comfortable and rewarding life on a 160-acre homestead. A popular technique in many immigration pamphlets was to contrast a farmer's progress in his first five or six years of operation through a succession of annual pictures which showed a homestead transformed from a humble dwelling on unimproved land to a two-storey frame house surrounded by trees, livestock, and cultivated fields of wheat. The photographs or illustrations depicted a diversified farm of dairy, grain, and fruit, implying that each farmer could be self-sufficient. The emphasis was on economic success which in turn was based on the assumption that material comfort was a necessary prerequisite to spiritual well-being.

Immigration pamphlets stressed the good quality of the soil on the prairies as the foundation of successful farms. A delegate for a potential group of Mennonite settlers visited an already established Mennonite community in western Canada and reported: "The nature of the ground is black soil, with heavy clay sub-soil, and, therefore, very fertile. The grass grows very close, and the growth is wonderfully nutritious, which is seen by the fat cattle in the neighbourhood."[13] George Grant described the soil as "capable of raising anything." His only complaint was its excessive richness, which "left the farmer with nothing to do with his manure except dump it in the nearest river."[14] Pamphleteers described the soil in terms of successful wheat growing. The West was "the granary of the British Empire." "The richness of the soil," Alexander Begg, the resident historian of the Red River community, wrote in 1881, "produces immense crops, from twenty-five to forty bushels to the acre being the common average yield, and good crops have even been obtained from the first turning of the sod."[15] George Bryce, a Presbyterian minister and second principal of Manitoba College, the forerunner of the University of Manitoba, gave a more colourful description in his *Manitoba: Its Infancy, Growth and Present Condition* (1882): "The waving fields of grain through which the writer has gone remained impressed on the memory. From forty to a hundred acres of yellow wheat, seemingly as dense as it can be, waving slowly back and forward on a summer's day, is a most beautiful sight."[16]

Even Palliser's Triangle became a potential site for successful homesteading. In *Manitoba and the Great North West*, the report of his 1880 expedition, Professor John Macoun, the dominion government botanist, dismissed Palliser's negative image of the southern prairies as barren country.[17] Barren could only apply to the absence of wood, not soil, and was caused by artificial not natural causes, Macoun contended. "A perusal of my own journal and that of Mr. Wilkins shows that this region, although not everywhere suited for agriculture, possesses many fine tracts fit for the plough, and always good pasture."[18] Macoun was the true optimist, bubbling over with enthusiasm about the Canadian West. Sandford Fleming had a chance meeting with Macoun while on the boat that took the two of them from Collingwood to the lakehead, and describes "the Botanist": "At whatever point the steamer touched, the first man on shore was the Botanist, scrambling over the rocks or diving into the woods, vasculum in hand, stuffing it full of mosses, ferns, lichens, liverworts, sedges, grasses and flowers till recalled by the whistle that the captain always obligingly sounded for him."[19]

Immigrants were constantly reminded that on the prairies they need not struggle to clear densely forested land in order to homestead. An individual could arrive one day and begin farming the next. As Thomas Spence reminded prospective homesteaders: "The settler [in the East] expends . . . *ten or fifteen years of the best of his life*, in toilsome struggles to convert his farm into such proportions of open and wooded land as the settler on our partly wooded prairie lands finds his when he first goes on it; in other words, he actually receives from the Government the free gift of a ready-made farm of the richest kind."[20] As the Department of Agriculture pointed out in 1877: "Nature has done her share, and done it well and generously; man's labour and industry are alone required to turn these broad rolling prairies to good account."[21]

Prairie Utopias

Such utopian imagery spawned a number of utopian settlements on the prairies.[22] People actually came to believe the mythology of the West as a land of promise where anything and everything was possible. Many attempted to bring the dream into reality by creating utopian communities in this last unsettled area of North America. The open spaces and the absence of established institutions and values made the West a *tabula rasa*, an ideal locale in which to conduct experiments in communal living. If new societies could succeed anywhere, it was here in the idyllic conditions of the West. As historian Anthony Rasporich notes: "The image of the West in central Canada and Great Britain progressed rapidly from the *outopia* 'nowhere' or *terra incognita* to *eutopia*, a 'somewhere' or 'good place' of unlimited progress, enterprise, and development."[23] The aims and nature of these communal settlements varied widely, from sacred to secular, aristocratic to academic, authoritarian to democratic, and from conservative to socialistic, but the common ideal was to create a perfect society on the virgin prairies. The new millennium, in other words, would be inaugurated in the West.

Two such utopian communities that sprang up on the prairies during the settlement period were Cannington Manor and Harmona. Cannington Manor was a genteel English settlement south of Moosomin; it was established in 1882 by Captain Edward Mitchell Pierce, a British "gentleman and soldier" ruined by a London bank failure. He advertised in an English newspaper for "young men of good birth and education" who would learn the art of farming under his supervision. What he received was a group of remittance men who wanted to lead the life of a gentleman farmer in the "colonies." Alice Hewlett, a founding member of the colony, described the romantic enchantment that surrounded its beginning: "Once upon a time there was magic in the name of Cannington Manor, and there was magic there. . . . In those days it was a gallant adventure upon which the early settlers set out. The railway had come no nearer than Brandon; reports were all they had to go upon, reports of a fair land where milk and honey could be made to flow. So they set forth, from England and Scotland and from Ontario, and by devious paths found their way to the virgin prairie east of the Moose Mountains."[24]

Soon a communal village formed which included a grist-mill, blacksmith's and woodworker's shops, a co-operative cheese factory, a hotel, a post-office, a church, and an Assembly Hall which operated as a school. Work was frequently interrupted by leisure activities such as choral music, painting, poetry reading, and "scientific" discussions of agriculture and politics, and outdoor activities such as tennis, cricket, and fox-hunting. Hewlett described a typical summer day at the Manor: "Tea was served on Tennis Courts by the Ladies, and indeed it was a bright and happy scene. Intermingling with the pretty summer frocks of the ladies could be seen young men in flannels wearing the blazers and colours of all the best known English and Scottish public schools and even varsity blues. . . . Then back usually in a buckboard home to dress for dinner, to dine with friends or attend some public or private dance, card party, midnight frolic, drive or ride to the lake."[25] Without a solid economic base to sustain such frivolity, and when the railroad bypassed it by ten miles, the settlement declined. Some bachelors married local Ontario and English women, while others returned to England or pursued other schemes such as saving the British Empire by serving in the Boer War, or by searching for gold in the Klondike.

The Harmony Industrial Association, a radical socialist utopia, provided a striking contrast to Cannington Manor. Inspired by the writings of British utopian socialists John Ruskin, William Morris, and Edward Bellamy, a group of Manitoba radical Protestant farmers formed in 1895 a co-operative community at Beulah, Manitoba, called "Harmona"– named, according to one founding member, after one of the "Cities of Refuge in Israel [which] means a multitude," and inspired by the doctrine of Christian social co-operation. Each individual pursued the economic interests that he or she performed best while working for the common good of the community. All would share the fruits of their labour "to insure its members against want or fear of want." Their aim, as set out in the preamble to their constitution, was "to own and operate factories, mills, stores, etc. To provide educational and recreative facilities of the highest order and to promote and maintain harmonious social relations on the basis of co-operation for the benefit of its members and mankind in general."[26] Members were expected to be of "good moral character" and to be motivated by principles of "social co-operation" rather than individual needs. Such stringent demands appealed to a limited few only, and the colony never numbered more than fifty persons. Unfortunately, practical economic considerations got in the way of the colony's ideals, and the association disbanded after it failed to develop a staple export base or to achieve a railway link to the outside world.

The pastoral image of the West inspired other utopian settlement schemes. A group from the Parry Sound district of Ontario was inspired by immigration agent Thomas Pearce's glowing descriptions of the West to leave their unproductive farms near Georgian Bay in 1892 to travel over two thousand miles to Fort Saskatchewan where "the Promised Land" awaited them.[27] W. C. Pollard, the main chronicler for the group, captured the vision that inspired some six hundred Perry Sounders to begin anew in his book *Pioneering in the Prairie West* (1926): "Did humanity ever set for itself a nobler task than that of pioneering in a new and virgin territory? There the work of Nature can be seen on every side, and there avarice and selfishness are almost unknown, and all are engaged in man's primitive occupations: tilling the soil, guarding the flocks and herds, fishing in the waters, hunting in the wilderness, and mining under the ground. There the brotherhood of man is amplified, and common interests cement together social ties and friendships, and there the works of the Creator are seen before man makes any contributions or contaminations."[28] The reality was a far cry from Pollard's dream, as the Parry Sounders discovered, struggling to eke out an existence in adverse conditions.

Pollard's vision of "the building of Jerusalem in this pleasant land" was similar to Isaac Barr's dream for his colony of some two thousand British immigrants who settled the Lloydminster area at the turn of the century.[29] "Barr's lambs," as his followers were dubbed, believed that they were leaving the "dark Satanic mills," as the poet William Blake described industrial England, to farm the "pastoral land" of the prairie West. This ideal urged them on through the most horrendous difficulties—overloaded ships, storm-tossed seas, rickety colonist cars, and a two-hundred-mile trek from Saskatoon to present-day Lloydminster under the most adverse conditions. Many never made it to "the promised land," and those that did were reminded more of Jacques Cartier's description of Canada as the "land that God gave Cain" than of Lot's fertile valleys in the biblical story.

A number of religious utopian settlements sprang up in the virgin West where the inhabitants were promised religious freedom and the right to continue their unique lifestyles in isolation from the temptations of the "outside" world.[30] The Doukhobors (Spirit Fighters), the Mennonites, the Hutterites, and the Mormons, to name but a few of the more well-known religious communities on the prairies, came because they believed in the utopian image of the West as the place where they could establish their own vision of "the new Jerusalem." This Edenic quest for paradise was certainly in keeping with the utopian image of the West presented in the immigration propaganda.

A much later utopian scheme was Coalsamao (pronounced Co-al-sa-ma-o) from E. A. Partridge's *War on Poverty* (1926). It got its name from the first two letters of the names of the western provinces of (British) Columbia, Alberta, Saskatchewan, and Manitoba, with the final "o" for that part of northern Ontario also included. Partridge, "the sage of Sinatula" who had championed farmers' rights as first president of the Grain Growers' Company and as first editor of its "bible" of agrarian radicalism, *The Grain Growers' Guide*, believed his utopia improved on others that had gone before him by applying to a "definite locality with known natural characteristics," and "to a definite group of real people, with real political, social and economic entanglements internal and external, to contend with." This region was to be an autonomous political entity, regulated by a "High Court of Control" and governed by the principles of "co-operative action." "The care of each must be the concern of all," Partridge insisted, so that poverty would be destroyed, and all would live comfortably and equitably. Partridge failed to persuade enough westerners to, figuratively speaking, "'come out of the land of Pharoah'— the thieves' resort and gambling den known as 'The Business World'," to bring his dream into reality, and it remained a vision only on paper of a "new Jerusalem."[31]

The Perfect Prairie City

Utopianism was not restricted to the pastoral ideal. Although Sifton advertised for farmers only, many of the immigrants settled in towns or cities, or else moved there after unsuccessful attempts at farming. Towns and cities grew by an astonishing 700 percent in the pre-war decade. Where there had been only one prairie city—Winnipeg—in 1896, there were over twelve by 1914, not to mention the numerous towns that dotted the prairie landscape. These cities and towns vied for positions of dominance in the heady days at the turn of the century. Civic leaders attempted to persuade potential inhabitants that theirs was the best of all possible urban centres. In a region noted for its uniform physical appearance and its lack of distinguishing geographical features that could give one town or city a natural advantage over another, success was often judged in terms of the ability of civic leaders to "sell" their town or city. Boosterism—a popular form of the nineteenth-century concept of "progress," and based on the belief that a particular town or city was superior to all others—was used to convince people that in the urban centres of the West they could find the ideal setting to live a happy, prosperous, and contented life.[32] Each urban centre had its unique qualities to offer, its particular slogan, its unlimited promises of what it would provide and do for its citizens. John Foster Fraser reported in 1905 that "there are not a half dozen wooden shacks on the prairie, called a 'town,' where the inhabitants do not believe that in a very few years that town will be one of the most famous and prosperous cities in the entire Dominion."[33]

"The eyes of the world are upon the West," one pamphlet proclaimed, "half conscious, yet marvelling at the unbounded wealth being taken from the rich, black land of its fertile prairies. . . . Regina is at the centre of this rich land and offers unlimited opportunities for industrial development to the commercial and financial countries of the world."[34] Wolseley was billed as "the Grain Golden city of the Central West." Although only having a population of one thousand, its "tributary" population was five thousand and its setting "the prettiest of Western Canada." "The orderly arrangement of the business thoroughfares, the fine stores that stand upon the principal streets, the artistic residences in which the citizens live and the beautiful surroundings of the town, all conspire to make Wolseley far better fitted to call itself the City-Beautiful, than many another town, that has done so with a loud voice. . . . The country all around is a veritable Garden of Eden during four months of the year." (The pamphlet failed to describe what conditions prevailed for the other eight months.)

Alix, Alberta was "the centre of Alberta, the Garden of the West." Its founding father, Joseph Todd, chose the site for the town, we are told, because "travel as he might, he could find no more desirable place to settle. Indeed, what more could be wished for in a new country. Fertile soil, grass in plenty for unnumbered thousands of cattle, sufficient timber with which to build his home, scenery that is unsurpassed on the American continent and fuel in plenty, both from the patches of timber and from the coal beds of the Red Deer River but a scant half dozen miles away." Many western towns likened themselves to their American counterparts: Winnipeg was "the Chicago of the North"; Okotoks was the "Eldorado of South Alberta"; Saskatoon was "the Minneapolis and St. Paul of the West"; and Calgary was "the Banner City of the Last Great West."

Few if any western communities could match Saskatoon for its boosterism. Only superlatives would do. Saskatoon was described on different occasions as "the fastest growing city in the world," "the eight-year-old wonder of the British Empire," "the Largest City in the World for its Age," and "the greatest example of town and city building in the world's history." "Nowhere will you find a happier people," one pamphlet boldly proclaimed. Why? "Simply because prosperity has lifted the lack of money out of life and thereby annihilated nine-tenths of human tribulation." Another pamphlet encouraged people to "come to Saskatoon, where, of all places in the West, your success is most fully assured; where no deserving man has ever yet failed; where there are no poorhouses because there are no poor, where there is comfort, happiness and prosperity and an unlimited field for your intelligence and energy." Still another pamphlet attributed Saskatoon's amazingly rapid success to "*no old inhabitants* to hinder progress" and to a sixteen-thousand-strong population "moved but by one impulse—the city's good."

Booster literature talked only in terms of economic growth and material success. What made a town or city great was size: the size of its population, the size of its acreage, the magnitude of its homes, the extent of its industry, and the potential of its citizens to get rich fast. Bigger was better. Few boosters thought in terms of selling the cultural qualities of their towns and cities. Such "extravagancies" were by-products of wealth that reflected a city's prosperity rather than led to its enrichment. The utopia envisioned in the booster literature was of a material world where all would live prosperous, contented, and comfortable lives.

Prairie Utopias Envisioned

It was left to the early western Canadian writers such as Charles Gordon (Ralph Connor), Robert Stead, Nellie McClung, Emily Murphy (Janey Canuck), and artists such as Washington Lynn, Inglis Sheldon-Williams,

James Henderson, and Augustus Kenderdine to capture in print and on canvas the quality of this new western society, to show to what extent the ideal presented in the propaganda literature had become real. Believing that they were simply describing the West, these individuals actually created their own mythical West that was as utopian as that depicted in the propaganda literature.[35] By setting their romantic stories in the physical locale of western Canada, and painting life-like yet idyllic scenes of the prairies, these writers and artists made people believe that the West they depicted was the "real" West. The ideal became real; the pastoral West was removed "from literature into history, from form into reality,"[36] from the imagination to a physical setting.

Their West was, physically, a land of milk and honey, an Eden of flowers, trees, wheat, fruit, and cattle, with plenty for everyone. Emily Murphy writes of the prairies: "Yesterday was brimful of liquid sunshine. It was as good as gold — indeed much better than gold. Since coming here, I have lost my old habit of insomnia, and am beginning to like the place better. It reminds one of Winthrop's description of Acadia —'a land where sunshine never scorches and yet shade is sweet; where simple pleasures please; where the sky is bright, and green fields satisfy for ever.'" At another point she exclaims: "The whole land is a paradise of blossoms — a very garden of the Lord."[37] Ralph Connor describes the foothills country thus: "On the hillsides and down in the sheltering hollows we could see the bunches of cattle and horses feeding upon the rich grasses. High above, the sky, cloudless and blue, arched its great kindly roof from prairie to mountain peaks, and overall, above, below, upon prairie, hillsides and mountains, the sun poured its floods of radiant yellow light."[38] Nellie McClung recalls her first glowing impressions of the prairies as her family moved West: "Never had I experienced as great a moment as came to me, when the oxen's heads were turned west on Portage Avenue and the long trail received us unto itself. I felt that life was leading me by the hand and I followed on light feet. We would travel with the sun, until we came to that flower starred prairie where no stone would impede the plow; where strawberries would redden the oxen's fetlocks; where eight-hundred acres of rich black soil was waiting for us."[39] Here was "God's country," as James Oliver Curwood, the well-known British author, coined it, an image that for years came to be associated with western Canada.

Songs augmented novels and poetry in presenting a utopian image of the West.[40] These songs often pointed out the realities and difficulties of homesteading, but then went on to show the joys to be had in such hardship. In "The Homesteader," the Westerner is pictured as a man who has turned his back on the East for something new and exciting:

> On the distant lonely prairie,
>   In a little lonely shack,

New life the homesteader faces;
  On the world he's turned his back.

He's fifteen miles from a neighbour
  And a hundred miles from a town;
There are rolling plains between them;
  It is there he's settled down.

In the midst of God's great freedom,
  Under skies of fairest blue,
He is building broad foundations
  And a manhood strong and true.[41]

The image is reiterated in the final stanza:

With age-old wisdom behind him,
  And spurred by his own great need,
Thus he builds his broad foundations
  Free from custom and from creed.

Other songs talked of the joys and beauty of settling the West. One popular song, "O Prairie Land," began:

We've reached the land of pleasant dreams,
  Of level plains and deep ravines,
Where flowers abound on every hand
  In this, our lovely prairie land.[42]

Later stanzas talk about the different enjoyments to be found in this "Prairie Land."

Another song, "Harvest," captures in its title the essence of its stanzas, which go on to talk about the "tranquil golden sea" and "rippling wavelets" of wheat. Wheat is depicted as the symbol of progress, as farmsteads replaced buffalo herds, and of contentment, as homesteads "nestled in the amber light." The final stanza depicts Western farmers as "God's Chosen People" with a mission greater than that of the soldier or hunter:

Manitoba, from thy prairie,
  Won by God's especial grace,
To a nobler, fuller mission
  Than the battle or the chase,
Rises up the song of harvest
  As the thankful people raise
From the oat fields and the wheat fields
  Fervent notes of thankful praise.[43]

Some Western Canadian artists depicted the same opulent West through the effective use of European painting styles on selected prairie scenes.[44]

Using rich dark tones, restrained colours, and soft outlines, they set the mood of a peaceful scene. Then they chose familiar landscape settings—farmsteads, valleys, and trails—to convey a sense of the prairies as a pastoral land reminiscent of an English countryside or of a northern French landscape. James Henderson's depictions of the Qu'Appelle Valley in his "Summer in the Valley" and "Autumn Hillsides" are examples; quiet homesteads nestled in the valley convey the same image of the land as the western novelists created. Augustus Kenderdine's paintings of the Qu'Appelle region have a similar effect. Tranquil scenes, rich in trees and presented in subdued tones, present an image of the prairies which is a far cry from the wind-swept, drought-stricken prairies that many farmers experienced. Charles Comfort commented on Kenderdine's selective view of the prairies: "He interprets the Western landscape more imaginatively than circumstances would require, and a preference for softly modulated tones and colours in his composition suggests that of the quiet solitude of the French paysage rather than the breeze-swept plains of the Canadian prairie."[45]

Edward Roper, a writer of travel books, crossed Canada in 1887 by CPR and recorded his impressions in *By Track and Trail*. The trip also afforded him an opportunity to paint prairie scenes. The two records, his travelogue and his paintings, contrast greatly. His travel book conveys a desolate and lonely land, while his paintings present a picturesque land where settlers were successfully turning virgin soil into settlement. He concentrated on farmsteads and ploughed fields to convey a land of promise, contentment, and personal fulfillment.

Western writers, like the immigration propagandists, believed that this "garden of the West" would be the home of a new and better society, one more egalitarian, democratic, free-spirited, and co-operative than that which existed elsewhere. They delighted in contrasting this new land with older societies, particularly that of eastern Canada. As historian Gerald Friesen notes, the West, for these writers, was "young, not old; free, not restrained by convention; egalitarian, not caste-bound; virile, not feeble; close to nature, not urban."[46] Robert Stead in his novel *The Cowpuncher* (1918), a love story between an eastern girl and a western boy, played up this contrast of East and West.

> The following morning found Dave early on the trail, leading a saddled horse by his side. The hours were leaden for the girl all that day, and looking into the future she saw the spectre of her life shadowed down the years by an unutterable loneliness. How could she ever drop it all—all this wild freedom, this boundless health, this great outdoors, this life, how could she drop it all and go back into the little circle where convention fenced out the tiniest alien streamlet, although the circle itself might lie deep in mire? And how would she give up this boy who had grown so imperceptibly but so intimately into the very soul of her being; give him

up with all his strength, and virility, and—yes, and coarseness, if you will—but sincerity too; an essential man, as God made him, in exchange for a machine-made counterfeit with the stamp of Society?[47]

Arthur Stringer expressed a similar attitude in *The Prairie Wife* (1915), the first novel of his trilogy on the West. The protagonist claims: "Here we are out here without any of the refinements of civilization, and we're as much at peace with our own souls as are the birds of the air. . . . Culture, it seems to me as I look back on things, tends to make people more and more mere spectators of life, detaching them from it and lifting them above it. Or can it be that the mere spectators demand culture, to take the place of what they miss by not being actual builders and workers? We are farmers, just rubes and hicks, as they say in my country. But we're tilling the soil and growing wheat. We're making a great new country out of what was once a wilderness. To me, that seems almost enough."[48] Here in the new West, anything and everything seemed possible, if not today at least tomorrow in "next year's country." Optimism was the finest quality that westerners possessed. Emily Murphy observed "with what joy I ride over the land this morning! In God's great blue all things are possible, and all things are fair."[49]

The image was of a West full of romance and adventure where heroic individuals daily acted out a life and death drama of good versus evil on a majestic stage. Young virile men and modest maidenly women struggled to conquer the forces of evil so as to create the perfect society. Emily Murphy described the virile westerner in her *Janey Canuck in the West* (1910): "The real Westerner is well proportioned. He is tall, deep-chested, and lean in the flank. His body betrays, in every poise and motion, a daily life of activity in the open air. His glances are full of wist and warmth. There is an air of business about his off-hand way of settling a matter that is very assuring. Every mother's son is a compendium of worldly wisdom and a marvel of human experience. What more does any country want?" She notes: "It is a great place this Canadian West—the country of strong men, strong women, straight living, and hard riding. Tut! Who wants to go to heaven?"[50] Ralph Connor described in *The Sky Pilot* (1899) the high adventure that he believed characterized the West: "Here [in the foothills] are the homes of the ranchmen, in whose wild, free, lonely existence there mingles much of the tragedy and comedy, the humor and pathos, that go to make up the romance of life. . . . A country it is whose sunlit hills and shaded valleys reflect themselves in the lives of its people; for nowhere are the contrasts of light and shade more vividly seen than in the homes of the ranchmen of the Albertas."[51] Robert Stead projected the heroic image of the westerner in a stanza of his poem "The Homesteader":

> For here, on the edge of creation,
> Lies, far as the vision can fling,
> A kingdom that's fit for a nation —
> A kingdom — and I am the king![52]

This sense of the heroic is well conveyed in Inglis Sheldon-Williams's early paintings of the West. He did a series of drawings for the *Daily Graphic* in 1890 which depicted farm scenes full of activity while his paintings captured dramatic scenes of adventure on the wind-swept prairies. They were exciting narratives, paintings that depicted the heroic conquest of the West in epic proportions. In wintry blizzards and blinding lightning storms, Sheldon-Williams conveyed the excitement of western settlement. The foreground was full of action, the landscape a mere backdrop to show that the setting for the heroic feat was the West. Sheldon-Williams was simply trying to capture on canvas his idealized picture of the prairie that had first attracted him to western Canada and then to the utopian settlement of Cannington Manor. He described the settlement as "a parklike place of lakes abounding in all manner of wild fowl, rolling ridges crowned with poplar and willow groves and pleasant open spaces for building and cultivation. . . . I lived in the atmosphere of Virgil's Georgics."[53]

Western writers and artists, like the immigration pamphleteers, believed in the magical quality of the West to turn ordinary individuals into superior beings. "How wonderful the power of this country of yours to transform men," proclaimed one of Ralph Connor's characters.[54] In *The Sky Pilot*, Connor described the impact of the environment on British immigrant cowboys in the Alberta foothills: "These young lads, freed from the restraints of custom and surroundings, soon shed all that was superficial in their make-up and stood forth in the naked simplicity of their native manhood. The West discovered and revealed the man in them."[55] Nellie McClung described her heroine, Pearlie Watson, in terms of her prairie spirit coming out of the new land. Pearlie is "like the rugged little anemone, the wind flower that lifts its head from the cheerless prairie. No kind hand softens the heat or the cold, nor tempers the wind, and yet the very winds that blow upon it and the hot sun that beats upon it bring to it a grace, a hardiness, a fragrance of good cheer, that gladdens the heart of all who pass that way."[56]

The idealized West was rural and pastoral. The heroes and heroines of western novels were homesteaders and farmers or farm wives, or else the bearers of civilization, such as the mounted police, or ministers who espoused rural western values and threw off the shackles of their eastern upbringing. Early western artists painted scenes of prosperous farm life and homesteading, frequently with a man "breaking the land" or tending to his cattle as his wife and children look on in contentment. The qualities highlighted were hard work, honest toil, and simple living.

The image of a western Canadian pastoral utopia so prominent in the immigration propaganda, the booster literature, and art was a strong incentive to western settlement between 1880 and 1914. Not only did it spur a host of explicitly utopian communities—possibly more than in any other region in North America—the image also attracted hundreds of thousands of immigrants in search of a better livelihood or a new land where they might create the idyllic conditions that are a part of every man's and woman's dreams. Immigrants wanted to believe that here, in this isolated wilderness, the conditions were perhaps right for the creation of a perfect society. It was this utopian image and the subsequent disillusionment when the ideal clashed with reality that contributed to the rise of a western Canadian consciousness and that helped fuel the agrarian protest movements of the early twentieth century.

Agrarian Paradise

Homes for Millions (1891)
Nicholas Flood Davin, ed.

The following pages are addressed to the farmers and farm labourers of Europe. They show them where they can have fruitful land for nothing; happy homes; independence; where careers are free; where there is no landlord to grind the tiller of the soil; no military conscription; no gilded idleness to cast a slur on labour; no aristocracy; where the phrases "lower classes," "humbler classes" are unknown. . . .

All over Assiniboia, Alberta, Saskatchewan, will be found men who came in within ten years with little or no money, but who had will and work in them, who are now rich farmers. Work and stick to it—this is all that is necessary to become independent. . . .

A country richer in agricultural capacity, in minerals, in beauty, in health-giving qualities than Australia, than in fact any country to be found in the world, is thrown open. All you need to win its advantages—the strong arm, the strong will, intelligence. You can be carried into the heart of this great country on the Canadian Pacific Railway, the greatest railway in the world from every point of view, without discomfort, nay, with all the conveniences of an hotel on rails.

Choose where you may to settle you cannot make a mistake; for the blessings of independence, and wealth, and freedom, everywhere await the farmer or farm labourer who brings with him the virtues of honesty, thrift, sobriety, energy. Vast as our fields are, the day is at hand when they will all be taken up. [pp. 3–4]

All the charms that belong to youth, hope, energy, are found in the North West, and the bracing influence of the new free land on mind and character is remarkable. The Ontario farmer is a fine specimen of the yeoman, but three years in the North West raises him higher on the scale of manhood—while a commensurate improvement is noted in all classes and races from Europe who have come amongst us, having the essential qualities of capacity for work, perseverance, sobriety and intelligence. [p. 6]

The Plough (1923)
Robert J. C. Stead

. . .

Where yesterday the lazy bison lay
A city glitters in the sun to-day;
His paths are turned to streets of wood and stone,
And thousands tread the way he trod alone;
The mighty hum of industry and trade
Fills all the place where once he held parade,
While harnessed Vulcan, mightier than Mars,
Leaps through the dark and strews the night with stars!

The sound of trade is heard on every hand,
And sturdy men rise to possess the land;
A thousand towns and hamlets over night
Spring up to greet the early morning light;
A thousand hopes are born where hope was not,
And children play where Indian wars were fought;
And millions, knowing neither how nor why,
Sit down to eat of that thou dost supply.

Where once the silent red-man spurned the ground,
A land of peace and plenty now is found,
A land by Nature destined to be great,
Where every man is lord of his estate;
Where men may dwell together in accord,
And honest toil receive its due reward;
Where loyal friends and happy homes are made,
And culture follows hard the feet of trade.
[pp. 31–32]

The Prairie Lands of Canada (1880)
Thomas Spence

The future citizen of the North-West of Canada will have Norse, Celtic and Saxon blood in his veins. His countenance, in the *pure, dry,* electric air, will be as fresh as the morning. His muscles will be iron, his nerves steel. Vigor will characterize his very action. . . .

Situated where the great stream of human life will pour its mightiest flood, beneficiently endowed with nature's riches, and illumed by such a light, there will be no portion of all earth's domain surpassing in glory and grandeur the future of Canada's North-West. [p. 6]

It is the glory of Canada that the territory she acquires by purchase she offers to distribute among the landless of old nations, extending to them a cordial welcome to come and partake of the bounties which the enterprising and industrious may secure, and when it is considered that here also may be possessed the perfect health requisite for their highest enjoyment, it is not too much to claim that the Canadian North-West Prairie Lands present unequalled inducements to those in search of new homes. [p. 9]

Great as are the unquestionable advantages which a union of money and industry possess, there is no country under the sun where unaided muscle, with a plucky purpose, reaps greater rewards than under the bright skies and helpful atmosphere of this fair land.

Feeling himself every inch a man, as he gazes upon the unclaimed acres which shall reward his toil, the settler breathes a freer air, his bosom swells with a prouder purpose, and his strong arms achieve unwonted results. Any man whose capital consists on his arrival of little but brawny arms and a brave heart, may do as others have done before him, select a homestead in some of the many beautiful and fertile regions westward, and into which railroads will rapidly penetrate, after which, being allowed six months before settling upon the land, he may work upon the railroad and earn enough of money to make a start in a small way; and by the time he produces a surplus, the railway will be within a reasonable distance to take it to market; he finds himself the proud possessor of a valuable farm, which has cost him little but the sweat of his brow. [p. 10]

All intending emigrants should remember that a new country like this is not the idler's paradise, that all its mines of wealth are surrounded by bustling difficulties. Its great superiority is that it is a *land of opportunities*.

Here as in no other portions of this continent are *openings* to-day that yield their wealth to brains, energy, pluck, whether with or without capital, more than is actually necessary to start with fairly; and if a man wants to work honestly for what he has, he can do it as well here as in any land beneath the sun. In a few short years our yet undeveloped wealth will astonish the world, when our coal and iron mines are laid bare, when our vast plains and hills are covered with flocks and herds, when our valleys supply grain to Europe and the East, and the great Canadian Pacific Railway links England, Canada, Japan, and China, in one great belt of commerce and mutual prosperity. [p. 30]

The Lady Bountiful (1906)
The Last West
George Livingstone Dodds

One hundred million acres of grazing land is shown,
    With herbage most nutritious in Western Canada alone.
    Eighteen hundred flour mills already dot the land,
    And twenty thousand ranches are under her command.
    Nearly two million acres were sold in '94
    At four and a fifth per acre that now are worth a score.
    The wheat that Western Canada, so generously supplies,
    Was awarded, at St. Louis Fair, the coveted first prize.
    In all the old world's markets, if their reports you scan,
    You will find Canadian wheat and flour from England to Japan.
    Surely these well-proven facts most certainly disclose
    That she is Lady Bountiful, not The Lady of the Snows.

The Canadian West (1906)
The Last West
George Livingstone Dodds

Hail to the World's great garner,
    The fair Canadian West,
Where the golden grain on the boundless plain
    Heaves like an ocean's crest.

Star of the British Empire,
    The haven for those who roam,
The refuge for stranger exile
    Who seeks for a friend and home.

The brightest gem of the Occident
    Has ceased to be but a dream,
As to east, to west, to north, to south,
    She empties her golden stream.

Food for the great world's millions
    She pours from her fertile breast;
This land with a mighty future,
    The fair Canadian West.

G. L. Dodds, real estate dealer and appraiser for the North of Scotland Canadian Mortgage Company, Limited, for twenty years at Wolseley, Saskatchewan, and Melita, Manitoba. "I Have a Message: 'Western Canada Is Beckoning To You Now.'"

Read this Pamphlet on Manitoba, the N.W.T., Provinces of Ontario and Quebec (1883)
Department of the Interior

I must confess, that though I have travelled very extensively in this great country, I have never yet been enabled to realize its vastness. Millions and millions of acres of the finest grain-growing land in the world; in fact, an ocean of land, if such an expression is allowable. As I stood on the platform of the railroad car, as we were running along, and looked first on one side and then on the other of the track, the immense tracts of land extending on each side as far as the eye could reach; and then, when we left the track, and drove by stage for long distances, still the level prairie stretched out to an almost boundless extent. As I remarked to a friend with whom I was conversing on the subject, "here is a home for the surplus population of Europe for the next fifty years." [p. 21]

Western Canada (1899)
Department of the Interior

"Westward the Star of Empire Takes Its Way"

This saying never had a more fitting exemplification than in Manitoba. As large as England, Scotland and Ireland put together, with its 116,021 square miles, its 74,000,000 acres, with a population of over 200,000, settled there within the past few years, it has made marked progress. Its population is largely English-speaking, many from the United States having made their homes there, for reasons which are best set out in the testimony they offer. Mennonites, Icelanders, Scandinavians and Germans are also there. Some of these are in colonies, while others have preferred casting their lot with the English-speaking people.

As a rule, people with means, and those satisfied with the existing conditions, do not move; and it will, therefore, not be surprising to learn that most of those who have gone to Manitoba to settle were not accompanied by very large bank accounts. This is referred to so as to emphasize by contrast the condition in which most of them are found to-day. The farmer who has continued his farming operations for from six to ten years is in circumstances which many settlers in older countries were unable to reach after a life-time of toil. The laborer is happy and contented; he is only waiting for an opportunity to get a farm of his own and become as independent as his employer. With a farm free from debt; his fields of ripening grain ready for harvest; with herds of cattle on his pasture lands, and flocks of sheep feeding on the hillside; dairy and poultry providing the household with groceries and many other comforts; schools for his children in the immediate neighborhood; churches close at hand, and such other social advantages as he desires within easy reach—what more is required for a happy existence? And that is the condition of the average Manitoba farmer to-day. As a rule, he has had experience elsewhere; and if he is asked the question, the reply in almost every case will be, that he would not leave the country. [p. 38]

The Western Plains of Canada Rediscovered (1903)
Isaac Cowie

In the ample space blessed with universally fertile but various kinds of soil, selectors of all tastes may be suited. The old saying that one might put in a plough at Winnipeg and never touch anything but good soil all the way to Edmonton, for a thousand miles, is now known to be no longer a figure of speech but a solid, indisputable fact. [p. 18]

Farming and Ranching in Western Canada (1890)
Department of the Interior

The Country to Settle in

Those who honestly doubted, and those who wished the public to disbelieve, the reports concerning the fertility of the Canadian North-West have ceased to be heard; the first have been converted into warm advocates of the country's merits, the others are silent for very shame sake, and because no one will now believe them.

The superior quality of the wheat and other cereals grown upon these lands and the greater yield per acre, when compared with any other portions of the continent, is now universally acknowledged, and, while the crops obtained are greater, the amount of labor required to produce them owing to the nature of the soil is less than in any other country. The climate and natural pasturage are both highly favorable to stock-raising, and as a result no finer cattle are to-day shipped across the Atlantic to the English market, than those which have matured upon the plains of Manitoba and the North-West territories.

It is no longer a question whether it is a good thing to go to the Canadian North-West, but simply in what part of that great country it will be best to make a home. [p. 3]

A farmer can come in about the middle of March, select his land and build his shanty; he can commence to plough about the fifth of April; he can break ten acres and put it under crop on the sod; he can continue breaking for two months after he puts the ten acres under crop, and can break thirty acres, and backset the forty acres in the fall ready for crop in the spring. He can raise enough on the ten acres to give him a start; he can cut hay enough for his oxen and a cow in July, and it will cost him about $60 additional to seed the forty acres in the spring.

Suppose he puts in 30 acres of wheat, and raises only 25 bushels to the acre, at 80 cents per bushel, it will be worth $600; say 5 acres of oats at 40 bushels per acre at 35 cents per bushel, $70; say 1 acre of potatoes, 200 bushels, at 40 cents, $80; 3 acres of barley, 40 bushels per acre, worth 40 cents, $48; and 1 acre of garden stuff at $120; total $918. After deducting expenses of harvesting and the whole original outlay the farmer will still have something to the good to start with next year.

It must not be forgotten, however, that hundreds have arrived in Winnipeg without any money, and by first working on wages have prospered and become substantial farmers. [p. 7]

Western Canada: How to Get There; How to Select Lands; How to Make a Home (1902)
Department of the Interior

Settlers' Testimony

Birtle, November 20, 1901.

I came to this district in 1887, from near Boston, Lincolnshire, England. My earthly possessions at the time I reached this place were $1.75, a wife and seven children. I rented a farm, got work around where I could for myself and my boys and started in and ever since we have worked hard and faithfully, and today I am the owner of 800 acres, and I think as fine a residence as there is in this district, a large frame house, plastered and painted, well furnished, heated by furnace; and frame and log stabling for 100 animals. On my farm I have 520 acres under cultivation and nearly all fenced, and I have just finished threshing, having threshed 8,230 bushels of grain. I own 12 horses, 81 head of cattle, 15 hogs and all the equipment necessary for a farm. We are now enabled to live comfortably and easily, and my total liabilities are but small. We are convenient to railway station, creameries, mills (both lumber and flour), schools, churches and all conveniences as are found pretty generally in every part of this Province now.

My position is only that of many others and a position that any man may in a few years work himself into in this country by steady work. There is, as you will imagine, not much time for idling, at least until after one has got himself in a fair position. The climate here is excellent. The soil is rich and productive and for garden stuff and vegetables I have never seen its equal in any part of the world.

My advice to small tenant farmers at home and to the laboring class, particularly of agricultural districts, is to come to this country and make it their home if they are willing to work hard for a few years. A man should have a little capital with him, which would make it much easier for him. A man with from £200 to £400, coming to this country, working hard, and using good judgment in the expenditure of his money can soon put himself in easy circumstances.

W. E. Cooley

[pp. 19–20]

Canada—the Hope of the World: An English Lady's Opinion of the Opportunities of the West (1910)
Mrs. Walter Parlby

To a vast majority of the untravelled, and less well read, public in the old country, the Canadian West is still a place of wild and woolly ways, a land given over to broncho busting, grizzly bears, and picturesque cowboys; an illusion fostered by the oft-recurring "Wild West" shows, with their lurid presentments of Red Indian warfare, broncho-busting and shooting; a most thrilling entertainment, I have no doubt, to the peaceful dwellers in the British Isles, but how very far removed from actual facts I should very much like to show, feeling, as I do, that the emigrants we want would come in far greater numbers than they do, could they once realize that in coming to this land of boundless prosperity, they are not leaving all the comforts and good things behind them, to face a life of peril and hardship, such as our forefathers had to endure in the brave old pioneering days.

On the contrary, they come to a country thickly settled with peaceful, hard-working farmers of all nationalities, where they will find, among other things, an excellent government—most paternal in the way it looks after the interests of its population—first-class education for their children, and that wonderful equality of opportunity which is the common birthright of all in these new lands.

For the retired army or naval man, or to the many hundreds of people living on small pensions of, say, £400 or £500 a year, I can imagine no better country than this, where their income—in England a mere pittance—would mean a comfortable existence, with the added satisfaction of owning their own homes, with good shooting, with horses, as many as they cared to keep, and with countless opportunities of doubling and trebling any little capital which they might possess, by wise investment; to say nothing of the opportunities for starting in the world a growing family of sons and daughters. To the many unmarried women of the old country also, leading aimless, empty lives, what a prospect this country opens up! True, the government does not allow women to homestead (except widows with families to support), but then a comparatively small sum would suffice to buy a home and a few acres and set up a small poultry farm or other paying hobby.

Things move so quickly in these new countries that even those living on the spot often feel inclined to rub their eyes and wonder if they have not just awakened from some Rip Van Winkle sleep, and in a few years' time the opportunity for so many, that is now here, may have passed away, and we from the old country hate to see all these wonderful offerings being callously disregarded by our kinsfolk beyond the seas, to fall into the hands of every nationality but ours. . . .

We in Canada have been accused of being too optimistic, but that does not trouble us in the least; we glory in our optimism! We defy anyone to be other than an optimist, living in this glorious sunshine, breathing this crisp, exhilarating air. We set no limits to our imaginings, to our ambitions, of what this wonderful country is going to become, or to the magnificent futures awaiting the children that are growing up around us. All we want is for more of our old country kinsfolk to come and join us in our optimism, to take advantage of all the goodly things this Canada of ours is offering so freely, to listen to the call of the West, to leave their little island to its fogs, and its factions, and to throw in their lot with a mighty continent flooded from ocean to ocean with the golden light of unbounded prosperity—with Canada, "the hope of the world."

Why I Emigrated
Land, A Living and Wealth (1913)
Walter Noble Burns

"Why did you emigrate from the United States?" I asked a farmer in Western Canada.

"I believed Western Canada was a land of opportunity for a poor man," the farmer answered. "I have found it a poor man's paradise."

The farmer was a pioneer. Five years before he had trekked across country from Iowa. He had settled upon a virgin prairie. Now he was the owner of a landed estate which spread out before me in league upon league of billowing wheat. His stalwart, bronzed figure had for impressive background his farm itself, visible embodiment of his labor and achievement — a fine two-story farm house, a great barn in the midst of a small village of granaries and outhouses, an orchard weighted with fruit; horses, cattle, sheep and hogs in the pastures, and on all sides to the horizon wheat, nothing but wheat. [p. 18]

Putting a Town on the Map
Land, A Living and Wealth (1913)
William J. Shanks

We were coming back to the three-year-old town on the Grand Trunk Pacific's Winnipeg-Edmonton line, after a twenty-mile motor trip through surrounding wheat fields. Our chauffeur pointed ahead to the distant lines of buildings, the smoke from railway yards, the tall elevators, the church spires glistening in the afternoon sun.

"Three years ago," he said, "there was no town — only the level prairie like we are going through now. When the townsite was placed on the market the people were waiting for it. It went with a rush, and though new towns are springing up on all sides, its growth is more rapid than ever. We are proud of our three-year-old."

At other points we were entertained in towns much less than three years old — in one less than a year old, with its Board of Trade, its leading hotel, its banks, stores, warehouses, and the ubiquitous elevator. These prairie towns seem to have no baby-hood. They scorn adolescence. The impressionist town-builders put their brush on the map, and the picture is complete. They will grow, of course, but in all the elements of solidity they are mature at birth.

Ordinarily a village or town grows like a plant from the seed — by easy stages. In Western Canada, they are made to order. At the opening of one season, a slice of vacant prairie is taken for a townsite. Before the season's close there is an embryo city with business streets, stores, banks, a warehouse or two, a huge grain elevator. A new city has been born, full panoplied. Before it is a week old, it has its newspaper, and foundations are being dug for a school, a church and a town hall. At the season's end it is no longer a pioneer community. There are still newer ones on the heels of the railway builders. [p. 37]

Into the World: Letter from an Emigrant (1927)
Frans van Waeterstadt

I have, in my short life, cherished a considerable number of illusions, more than I could now possibly remember. Most had a brief existence, and died out by themselves only to be quickly replaced by new ones. Others took possession of years of my life, again and again they formed the themes of my deepest thoughts and were the cause of many dreams. But slowly and surely I got older. I came to understand the reality of life . . . and that reality shattered my most beautiful illusions into shards.

There's one fantasy which I've carried with me practically all of my life. I wanted to leave Friesland's flat countryside which becomes after a while, even for the Frisian, a monotonous landscape. Away from this little piece of the world where everybody is the same. I wanted to have adventures, into the world! I wanted to see strange people, Indians, Chinese, Arabs and even Hottentots, as long as they looked different than the people who crossed my path everyday. Wild mountainous landscapes, thundering untamable waterfalls, primeval forests, where the lion and the tiger were still masters. Into the world! That was my great dream. Now my dream, at least in part, is going to become a reality, a hard drab reality, with necessity as its background. Now I have to go into the world, now I have to—in order to find a decent existence.

How many are there in these districts who, like me, find the struggle for existence increasingly difficult? How many are there like me who longingly envision a land where one gets an opportunity to work and through that work a decent existence? I'm going to give it a try in Canada. I believe that Canada offers a man a chance, a chance to show what he can do, a chance to roll up your sleeves, a chance to succeed. O, that success must be wonderful! Here I notice the sympathetic and, more often than not, contemptuous glances of my acquaintances. I hear their scornful gossip and scheming, niggling whispering about "that Frans, who can't get into his stride." That's the terrible torment which I'm now going to escape. I'm going into the world!

Canada has no use for dreamers, only people with a practical spirit and a pair of strong hands. It needs those people for its agriculture. In Canada there are not just thousands but millions of arable hectares of land waiting for the industrious hand to liberate them from the wild bush and tree cover, from the dry woody prairie grasses. The ground must come in contact with the air bringing to it the marvellous nitrogen which causes the grain kernel to germinate and magically transforming it into a mighty, heavy, bending grain stalk. With tenacious patience and concentrated work the arid, but by nature fruitful, Canadian prairies must be changed into rolling seas of grain. Agriculture—there lies the future of this young land.

Rupert Brooke in Canada (1913)
S. Martin and R. Hall, eds.

Winnipeg is the West. It is important and obvious that in Canada there are two or three (some say five) distinct Canadas. Even if you lump the French and English together as one community in the East, there remains the gulf of the Great Lakes. The difference between East and West is possibly no greater than that between North and South England, or Bavaria and Prussia; but in this country, yet unconscious of itself, there is so much less to hold them together. The character of the land and the people differs; their interests, as it appears to them, are not the same. Winnipeg is a new city. In the archives at Ottawa is a picture of Winnipeg in 1870 — Mainstreet, with a few shacks, and the prairie either end. Now her population is a hundred thousand, and she has the biggest this, that, and the other west of Toronto. A new city; a little more American than the other Canadian cities, but not unpleasantly so. The streets are wider, and full of a bustle which keeps clear of hustle. The people have something of the free swing of Americans, without the bumptiousness; a tempered democracy, a mitigated independence of bearing. The manners of Winnipeg, of the West, impress the stranger as better than those of the East, more friendly, more hearty, more certain to achieve graciousness, if not grace. There is, even, in the architecture of Winnipeg, a sort of gauche pride visible. It is hideous, of course, even more hideous than Toronto or Montreal; but cheerily and windily so. There is no scheme in the city, and no beauty, but it is at least preferable to Birmingham, less dingy, less directly depressing. It has no real slums, even though there is poverty and destitution.

But there seems to be a trifle more public spirit in the West than the East. Perhaps it is that in the greater eagerness and confidence of this newer country men have a superfluity of energy and interest, even after attending to their own affairs, to give to the community. Perhaps it is that the West is so young that one has a suspicion money-making has still some element of a child's game in it — its only excuse. At any rate, whether because the state of affairs is yet unsettled, or because of the invisible subtle spirit of optimism that blows through the heavily clustering telephone-wires and past the neat little modern villas and down the solidly pretentious streets, one can't help finding a tiny hope that Winnipeg, the city of buildings and the city of human beings, may yet come to something. It is a slender hope, not to be compared to that of the true Winnipeg man, who, gazing on his city, is fired with the proud and secret ambition that it will soon be twice as big, and after that four times, and then ten times. . . .

> Wider still and wider
> Shall thy bounds be set,

says that hymn which is the noblest expression of modern ambition. *That* hope is sure to be fulfilled. But the other timid prayer, that something different, something more worth having, may come out of Winnipeg, exists, and not quite unreasonably. That cannot be said of Toronto. [pp. 85–86]

THE ONLY DRAWBACK.

UNCLE SAM = (Looking over Canadian West with Mr. Bull) THEY SAY ITS A FINE LOOKIN' COUNTRY, JOHN, BUT DURN IT ALL, YOU CAN'T SEE IT FOR THE WHEAT.

Spelling out success.

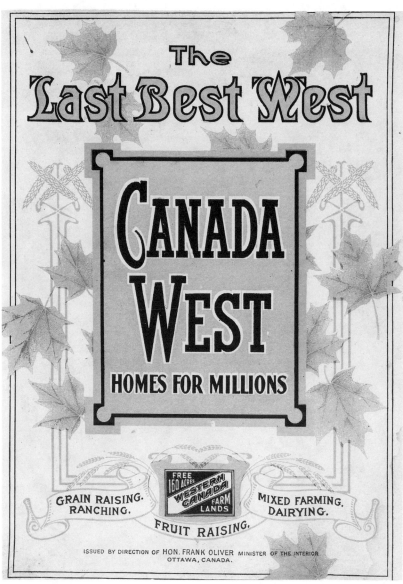

The self-sufficient West.

WESTERN CANADA

THE GRANARY OF THE BRITISH EMPIRE

Breadbasket of the world.

Manitoba: Its Infancy, Growth and Present Condition (1882)
George Bryce

One remarkable feature of settlement in the Northwest is the large number of those "well-connected," who are making Manitoba a home. Persons connected with the British nobility, relatives of principals and professors of college, sons of Canadian cabinet ministers, sons of wealthy capitalists, country gentlemen from Britain, who have been compelled by adverse circumstances to seek the New World, officers of the army and navy, all come up to the mind of the writer, as having been seen by him engaged in farming in his visits to different parts of the country; and a settler of three years' standing, one compelled to emigrate by the failure of the City of Glasgow Bank, has lately been chosen a member of the Provincial Legislature. In one settlement, 100 miles west of Winnipeg, are no less than four or five retired clergymen, of different churches, who have been unsuccessful in spiritual husbandry, and have become tillers of the soil. [p. 317)

Ocean to Ocean (1873)
George M. Grant

It is no wonder that these settlers speak enthusiastically of the country. The great difficulties a farmer encounters elsewhere are non-existent here. To begin with, he does not need to buy land, for a hundred and sixty acres are given away gratuitously by the Government to every *bona fide* settler; and one-third of the quantity is a farm large enough for any one who would devote himself to a specialty, such as the raising of beets, potatoes, or wheat. He does not need to use manure, for, so worthless is it considered, that the Legislature has had to pass a law prohibiting people from throwing it into the rivers. He has not to buy guano, nor to make compost heaps. The land, if it has any fault, is naturally too rich. Hay is so abundant that when threshing the grain at one end of the yard, he burns the straw at the other end to get rid of it. He does not need to clear the land of trees, stumps or rocks. Very little fencing is required, for he can enclose all his arable land at once with one fence, and pasture is common and illimitable. There is a good market all over Manitoba for stock or produce of any kind, and if a settler is discontented he can sell his stock and implements for their full value to new comers.

And what of the Indians, the mosquitoes, and the locusts? Neither Crees nor Sioux have given those settlers the slightest trouble. The Sioux ask only for protection, and even before Governor Archibald made the Treaty with the Salteaux and Crees by which they received a hundred and sixty acres of land per family of five, and three dollars per head every year for their rights to the country, they molested no one. Poor whites, were they about in equal numbers, would give ten times as much trouble as the poor Indians, though some of the braves still paint ferociously and all carry guns. And the mosquitoes, and the grasshoppers or locusts, no one ever spoke of, probably because the former are no greater nuisance in Manitoba than in Minnesota or Nova Scotia, and the latter have proved a plague only two or three times in half a century. [p. 93]

Manitoba and the Great North West (1882)
John Macoun

Regarding the country in the immediate vicinity of Battleford, I am quite aware that what I have to say flatly contradicts what appears to me to be the general impression concerning it. Before coming here I was told that Battleford was in the midst of a sterile, dreary waste of sand, but I wish we had a few hundred square miles of just such dreary wastes of sand in Ontario and Quebec. The soil is not the deep, black loam which I have seen in other portions of the North-West, but at the same time that it is not unproductive I shall presently produce abundant proofs. It is a rich and very friable soil, in which there is unquestionably some sand, but for all that it is deep, strong, warm and extremely productive. . . . [p. 100]

We are now 890 miles by cart trail northwest from Winnipeg, and over this immense distance pits, four feet deep and twenty miles apart, have been dug, and a careful examination of the soils shows that only about five per cent of the whole distance is unfit for agriculture and classed as third class soils, when compared with those of Prince Edward County which is one of the most productive districts of Ontario. The extent of these fertile lands cannot be realized by any person reading the accounts published in newspapers or blue books, nor even in passing over the trails as these are only particular lines. But having traversed the country in every direction I am enabled to grasp their immensity, without realising in any appreciable degree their influence upon the future of the civilized world. Seeing millions of acres of arable lands lying without inhabitants in one part of the British Dominions, and learning that in another part people on the brink of starvation are murdering each other for the privilege of renting a potato garden, causes one to exclaim against the shortsightedness of Governments, in not assisting emigration, and on the other hand against the foolishness of people remaining where their normal state for generations has been and *will* be one of poverty. [pp. 113–14]

Peter Rindisbacher, *Blackfeet Hunting on Horseback [untitled]* **(1833)**
Indians on the hunt; the struggle to survive in a harsh land.

Peter Rindisbacher, *The Murder of David Tully and Family by the Sifsatoons Sioux, a Sioux Tribe* **(ca. 1823)**
Settlers unwelcome: Red River settlers en route to the United States.

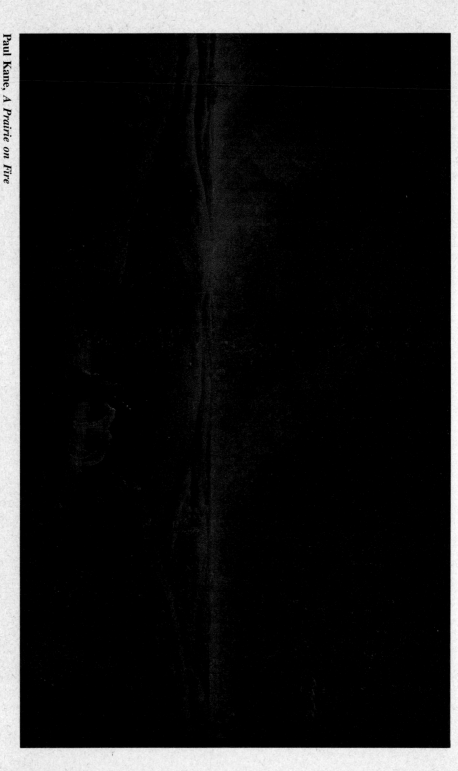

Paul Kane, *A Prairie on Fire*
A spectacular prairie scene.

Frederick Verner, *The Last Buffalo* (1893)
Nostalgia for a lost Eden.

W. G. R. Hind, *Buffalo Magnified by Mirage* (1862)
An advancing civilization.

William Armstrong, *Fort Garry* **(1857)**
Civilization meets the wilderness.

A "Home for Millions."

Edward Roper, *Some Prairie Flowers and a Prairie Dog* **(1887)**
The Prairies: a cornucopia of beauty.

Reta Cowley, *Potash Plant and Wolf Willows* (1968)
Beauty in the eyes of the beholder.

Illingworth Kerr, *Straw Stacks, March Thaw* (1935)
Sketching a prairie identity.

William Kurelek, *Who Has Seen the Wind* **(1976)**
The least common denominators of land and sky—Saskatchewan prairie.

Prairie Utopias

Pioneering in the Prairie West: A Sketch of the Parry Sound Colonies that Settled near Edmonton, N.W.T. in the Early Nineties
W. C. Pollard

One of the colonies that left the country surrounding the beautiful little village of Magnetawan is the subject of this book. The members located near Fort Saskatchewan, about 30 miles east of Edmonton, in Alberta.

When the colony was first mentioned it was intended only to have members of the Church of England in Canada, and to settle at the mouth of the Moose Jaw River, but the agent of the C.P.R. soon opened the way for all to join and become members.

To see the stir among the people, and the number volunteering to go to what was then the far west, brought to mind the fact that "There are lives that are erring and aimless," as most of them did not know what was ahead of them in entering a new country, void of capital, and in many cases without a sufficient grubstake to carry them for even a few months under new and strange conditions. They were accustomed to earning a livelihood in lumbering operations in the backwoods of Ontario.

However, in the excitement it was not a question of going—the only question was when: this year or next?

When the majority realized just where they were, and in the light of prospects ahead, they marveled that they had ever attempted to remain among the rocks and the beautiful scenery in the Parry Sound District. This was the more forcibly brought home to them when they discovered that the lands they had cleared so laboriously were worth little or nothing in the market, as so many wanted to sell at once.

The slogan was, "All for the West. All aboard; if you can't get a board get a slab; but go anyway and anyhow, ready or not ready!! Everyone must go to the Promised Land!!" [pp. 7–8]

Letter from a Barr Colonist (1904)
Alice Rendell

We are much amused at the reports that reach us from England as to the terrible plight we are in even to the verge of *starvation*. Please once and for all disabuse your minds of any such ideas. We are quite happy and contented, very much better off than we were in England, whilst as to food we live quite as well as ever we did. We have two butchers on the town site. Our meat is delivered at the door and is of the very best quality. Certainly we have had difficulties to surmount and hardships to endure but we quite expected we should before we left England and we treasured up a reserve fund of determination and pluck which stood us in good stead when the need came. I would never advise anyone to come out here who is the least afraid of work. They are better off at home. There is plenty of room to breathe in this country and if the work is hard the freedom, which is the indispensable attribute of the life here, makes one far less susceptible to physical fatigue than in England where one seems to have such a feeling of weighty oppression to handicap one's energies. Here one feels that each week's work is a step onward whilst also in the old country oftentimes a year's hard toil brought nothing but disappointment and additional anxiety. [pp. 24–25]

The Perfect Prairie City

Saskatoon (1911)
Saskatoon Board of Trade

If undecided as to whether you ought, or ought not to "Go West," just ask yourself the following questions and answer them thoughtfully and honestly:

Frankly, am I content with my progress in a worldly sense, – or have I stagnated?

Am I disheartened by the knowledge that others, no more favorably equipped, are elsewhere winning splendid success while the passing of years finds my position unaltered?

If I continue here, what are my future prospects? Are they worth the present toil; – or, have I nothing brighter to hope for? And what is

my condition likely to be five, ten or twenty years hence? How much
better;—or, how much worse?

Does my present employment call for my highest ability; or, do I know
and feel myself qualified for far bigger, better things—had I but the
chance?

Honestly,—am I satisfied; or, am I dissatisfied and discouraged?

Now, if you have stagnated, have no brighter prospects for the future
and are consequently dissatisfied and discouraged, and if you feel able
for better things, desire them and are willing to strive for them,—then,
as an intelligent man, you have no excuse for indecisions,—Come West!
Come to Saskatoon, where, of all places in the West, your success is
most fully assured; where no deserving man has ever yet failed; where
there are no poorhouses because there are no poor; where there is
comfort, happiness and prosperity, and an unlimited field for your
intelligence and energy. [p. 1]

In coming here, do not forget that the country is new to you even
as you are new to the country. Therefore, it is quite possible that, at
the outset, some slight discouragement may be your lot. If so, merely
accept it as the brief and trifling travail of your birth into the fuller, fairer
life that most certainly will be yours in this great land. IF YOU ARE STEADY,
HONEST, INTELLIGENT AND HARDWORKING, YOU CANNOT FAIL. Each year
your condition will improve. From the moment you arrive with us, you
can pluck from your heart all dread of the future and cast it forever from
you into the hopelessness of other days. Cling to this truth. Let it cheer
you to forgetfulness of whatever little difficulties you may at first
encounter. [p. 2]

The Psychology of Saskatoon (1908)
Saskatoon Board of Trade

Saskatoon possesses an ineffable charm peculiarly its own. The
stranger is obsessed by it within the first hour of arrival. Nor does this
charm arise merely from the responsive joy of the heart in those things
of beauty which so delight the eye,—not from the glorious freeness of
the prairie, nor from the pure, tender breath of its wandering winds;
not from the strange, quiet softness of the summer sky, nor from the
river winding at its own sweet will between wooded banks—winding
through the very heart of a picture which beautifully gives the lie to
popular conceptions of a prairie town. No, this singular charm is not
of these things: It is something deeper, subtler, more wonderful; it is
the charm of an all-pervading spirit of Prosperity! And nowhere else

in this whole wide Western Country is it so palpably present as in Saskatoon City.

Indications of prosperity are everywhere in Saskatoon; one seems to breathe prosperity. It permeates the whole community. Its influence outcrops continually—even in the common acts of the simplest citizens. It is beautiful and it is good.

Nowhere will you find a happier people. Men treat men kindly. The "Good Morning" greeting is unmistakably sincere,—so is the handgrip. These simple courtesies, so meaningless, so conventional in older parts, do here convey their literal significance. They are genuine. There is a smile in the heart of our people, and a smile through their lives. It is omnipresent,—WHY?

Simply because prosperity has lifted the lack of money out of life and thereby annihilated nine-tenths of human tribulation.

And, yet, how many are there who came here poor and discouraged, but a few years ago, whose beautiful homes or splendid farms to-day lend their tribute of adornment to this fair young city and district! There is no success anywhere for the man who fails here. But we have few failures. There is no room for the idler. The idler soon discovers this fact to speedily assume the universal earnestness and energy. [pp. 1–2]

Saskatoonlets (1911)
Saskatoon Board of Trade

Admitting the general development of a city and its district to be in proportion to the demonstrated value of the latter's natural resources; admitting also that the greater these resources the swifter such development;—and, further, agreeing that development involves population which in turn means business, does it not follow that any centre of supply—such as Saskatoon—should recommend itself for the establishment of wholesalers and manufacturers merely in proportion to the swiftness of its growth?

NO CITY IN THE ENTIRE BRITISH EMPIRE CAN SHOW ANYTHING LIKE SASKATOON'S EXTRAORDINARY RECORD OF PROGRESS!!

NOTE—Kindly re-read the above, and write Commissioner Board of Trade, Saskatoon, for all information. [p. 2]

Prairie boosterism envisioned.

Prairie Utopias Envisioned

Sowing Seeds in Danny (1908)
Nellie McClung

The prairie lay sere and brown like a piece of faded tapestry beneath the November sun that, peering through the dust-laden air, seemed old and worn with his efforts to warm the poor old faded earth.

The grain had all been cut and gathered into stacks that had dotted the fields, two by two, like comfortable married couples, and these in turn had changed into billowy piles of yellow straw, through which herds of cattle foraged, giving a touch of life and colour to the unending colourless landscape. The trees stood naked and bare. The gardens where once the corn waved and the hollyhocks flaunted their brazen beauty, now lay a tangled litter of stalks, waiting the thrifty farmer's torch to clear them away before the snow came. The earth had yielded of her fruits and now rested from her labour, worn and spent, taking no thought of comeliness, but waiting in decrepit indifference for her friend, the North Wind, to bring down the swirling snow to hide her scars and heal her unloveliness with its kindly white mantle.

But although the earth lay sere and brown and dust-laden, the granaries and elevators were bursting with a rich abundance. Innumerable freight-trains loaded with wheat wound heavily up the long grade, carrying off all too slowly the produce of the plain, and still the loads of grain came pouring in from the farms. The cellars were full of the abundance of the gardens — golden turnips, rosy potatoes and rows of pale green cabbages hanging by their roots to the beams gave an air of security against the long, cold, hungry winter. [pp. 294–95]

Clearing in the West (1935)
Nellie McClung

I had walked proudly behind my father, in the clean new furrows in my bare feet, as he broke the new sod on our farm, and as the coulter cut the sod, and the share turned it over, I knew he was doing something more than just plowing a field. I knew there was a significance in what he was doing, though I had no words to express it. I knew this was what the land had been waiting for all these long years. It was for this that the rain had fallen on it in summer and the snows had covered it in winter. It was for this the grass had grown on it, withered, and grown again, that some day someone would come and claim it, not for himself alone but for all people, claim it in the name of humanity and press it into humanity's service, stamping and sealing it forever with the broad signature of the plow. [p. 116]

Janey Canuck in the West (1910)
Emily Murphy

> "Where there's more of singing and less of sighing,
> Where there's more of giving and less of buying,
> Where a man makes friends without half trying
> That's where the West begins."
>   . . .

How the sun shines here in Winnipeg! One drinks it in like wine. And how the bells ring! It is a town of bells and light set in a blaze of gold. Surely the West *is* golden—the sky, flowers, wheat, hearts.

Winnipeg is changing from wood to stone. She is growing city-like in granite and asphalt. Hitherto, banks and hotels were run up over-night, and had to pay for themselves in the next twenty-four hours.

Winnipeg has something western, something southern, something quite her own. She is an up-and-doing place. She has swagger, impelling arrogance, enterprise, and an abiding spirit of usefulness.

"What I like," says an American to me, "is the eternal spunk of the place."

Winnipeg is another name for opportunity. The wise men did come from the east. They are all here. Winnipeg is a city of young men, and youth is ambitious. It is called the bull's-eye lantern of the Dominion, and the buckle of the wheat belt. If you want to please a Winnipegger, tell him the city's growth is steady and healthy—not a bit of a boom about it. You will be telling the absolute truth at the same time. [pp. 10–11]

Edward Roper, *Sulky Ploughing near Carberry Mountain, Manitoba* **(1887)**
Transforming the land from wilderness to homestead.

Inglis Sheldon-Williams, *Man Ploughing with Two Horses* **(ca. 1930)**
Breaking the land.

Gus Kenderdine, *Land of Promise* **(1923)**
The promised land.

Harvest

1. Ma-ni - to - ba, Ma-ni - to - ba, Fair thy fields of har-vest stand, Mel-low light of ear - ly au - tumn Steal-ing down a - cross the land; Laugh-ing up from far off mea - dows, Comes the south wind bold and free, Bend-ing

in-to   rip-pling wave-lets All the   tran-quil gol-den   sea.

Manitoba, Manitoba,
   Fair thy fields of harvest stand,
Mellow light of early autumn
   Stealing down across the land;
Laughing up from far off meadows,
   Comes the south wind bold and free,
Bending into rippling wavelets
   All the tranquil golden sea.

Manitoba, on thy prairies
   Yesterday the buffalo fed,
And the trembling plains re-echo
   With the thunder of their tread.
Now they sleep in earth's oblivion
   And the golden harvest waves,
In its wealth of autumn splendour
   O'er their long-forgotten graves.

Manitoba, peaceful homesteads
   Nestle in the amber light,
Where of old the tribes have gathered
   For their fierce and deadly fight.
And the Indian by the river,
   Standing at his tepee door,
Gazes sadly at the country
   He may cross in hunt no more.

Manitoba, from thy prairie,
   Won by God's especial grace,
To a nobler, fuller mission
   Than the battle or the chase,
Rises up the song of harvest
   As the thankful people raise
From the oat fields and the wheat fields
   Fervent notes of thankful praise.

The Poor Little Girls of Ontario

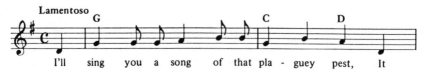

I'll   sing   you   a   song   of that pla-guey   pest,   It

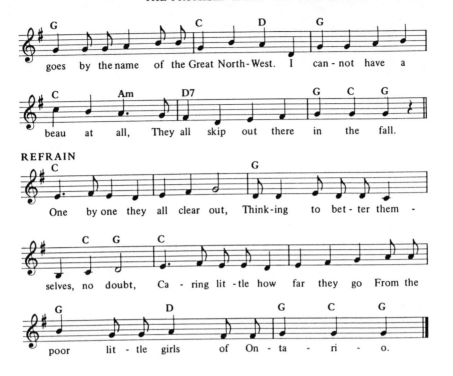

goes by the name of the Great North-West. I can-not have a
beau at all, They all skip out there in the fall.

REFRAIN

One by one they all clear out, Think-ing to bet-ter them —
selves, no doubt, Ca - ring lit -tle how far they go From the
poor lit - tle girls of On - ta - ri - o.

2. First I got mashed on Charlie Brown,
      The nicest fellow in all the town.
   He tipped his hat and sailed away,
      And now he's settled in Manitobay.
           Refrain

3. Then Henry Mayner with his white cravat,
      His high stiff collar and his new plug hat,
   He said if he stayed he'd have to beg,
      And now he's settled in Winnipeg.
           Refrain

4. Then my long-legged druggist with his specs on his nose,
      I really thought he would propose,
   But he's sold his bottle-shop and now he's gone
      Clear out to little Saskatchewan.
           Refrain

5. I'll pack my clothes in a carpet sack,
      I'll go out there and I'll never come back,
   I'll find me a husband and a good one, too,
      If I have to go through to Cariboo.

Last Refrain   One by one we'll all clear out,
               Thinking to better ourselves, no doubt,
           Caring little how far we go
               From the old, old folks of Ontario.

5

WESTERN REALISM
1880–1940

Disillusionment was implicit in the utopian image of the West, as settlers arrived to discover that the conditions on the western frontier did not match the image in the propaganda and the ideal in their minds. They lashed out at the image makers, while at the same time they made the painful adjustment to the realities of their new environment. They adjusted in two ways. They attempted to change reality into their ideal, to make the region over into the utopian image that had attracted them in the first place. The agrarian protest Movement, which grew rapidly in the prosperous years of prairie settlement through such co-operative organizations as the Grain Growers' Associations, and which erupted in the 1920s into the Progressive movement, aimed at creating a farmer-dominated third party, was one attempt to transform reality into agrarian utopian imagery. More often, westerners came to accept the realities of the West, with its harsh climate, geographical limitations, and social isolation, if for no other reason than to have a greater appreciation of the real environment in which they lived. Many poked fun at the region's foibles in song and verse. As well, a "literature of realism" appeared in the 1920s, following the disillusionment of the First World War, which went beyond the earlier romantic and utopian literature of the settlement era to create a literature that was more closely attuned to the region's environmental conditions and cultural characteristics and that was as well vastly superior in literary quality. Artists in the interwar years attempted for the first time to paint the realities of prairie landscape –

its flat land and its large sky—rather than impose European or eastern Canadian images onto western scenes. In history, a new interpretation of Canada—the metropolitan thesis—viewed the West as a hinterland to eastern metropolitan forces, a region subservient to the will and wishes of central Canadian business and urban interests. The catastrophic conditions of the Depression of the 1930s imposed its own realistic image on the prairies and destroyed any remaining vestiges of the West as "a promised land." Here were Palliser's worst predictions come true.

The Reality of Prairie Homesteading

Disillusionment and dissatisfaction were built into the settlement process.[1] The immigration literature had promised a "land of milk and honey" there for the taking. Propagandists played down the difficulties in the West or ignored them completely in their quest for settlers. As a result, immigrants could not help but be unhappy when the reality did not match their expectations.

There naturally arose a reaction to the utopian image presented in the immigration propaganda. One immigrant, who began a book on "My Four Years Experienced in the North West of America: Roughing It in the Far West," explained in the preface to his manuscript why he was writing it: "This book is not written for the purpose of running down America but for the purpose of letting any who are thinking of immigrating to America know what they may have to go through." He then began his first chapter:

> So many books, pamphlets etc. (mostly untrue) have been written about the charms and beautiful climate of the North-West of Canada and none about the hardships that have to be endured there that I think it high time someone should let the public know the true state of affairs in that region of the world. . . . I have before me the latest pamphlets on Manitoba and the North West and all I can say is that the ones that are not a pack of lies are a pack of rubbish, but rubbish or no rubbish I know perfectly well that they have been, and in future will be, the means of enticing people to immigrate to the North West.[2]

In the remainder of the manuscript he went on to recount the misfortunes that befell him from the moment he arrived until he decided to leave.

Adam Shortt, a professor of political economy at Queen's University in Kingston, wrote a critical two-part article on the West for the *Queen's Quarterly* journal based on his impressions of the region from teaching a summer course in southern Alberta in 1894.[3] He pointed out the need to balance the distorted image of the West in the propaganda—achieved, he claimed, through "a little well-placed exaggeration, effective use of half truths, and the prominence given to advantages when the modifying disadvantages are carefully ignored"—by presenting a realistic image of the West. He began: "The Great North-West, as a name at least, commonly surrounded with a halo of superlatives, has become familiar enough to most Canadians for a considerable time. Yet there are probably few names so familiar which convey so imperfect an ideal of what they represent."

Shortt argued that the chief limitations of the West could be attributed, ironically, to the immigration propagandists. In their attempt to create an ideal society, they ended up with a society that was far from ideal. He pointed out, for example, that the propaganda had failed to attract the hardy, independent, hard-working yeoman farmer depicted as the ideal, but instead attracted "the thriftless, unstable, mortgage-eaten and poverty-stricken elements, willing enough to have prosperity thrust upon them but without capacity to achieve it for themselves." The remittance man was the worst and the most extreme example of the dreamer who came west expecting to create idyllic conditions without toil or sacrifice. But thousands of city-bred immigrants who lacked farming experience— greenhorns—had also come, under the illusion that ranching or farming in the West only required that nature be allowed to take its course. Shortt claimed that they "are almost as helpless as a limb severed from the body. They know little of what it means to provide the greater part of their living for themselves, and still less of how to make a living out of ranching alone. They have come out expecting to do some work of course,— though not very much in so rich a country,—but mainly to enjoy the charm and freedom of nature, to ride horses, to indulge in field sports and, quite generally, to enjoy all those beautiful, poetic and aristocratic privileges promised them by the honey-tongued immigrant agent and the reliable settler's guide." As a result, Shortt argued, the West was populated in general by a class of people who lacked the physical skills to succeed at their new occupation and the social characteristics to live together in society. Rather than independent, they were highly dependent on the government for assistance; rather than socially responsible, they were "wild and woolly," believing that freedom on the frontier meant "to do as one pleases" irrespective of other people.

Furthermore, he claimed that the "intensely dreary aspect of the prairie during most seasons of the year and the oppressive *ennui* of the lonely life on the prairie" led to an excess of drinking, while few westerners found "spiritual consolation and enlightenment in religion." Shortt concluded, therefore, that the West was not being populated by a superior class of people, as the propagandists and the early literary writers had depicted. Instead, the area attracted a class of undesirables who were not capable of succeeding and who lowered the level of citizenry to a base common denominator that was far from ideal.

Shortt overstated the case, but certainly all new settlers in the West experienced difficulty adjusting to their new home. They felt like strangers in a strange land.[4] Immigration and settlement accounts abound with examples of the painful adjustment. For some, the cold reality confronted them from the moment they set eyes on the desolate prairie itself; for others, it was their first view of their 160 acres on the bald prairie of the southern plains or in the densely-forested region of the park belt, far from neighbours. Then they experienced the chilling realization that they had only themselves to depend on in order to survive. For still others, the adjustment came when they realized that they could not hope to succeed on a quarter section alone. As historian Lewis G. Thomas notes: "The complaints of the western farmer about his exploitation by eastern business stem ultimately from the hard fact that he was attempting what was next to impossible even on the best of western farm land and under the most favourable of prairie climatic conditions. None but the most exceptionally fortunate and the most exceptionally provident could make the quarter section family farm a continuing financial success; the unit was too small to begin with and it could not generate sufficient additional capital to permit its enlargement to an economic size by consolidation with adjacent small properties."[5] Other immigrants, especially from foreign countries, felt the difficulty of adjustment when they realized that they had to abandon their traditional cultural practices from the old country in order to survive in the new. Novelist Adele Wiseman, herself the daughter of Jewish immigrants, found "the environment . . . socially, rather than climatically, hostile."[6] Sunken hearts, tears, doubts, and disappointment were the standard reaction of the new immigrant to the West.

This realistic image of the West is evident in a series of articles done for the *Grain Growers' Guide*, the newspaper of the Grain Growers' Association, in the 1920s.[7] The editor of the newspaper asked home-steaders to contribute to a special issue on their "Homesteading Experiences." He printed the best accounts in the paper, while A. S. Morton of the University of Saskatchewan's history department copied the remainder and deposited them in the Archives. One is struck in reading these reminiscences by the difficulty the immigrants had in adjusting, largely because of the high expectations with which they had come to the West. Indeed, the contrast between their ideals and the reality became the crucible out of which a new, more cynical, sober view of the West emerged in the early twentieth century. One account began:

> I was born in Yorkshire England. . . . Whilst away from home I met the man who now is my husband, [and who] often like myself read the literature which was distributed wholesale especially in rural parts of England describing the beauties of Canada, showing pictures of cattle knee deep in prairie grass, miles of golden grain all just waiting for some one to come to take possession. . . . We arrived at Estevan, Saskatchewan about the first week of April 1907, any one who remembers that winter

and spring will surely feel sorry for the immigrant who left their own country of green hedges, green fields, primroses, snow drops out and found here huge banks of snow the likes of which we had never seen before, and zero weather, people muffled up to the eyes in furs. Certainly the pamphlets we read on Canada did not describe that side of the country to us.

A woman recalled the loneliness of homesteading for women: "There was always a ceaseless longing for the home land and old familiar faces, and it took many long years to overcome that lonesome feeling." Another woman wrote:

> When I look back over our homesteading days in Saskatchewan I have to laugh and cry at the same time. And I think all others who were among the first settlers on the prairies have the same feelings. When you think of how strange and different everything would be to one reared in a city, in the central [United] States, where there is very little snow and ice, where the thermometer never reaches the zero mark, where the grass is greener in the winter than it is here in summer (on account of the dead grass that is still on the prairie). . . . [My husband] came to Davidson in 1905. I did not come for a few weeks after Frank did, as we had three little girls, the youngest only three months old. So I could not come till the shack was built. . . . The country around Davidson did not look too bad for me, but the further north and east we came it got pretty rough and the knolls got steeper till they became hills. My heart sank. I could not imagine why anyone wanted to live in such a place for.

Welsh immigrant Evan Davies recalled the difficulty of adjusting to a strange new land like the prairie West: "I felt very low and I believe David James did too. This was so unlike what we had imagined back in Wales. We had visualized a green country with hills around, and happy people as neighbours—no doubt a naive outlook . . . but one common to many people emigrating at the time. . . . There was something so impersonal about this prairie, something that shattered any hope of feeling attached to it, or ever building a home on it."[8]

The Frederiksens, a Danish family who settled in Nokomis, Saskatchewan, before World War I, described the stark reality of home-steading on the prairies in a series of letters and reminiscences. On the impact of the prairies on them, Joanne Frederiksen wrote:

> It isn't easy to work up a farm here on the prairie without money, it takes all one's strength and time and even a lifetime to do it. . . . It is said that life is a struggle and if we did not know it before, we surely notice it here. Not as before a struggle against wild animals and man, but against nature's fury, the unyielding soil, the harsh climate [.] [I]t is a struggle for existence, a struggle against the loss of culture's benefits: church, school, parish, community. How deep roots a man has in his fatherland he may never know himself, until he loses them.[9]

Such accounts can be duplicated a thousand times over.

How typical are they? The cold statistics on the successes and failures of homesteading testify to the large number of people who did not fulfill their dreams in the "last best West." The rate of attrition—the failure of the homesteader to "prove up" and thus obtain a patent for his quarter section—was extraordinary. Almost half of those who tried to bring their dreams into reality had those dreams shattered in a nightmare of failure. For them, the prairie west was not "the promised land." Their story is often lost since it was unpopular to write about failure, especially in a land that had promised so much. They were denounced as "knockers" in a society of boosters.

John Donkin, a North-West Mounted Policeman, presented an equally negative image of homesteading experiences in the West as early as 1889 in his *Trooper and Redskin in the Far North-West*. In one passage he described a typical blizzard and its effect.

> The blizzard is a storm peculiar to the prairie regions, almost indescribable in its deathly power. It is the most terrible wind that rages upon earth; a cloud burst of powdered ice, accompanied by a violent hurricane, with the thermometer away below zero. I am utterly impotent to describe the cold. . . .
>
> In these terrible tempests, settlers have been known to have gone to feed their oxen in the stables, just a few yards from their own door; and have been seen no more, alive. Some have been discovered when spring has lifted the shroud of winter; their bones picked clean by the coyotes. Oxen have been frozen in their tracks. But any one can read the annual tale of devastation which is cabled across the Atlantic. It is utterly useless for the authors of emigration pamphlets to deny them. They do recur, and will continue to do so, in all the prairie lands, though in the dim future the increase of population may mitigate their severity.

Later on in the book he wrote:

> [A]ny degree of success, out here in the north-west, is only to be attained by stern determination, and rugged perseverance. The life of a pioneer is lonely and disheartening at first. And let him not hope to win a fortune from the soil. If he makes a living, he should rest content. This is, emphatically, a *hard* land to dwell in; and existence is a struggle.[10]

The Reality of the Prairies in Song and Verse

Folk songs provide a medium by which to understand the realistic image of the West in the settlement period.[11] Folk songs form an important part of the popular culture, since they describe common experiences and express the "gut feelings" of the common man. A rich literature of early western Canadian folk music exists. Many of these songs were sung to familiar tunes such as "Beulah Land" or "O Tannenbaum," and often they used earlier lyrics, only changing occasional words or phrases to reflect more accurately the reality being described. Indeed, a favourite technique was to take a popular song and substitute different words so as to alter completely the meaning of the song. This was especially true of those glowing accounts of the settlement experience which were a musical version of the immigration propaganda and which belied the reality that many homesteaders experienced.

One such song was the popular "Prairie Land," sometimes called "Alberta Land." An early version talked in glowing terms about settling "in this our lovely prairie land." In a later version (date unknown) the song starts out on a positive note, talking about "this great northwest prairie land," but by stanza four the image changes:

> We have no wheat, we have no oats,
> We have no corn to feed our shoats,
> We do not live, we only stay,
> We are too poor to move away.[12]

Another version, claimed to have been composed by the young people of Consort, Alberta in 1913–14 and entitled "Alberta Land," begins with a denunciation of the image makers:

> We've reached the land where we were told
> Was chocolate soil and full of gold
> And naught was known of storm nor cold,
> Alberta Land, Alberta Land.

For the stanza quoted from the earlier version has been substituted the following, which vividly portrays the reality of trying to survive on a homestead on the prairie:

> We have no wheat, we have no oats,
> We have no coin to pay our notes,
> Our credit's gone and we must pay,
> Oh for a harvest how we pray.[13]

Two later versions provide their own negative images of homesteading on the drought-stricken prairies. One, composed during the post-World War I depression, talks of an Alberta land "where nothing grows for man to eat." The other, written in the depths of the Great Depression, depicts the prairie as cruel, windswept, and parched, and its people as forlorn, starving, and downtrodden—a far cry from the utopian image in the immigration propaganda. It does end on a semi-positive note in its proverbial prairie faith in "next year country": "I'll tighten my belt, and have no fear, things will be better, I'm sure, next year."[14]

"Life in a Prairie Shack," first sung in the 1880s, complains about the fraudulent West—no doubt an indirect reference to the image makers.

It also pokes fun at the "tenderfoot" or greenhorn settler—particularly the remittance man—trying to make a living in the "raw frontier West." "The Alberta Homestead" describes the difficulties of travelling "through muskeg, mud, and mire" to come west only to find a desolate and cold region. The solution is to return to the United States where conditions were not so bad as one had imagined them. A song with a similar title, "The Alberta Homesteader," also depicts a West of endless problems, including the fear of "a-starving to death on a government claim." This song also ends with the person leaving the West:

> So farewell to Alberta, farewell to the west,
> It's backwards I'll go to the girl I love best.
> I'll go back to the east and get me a wife
> And never eat cornbread the rest of my life.[15]

One final homesteading song, "Hurrah for the Palliser," vividly describes the conditions in the triangular area of southern Saskatchewan and southern Alberta—Palliser's Triangle—and reinforces the fact that John Palliser was correct in his description of the area as a desert. The two choruses are particularly revealing:

> Hurrah for the Palliser, land of the free
> Land of the wheat rust, grasshopper, and flea
> I'll sing and I'll praise it, I'll tell of its fame
> While starving to death on my government claim.

> Hurrah for the Palliser, where blizzards arise
> Where the summer sun burns and the flea never dies
> And the wind never stops but it always complains
> 'Til it blows us all off our government claims.[16]

A Literature of Prairie Realism

In the interwar years there emerged in prairie literature a "realistic" tradition; it was a reaction against the sentimental and the romantic which had characterized prairie literature in the pre-World War I era. It was also a logical result of the disillusionment following the failed attempts at raising up the new millenium from the carnage of World War I as well as the immediate postwar depression.[17] In this new literature, the western landscape is depicted as harsh, foreboding, unyielding, and lonely. Martha Ostenso spoke of the loneliness of the prairies in her novel *Wild Geese* (1925):

> As he rode along, a mood of loneliness overtook him—the same cold feeling of belonging nowhere that he had had at night when he was a little boy, after the priest had put the light out and he lay listening to the rain on the glass of the window. . . . Suddenly Mark stopped his horse

to listen. He lifted his face up to catch the strange sound that was passing over him, a great summoning trumpet-call, that seemed to hollow out the heavens.

"Wild geese," he said aloud. "They sound as if they know something about it—something about being alone."[18]

In *Fruits of the Earth* (1933), Frederick Philip Grove depicted his protagonist, Abe Spalding, as struggling to conquer a land that was resistant to man's efforts:

> A few hundreds yards from the Somerville Line, as the east-west road was called, he reached that flat and unrelieved country which, to the very horizon, seemed to be a primitive wilderness. North, east, and west, nothing showed that looked like a settlement, and the impression of an utter loneliness was perhaps even enhanced by the knowledge that somewhere it harboured at least one man by name of Hall, half-crazed with work and isolation, destined to be Abe's neighbour. . . . But this immense and utter loneliness merely aroused him to protest and contradiction: he would change this prairie, would impose himself upon it, would conquer its spirit![19]

In his short story, "Snow," Grove depicted a winter on the prairie as a life-threatening experience. Absent is the utopian image of man gaining strength and satisfaction from the bracing air of a prairie winter; instead images of helpless, beleaguered man, a victim of his harsh environment, prevail:

> Nothing was visible anywhere; nothing but the snow in the first grey of dawn. Then, like enormous ghosts, or like evanescent apparitions, the trees of the bluff were adumbrated behind the lingering veils of the night. . . .
>
> A suspicion took hold of him; with a few quick reaches of his arm he demolished the roof of the drift all about.
>
> And there, in the hollow, lay the man's body as if he were sleeping, a quiet expression, as of painless rest, on his face. His eyes were closed; a couple of bags were wrapped about his shoulders. Apparently he had not even tried to walk! Already chilled to the bone, he had given into that desire for rest, for shelter at any price, which overcomes him who is doomed to freeze.[20]

The image is of a land in which man feels alienated. Unlike the earlier literature of Connor, McClung, and Murphy, where western man was depicted as living in harmony with Nature, the land, and himself, the literature of the interwar years depicted prairie man as struggling against a harsh and unyielding land that ultimately transformed him into a cold, calculating, and harsh character, like the land itself. The struggle required self-discipline, self-denial, and a sacrificial effort that carried over into other human relationships, creating the same lust for power and need to conquer and control that was required to subject the land itself. Frederick Philip Grove explains the theme, which dominated his own novels in the interwar years, as follows: To be successful, a pioneer had to be "dominant" and "rigid"; he had to have "a single-minded preoccupation with the specifically-pioneering task." Yet in his success in subduing the land, he comes to realize—too late—that "he has been working for a purpose which has defeated its end. He cannot, now, settle down to enjoy the fruit of his labour."[21]

Images of spirit-less man shaped by an equally inanimate land abound in prairie literature in the interwar years. In *Wild Geese*, Martha Ostenso describes her protagonist, Caleb Gare, as "a spiritual counterpart of the land, as harsh, as demanding, as tyrannical as the very soil from which he drew his existence."[22] In *Settlers of the Marsh* (1925), Grove depicts Neils Lindstedt, the central character, as a success in realizing his material ambitions but as a tragic figure in the realm of human relationships and in his inner spiritual self:

> Of his material success he had no doubt. Was he not slowly and surely making headway right now? While he was hibernating as it were? . . .
>
> Yet material success was not enough. What did it matter whether a person had a little more or less wealth? . . . [T]he accessories of life were really the essentials; they were what made the living worth while: the building up of a whole little world that revolved about him. About him? Not at all. . . .
>
> He himself might be forever a stranger in this country; so far he saw it against the background of Sweden.[23]

Sweden was symbolic of the spiritual element of life, the traditions of the old world; the prairies represented the materialism and progress of the new world. In contrast to earlier novelists who depicted the new, unfettered West triumphing over the traditional, staid East, Grove depicted the West in some of his writings as destroying what is good in the old world; the materialism of the new world overcame and eclipsed the spiritualism of the old.

In *Fruits of the Earth*, Grove has Abe Spalding realize in a flash of insight how he had become a slave to his land.

> . . . he was worried and restless. He was in debt. He worked frantically; he even pulled weeds again by hand, a thing he had not done for a year or two; and he did it alone now; for Ruth no longer kept him company. The crop did not promise so well that year; the flood had been slow in running out; and after that there was a drought; in patches the wheat was turning yellow before it had headed out. It was, of course, impossible to rogue three hundred acres of grain; he did what he could. Yet there were odd little twinges of a lack of confidence. With his thirst for conquest he lived dangerously, always assuming new debts before the old ones were paid off; he was discounting the future; he was selling himself into slavery.[24]

Arthur Stringer, in his trilogy of novels on prairie life as seen through the eyes of a woman, has his protagonist go through an evolution in her views of life on the prairies. In *The Prairie Wife* (1915), she is the joyous, optimistic, and enthusiastic new wife of a prairie dweller (see Chapter 4). In *The Prairie Child* (1922) she is a sober, callous, and beaten mother alone on the lonely prairies. The only virtue she can find in prairie women is their stubborn will to survive:

> A prairie mother *has* to be a great woman. She must be great to survive, to endure, to leave her progeny behind her. I've heard the Wise Men talk about nature looking after her own. I've heard sentimentalists sing about the strength that lies in the soil. But, oh, pioneers, you know what you know! In your secret heart of hearts you remember the lonely hours, the lonely years, the lonely graves! For in the matter of infant mortality alone, prairie life shows a record shocking to read.[25]

Sinclair Ross wrote of the heartaches of wheat farming on the prairies, in which man loses out to nature, whether in the form of insects, disease, or the intractable weather, in his moving short story, "A Field of Wheat." He uses Martha, the farmer's wife, as the medium to project the image of a malevolent West that destroyed body and soul:

> Martha was thirty-seven. She had clinched with the body and substance of life; had loved, borne children—a boy had died—and yet the quickest aches of life, travail, heartbrokenness, they had never wrung as the wheat wrung. For the wheat allowed no respite. Wasting and unending it was struggle, struggle against wind and insects, drought and weeds. Not an heroic struggle to give a man courage and resolve, but a frantic, unavailing one. They were only poor, taunted, driven things; it was the wheat that was invincible. . . .
>
> She had loved John, for these sixteen years had stood close watching while he died—slowly, tantalizingly, as the parched wheat died. He had grown unkempt, ugly, morose. His voice was gruff, contentious, never broke into the deep, strong laughter that used to make her feel she was living at the heart of things. John was gone, love was gone; there was only wheat.[26]

Yet the struggle between man and nature in prairie literature in the interwar years is more than just a struggle of man against the land or man in search of material success. It is a struggle of human nature— good versus evil—within the psychic wilderness of man himself. This inner spiritual struggle is most forcefully dramatized in Sinclair Ross's classic novel, *As For Me and My House* (1941). The arid conditions of the town of "Horizon" in the midst of the Great Depression are symbolic of the sterile spiritual and psychic conditions of the characters of the Bentleys themselves. The real drama is the battle between the two protagonists—Philip and Mrs. Bentley—acted out on a stage of prairie desolation befitting their inner turmoil:

> We've all lived in a little town too long. The wilderness here makes
> us uneasy. I felt it first the night I walked alone along the river bank—a
> queer sense of something cold and fearful, something inanimate, yet aware
> of us. . . . We shrink from our insignificance. The stillness and solitude—
> we think a force or presence into it—even a hostile presence, deliberate,
> aligned against us—for we dare not admit an indifferent wilderness, where
> we may have no meaning at all.[27]

In this respect, the realistic literature of the interwar years reflected the
reality of man's demonic nature—his irrational side—which Sigmund
Freud had "discovered" in the field of psychology and which the
destruction of a world war had laid plain for the world to see. Rational
man had become irrational man, and this new demonic being was as
evident on the Canadian prairies as he was in the urban setting of
European realistic novels. As the western Canadian literary critic Dick
Harrison notes in *Unnamed Country* (1977):

> Prairie realists represented man as spiritually alien to the plains, isolated
> and alone in a still unnamed country because he had transformed the
> prairie with his hands but not with the power of his heart or his
> imagination.[28]

A third image in prairie realist literature—besides alienated man and
demonic man—is what the literary critics call "the machine in the garden."
Prairie literature in the interwar years reflected the reality of a society
undergoing dramatic change from rural to urban living. Mechanization
of the family farm, which occurred to the greatest extent in the twenties,
was the chief reason for this revolutionary change. Prairie novelists often
dealt with the tensions inherent in a society of dramatic change, and
used the dichotomy of rural and urban as a means to comment on the
strengths and limitations of these two lifestyles. In other words, the
country and the city, the farmer and the urban dweller were symbolic
of two societies in tension—the rural, pastoral society, the garden of the
West, and the industrial, technological society, the mechanized civilization
of the East. Whereas in earlier western Canadian literature, the former
was always associated with the virtues of the good life and the latter
with the vices of modern living, in the realist tradition such a simple
black and white division did not occur.

Frederick Philip Grove came closest to perpetuating the pastoral myth
of a virtuous rural society and a debased urban society. In a way this
was ironic because Grove (born Felix Paul Greve) had spent his childhood
and youth in cities. He had grown up in Hamburg, been educated at
the University of Bonn, and travelled as a student to Munich and Rome.
His background had prepared him to see the city rather than the
countryside as the ideal society. Nevertheless, while Grove could be

critical in his depiction of rural society as harsh and exacting, he did see it as more desirable than urban living, in that it afforded man opportunities for spiritual development. Grove held the typical rural suspicion of urban society as one of materialism, debauchery, greed, and debasement.

In associating rural society with spiritual values, Grove accepted the western farmers' own image of themselves as "God's Chosen People."[29] The western farmer premised his fight against the East, big business, and urban encroachment on the idea that "God Made the Country, Man Made the Town"—that the family farm was the ideal social unit, and farmers the most virtuous and moral beings on earth. The agrarian West might not yield a better material life, but it afforded a better spiritual life. It was this image that had fuelled the agrarian protest movement of the 1920s, known as the Progressive Movement. It was one reaction to the realities of mechanization and urbanization: to challenge the idea that farming had ceased to be an occupation and had become a business— agribusiness—and to transform reality into an agrarian utopian dream by reasserting the prestige and ideals associated with agrarianism. Grove perpetuated this image in his novels.

If Grove associated rural society with spiritualism and urban society with materialism, however, he did not return to the simplistic black and white view of earlier prairie novelists. He realized that the new industrial and technological society was here to stay, and that people had to learn to balance the growing materialism with spiritual values. The "machine in the garden" presented a challenge to prairie man to hold fast to his spiritual roots in his quest for the promised land.

Surprisingly, Robert Stead, the romantic novelist of the prewar era, went furthest in his later novels in exploring the implications of the "machine in the garden" image. In *The Smoking Flax* (1924), he begins by setting a peaceful prairie scene in which a Ford car, the symbol *par excellence* of mechanization on the prairies, suddenly becomes the focal point:

> Long vistas of undulating prairies checkered in black, moist fields. Here and there a grove of green poplars; here and there a farmhouse, white and peaceful in their shadows. Grass, green and moist, with a purple carpeting of anemones. Water shining from many tiny lakes. Coveys of white clouds, like ruffled swans, afloat in an infinite sky.
>
> A long road, running straight on forever. Up and down the sweeping vistas of prairie-land; by the checkered black fields breathing deep the still sunshine of early May. . . .
>
> Over the ridge to the eastward an atom suddenly appears where the road leaps out of the sky. It grows rapidly, flashing a heliograph in the sunlight as it approaches. Presently it defines itself as that most familiar of all objects on the prairie trail, ouster of horse and saddle and buckboard and prairie schooner—a Ford automobile.[30]

Later in the novel Stead has his major characters, Cal and Minnie, leave the farm—not out of a feeling of melancholy and remorse but with an attitude of defiance and joy. Minnie comments: "I got fed up on the farm, so I quit it. If I get fed up on the office, I'll quit that, too." "And go back to the farm?" Cal asks. "No. Anything but that."[31]

In *Grain* (1926), the "hero" of the story, Gander Stake, although the son of a farmer and a farm boy, shows no love for the land. His first love is the machine. When Gander first hears the roar of the threshing machine, Stead writes:

> The steady pant of the exhaust, the rumble of the wheels, the voice of Bill Powers raised occasionally in caution or direction to his engineer — these were the accompaniments of that mechanical procession which on the morrow would thresh in a dozen hours the wheat to feed a hundred families for a year. . . . And although Gander was a boy not touched by the romance of books here was something that stirred him deeply — the romance of machinery, of steam, which at the pull of a lever turned loose the power of giants![32]

Gander found in the machine a love he could not find on the land or even in the woman he coveted, Josephine Burge. The machine is depicted by Stead not as an alien entity in the garden but rather as the means to transform farming from a mere occupation or pursuit to an industry — agribusiness. Thus, Stead characteristically has Gander go off to town to work as a mechanic at the end of the novel.

Absent from *Grain* is the romantic image of the rural West that prevailed in Stead's prewar novels. It was as though he himself had come to accept the reality of the new mechanized and urbanized West as having virtue itself. For him, the image of the utopian West as pastoral myth now seemed out of place, and he attempted in his novels of the 1920s to present a realistic image more in keeping with this new West.

Sketching the Stark Prairies

Some artists in the settlement period and especially in the interwar years attempted a more realistic portrayal of the West.[33] They wanted to see the landscape in its own terms, not through eastern eyes. One of the first prairie artists to attempt a more realistic portrayal of settlement life in the West was, ironically, Inglis Sheldon-Williams, the same artist who depicted the romantic, utopian life of Cannington Manor. In his later paintings — in which he was strongly influenced by the paintings of the Barbizon School of northern France, to which he was introduced when studying in Paris and London from 1896 to 1913 — he depicted the struggle of homesteaders against the elements of blizzards, storms, fires, and cold. These paintings conveyed the message that the prairie landscape was at best indifferent and at worst menacing, and thus, farming the prairies was a challenge, an act of defiance that took more than just a desire to succeed; it took courage, fortitude, and a good deal of luck. He dramatized prairie homesteading as a life and death struggle in which man did not always triumph. Such paintings offered a balance to the tranquil and pastoral scenes produced by the majority of prairie artists in the period. Unfortunately, just as Sheldon-Williams had come to experiment with realism in his paintings, he left for England in 1917, never to return.

C. W. Jefferys also painted in the realistic tradition in the settlement period. Born in England and raised in Toronto, Jefferys made numerous trips across the country between 1901 and 1924 in search of a landscape to which he felt an affinity as an artist; that landscape became the prairies. He once commented that all of Canada could be divided into two topographies for purposes of painting: northern and western. He described the latter as "a land of wide open spaces, of suave flowing lines, of harmonies of colour, of which the extreme type is the western prairie."[34]

The prairie West that he depicted was not a landscape of valleys, trees and lush vegetation, but of flat expanse, open spaces, and large azure skies. He understood why earlier artists had gravitated toward images of the garden in their paintings of the West: "In a new country like this, where life in general is crude, and regardless of little beyond material things, it is natural that the first conception of art should be that of the shelter garden, where the fairer spirits may dream awhile and forget the hurly burly." While sympathetic, he was also critical of this romanticizing because it distorted reality. As he wrote:

> Now with traditions and training such as these (i.e. French and English) how is the painter to deal adequately with an environment such as ours? Where can he find pigment that will fix upon canvas his response to the air and sunlight of a western wheatfield? . . . He who approaches rural and pastoral Canada with the expectation of finding Europe in North America misses entirely its peculiar spirit.[35]

For Jefferys, the "true West" was a landscape that could be reduced to the common denominators of earth and sky; this was the West that he wanted others to see. He found an approach suitable to the prairie landscape in impressionism. Impressionistic art emphasized space and light, and these were, in Jefferys' estimation, the essence of a prairie painting.

Jefferys seemed almost alone in the settlement period in his efforts to paint the prairies realistically. Not until the twenties did a new generation of artists appear who wanted to paint the landscape on its own terms. By this time, realism in western art became associated with another equally important concern of the period: the search for a regional identity. Artists such as L. L. Fitzgerald, W. J. Phillips, Illingworth Kerr, and Robert Hurley wanted to do for the West what the Group of Seven was doing at the same time for Canada in general: namely, discovering images of the land which could become symbols of identity.[36]

Lionel Le Moine Fitzgerald was born in Manitoba, the son of immigrant parents. He rose in the artistic society of his native province to become principal of the Winnipeg College of Art, and in 1932 he became a member of the Group of Seven, on the eve of their disbanding. Unlike other members of the Group, Fitzgerald preferred painting his native prairie to northern Ontario. He did share with members of the Group an affinity for the natural landscape as the soul of its people and the symbol of their identity, but it was the soul of the prairie people and the regional identity of the West through its unique landscape of earth and sky that fascinated him. His paintings, like those of Jeffreys, emphasized space and light to represent the open land and bright sky on the prairies. Land and sky, he claimed, were the unique physical characteristics of the West upon which a unique regional identity could be based.

Illingworth Kerr, born in 1906 at Lumsden, Saskatchewan, in the Qu'Appelle Valley, went even further than Fitzgerald in his quest for a regional identity. Kerr's paintings of the open prairies in winter were, according to art critic Ronald Rees, "the first to register the stark qualities of its light and lines and to convey a sense of its awesome, inhuman scale."[37] What Kerr and other prairie painters were attempting to do was to reduce the landscape to its bare essentials so that the landscape became in prairie art, as it did in prairie literature in the interwar years, symbolic landscape.

Robert Hurley felt an affinity for the prairies which neither Fitzgerald nor Kerr quite felt. Art critic Terry Fenton claims that Hurley was "the first genuine painter of the prairies."[38] Initially, this was not the case. When Hurley first arrived from England in 1923, he described the prairies as "a desolation – an abomination of desolation."[39] However, he grew to love the simplicity of the prairie landscape, and he had the ability to capture its essence on canvas. He broke with the romantic tradition in western Canadian art by shifting the iconography from streams and wooded valleys – uncharacteristic prairie landscape scenes – to flat prairie, railways, telephone posts, grain elevators, and an expansive sky – images that he stereotyped as symbolic of the prairies. He then used sharp, clean outlines and dominant colours to express the simplicity and vastness of this landscape. He was so successful at expressing what the majority of westerners felt about their region that his paintings sold in the thousands. As Percy Wright of the Saskatoon *Star-Phoenix* wrote of the prairie people: "It was as if they had been waiting for an interpreter who would point out to them the realities of their environment."[40] Hurley

became that artistic "interpreter" of prairie "realities." He contributed
to a new era in western Canadian art by shifting the artistic image of
the West from a promised land to a stark environment, thus forcing the
artist to seek its meaning in abstraction or symbolism.

The Exploited West

In keeping with the realistic image of the West in prairie literature and
art, there arose in the 1930s a new environmentalist approach to Canadian
history which was as harsh in its image of the West as that depicted in
the literature of the time.[41] The Laurentian thesis and its corollary the
metropolitan-hinterland thesis argued that central Canada—the Laurentian
Shield country—formed a commercial, political, and cultural empire that
through its metropolitan centres dominated and exploited the hinterland
regions, like the West, that came under its influence. Thus, the West
ceased to be seen as the creative centre of the nation which had constantly
thrown up new ideas and democratic movements (as in the frontier thesis)
and was depicted instead as a region subordinate to the metropolitan
centres of central Canada and essentially conservative and even
reactionary in its ethos. Historian J. M. S. Careless summarized the idea
this way:

> The Laurentian School . . . looked not from the forest-born frontiers for
> its perspective of Canadian history but from developing eastern centres
> of commerce and industry. Indeed, it primarily studied the effects of the
> East on the West, and largely regarded business men and conservative
> urban political elements as agents of national expansion who might well
> be more far-sighted in their outlook than were their agrarian opponents.[42]

Hopkins Moorhouse, an activist in the agrarian protest movement of
the 1920s, clearly presented the farmers' version of their inequitable
position in Confederation in his *Deep Furrows* (1918), and thus projected
the negative image of the West of the metropolitan-hinterland relationship:

> Admitting that the prosperity of Western Canada is essential to our
> national prosperity, it is not necessary to look far in order to understand
> why the farmers have taken this definite action. Western farmers and
> citizens generally are carrying extra burdens which offset the advantages
> of cheap and fertile land. Interest on mortgages and bank loans have been
> higher than in Eastern Canada. It is more expensive to distribute
> commodities West than East. On account of the lavish donations of
> Western lands to railway promoters the cost of railway construction has
> borne heavily on the West. Freight rates are about sixty per cent higher
> and express rates about sixty-six per cent higher than in Eastern Canada.
> Thanks to the protective tariff, Western people are paying high for
> everything they get without any return compensation.[43]

This realistic image challenged the utopian image of the prosperous, self-sufficient, contented western farmer. The agrarian protest movement was an attempt on the part of western farmers to correct their perceived inequitable position in Confederation in hopes of restoring the western farmer to his rightful place as the centre of the nation. But the reality of his position belied such a dream and fuelled his spirit of protest.

The realistic image of the West of the interwar years was a corrective to the utopian image that prevailed in the settlement period in the immigration propaganda, and in the art and literature of the period. But it had its own limitations in capturing the image of the West. Like earlier image-makers, the realists looked to the physical landscape for the images. There was a strong sense of environmental determinism underlying their perception of western Canada. There arose in the post-World War II era a generation of western Canadians who saw the West less as a physical entity that shaped one's outlook—whether optimistic or pessimistic—and more as a spiritual and mental concept. They looked inward, to the "landscape of the mind," to discover their images of the West.

The Reality of Prairie Homesteading

Some Observations on the Great North-West Immigration and Transportation (1895)
Adam Shortt

The Great North-West, as a name at least, commonly surrounded with a halo of superlatives, has been familiar enough to most Canadians for a considerable time. Yet there are probably few names so familiar which convey so imperfect an idea of what they represent. Before going out to see something of the territories for myself, I found that, in my own case, I had developed two quite distinct, and in some measure conflicting ideas answering to the name North-West. The one, corresponding to the great North-West with the retinue of superlatives, was obtained by reading Government pamphlets and settler's guides, C.P.R. literature of a similar type, and articles on the territories and the railroad, in various Canadian and English periodicals, from the pens of a number of enthusiastic writers who are the chief ornaments of the Canadian school of patriots. The other, a much narrower, more localized and much less splendid, but withal more human idea, was derived mainly from conversations with persons who had lived in widely different parts of the North-West, and who, while tolerably well satisfied with their lot, were not rendered arrogant by unusual good fortune. [p. 183]

To meet with some such families in their prairie homes, is an interesting though saddening experience. There we are likely to find a combination of wretched surroundings, ill-furnished and poverty-stricken shacks, yet with here and there a remnant from the happier estate of the past, such as an odd piece or two of fine old English table ware in china or silver, a few draggling ghosts of garments that once in their original brightness had probably shone in far off social gatherings, or perhaps a room ornament or two, looking most incongruous amid their present surroundings. Still, in the midst of these unpromising circumstances one may find people of charming manners and most enjoyable conversation. One cannot but feel that it was a shame to have lured such people out into the wilderness to make shipwreck of their lives. But failures of many kinds are too common there to attract much attention or excite much pity. If, however, they begin to give vent to their hardships in print and to accuse the Government or the Railroad of deception, they are styled "chronic kickers," and attempts are made to smother them out. They are abused as thriftless and incapable; and most of them certainly are when set out on the prairie. Why, then, encourage such people to come to the country by giving such an exaggerated and misleading account of it as to cause them to suppose that it is very easy to make a living and even to grow rich there? [p. 189]

Letter from Danish Immigrants in Western Canada (1911) "Scandinavian Experiences on the Prairies, 1890–1920: The Frederiksens of Nokomis"
Jorgen Dahlie

You must excuse me, it's been eight days and I haven't managed to write but we were all so exhausted . . . it has been difficult just to get food ready three times a day. . . . When we were set out in the middle of the night in the cold at the last station in a driving snowstorm, we all cried but then my husband was there. . . . Here it's still so desolate and frightening on the wild prairie. It is like the ocean. We are a tiny midpoint in a circle. . . . You will . . . understand that it looks terrifying, more than you can imagine. . . .

It certainly isn't too homey here yet but I believe it will be in time. It is to be hoped that there will be some comfort for the children inside these four low walls, if we are to survive. My husband has worked and struggled, his clothes are in tatters, he could hardly do without us and therefore we *had* to make the trip. . . . He is hoping to get work after threshing season in the fall, and that would be well paid. Everyone likes him and is willing to give him a helping hand. My duty will be to think as little about myself as possible and to do . . . all for him and the children — and with God's help — it *will* go well, such is the stand we take as we begin. [p. 107]

Prairie Settlers
Mary Hiemstra

The men went away after a while and Dad went to look at his land. Mother said he counted every blade of grass every day, which was an exaggeration, but he never tired of walking across his acres. He was terribly proud of this new farm, and he inspected it as a king inspects his kingdom. When he returned from a walk his face was always bright and his voice hopeful.

'I never saw owt to compare with this place,' he said when he came home that afternoon. 'It's fair surprising the way it warms up. No fog, no drizzle, just sunshine. If you stand still you can see the grass growing. Another week and the trails will be passable, then work on the railroad will start. Once that's finished, Sally, we'll be rich in no time.' He took off his cap, the one he had brought from England, hung it on a peg, pulled his home-made chair close to the packing-box table, and waited for Mother to pour him some tea.

Mother paused with her hand on the handle of the little blue teapot and looked sharply at Dad. 'I thought you said we were going home as soon as the trails were passable?' she said.

'Well . . .' Dad looked uneasily at the brown log walls and the green trees not far from the open door. 'I thought maybe we might try it a bit longer now that the weather's warm,' he said.

'It won't be warm for ever.' Mother filled Dad's mug with steaming brown tea and handed it to him. 'And there'll be other winters.'

'But not as bad as the last, and when we get some breaking done —'

'The prairie doesn't plough easy.' Mother put sugar in her tea. 'And it won't be ploughed in a day either. It will take years, and a lot of things might happen. Have you forgotten how we nearly lost Jack last winter? Next time we might not be so lucky.'

'I was thinking on buying a farm for him and for the lasses as well, one of these days.' Dad stirred his tea, though he hadn't put any sugar in it.

'They may not want a farm.' Mother stirred her tea carefully. 'Farming's a hard life for a woman.'

'You don't think you could stick it another year?' Dad stopped stirring, lifted the spoon out of the brown tea and watched the drops fall off the tip of the spoon back into the mug. They made soft little plinks in the silence.

'It's that lonely. All winter and hardly a word to another woman.' Mother picked up her mug of tea, but her hand trembled and she put it down again.

'We might go to Lloydminster next winter.' The warm glow was going from Dad's voice.

'And live in a tent and have scurvy?'

'There might be houses by then.'

'But it's more likely there won't.' Mother's blue eyes were beginning to look angry.

'It's a shame to lose the farm after we've lived on it a whole year.'

'It isn't as if it was one of the bairns.' Mother glanced at Jack, busy in the wood-box.

'If we go,' Dad said slowly, looking at his spoon, 'the rest of the colony might go too. I wouldn't want to start something like that.'

'You're making excuses, that's all.' Mother's voice trembled.

'No, I'm not. You heard what Watson said: nobody wants to be the first to go. They'll say we're running away.'

'I don't care what they say.' Mother flounced across the room and shut the door as if she couldn't bear the sight of Canada. 'I've had enough of this place,' she said.

'It's a shame to give up now,' Dad said. 'In another year the farm will be worth a thousand dollars, and when Jack grows up—'

'If we stay here he may not live to grow up,' Mother said. [pp. 50–51]

Not a Penny in the World

We come to Calgary in 1898 and then we moved out of there about 10 miles and then my father died, so my mother she took a homestead. Oh yes, a woman could take up land then, but not many did. Not many. I don't know how she did it or how she ever got the idea she could do it. A wonderful woman, my mother, wonderful woman. Even today I don't know how she managed.

See, she had no experience. We weren't farm people. We'd come from the Falkland Islands, and if you know them there's nothing there to farm.

I don't know how in the world she ever got along. Three children, two sisters, and myself and not a penny in the world. Somehow she got a roof over our heads. A neighbor or two helped but she did it all, mostly. That's the kind of women there were then. I wish I had a picture of her to show you. Not a big woman but all this spirit. She knew she had to provide a home for the three of us and that's how she did it, right out on the prairie. She would work 18 hours a day. Absolutely.

At first she'd hire to get a little bit of plowing done when she could get a dollar or two. She'd sell eggs in High River, and sometimes women in the town would hire her for a day. She'd walk in to town, work all day, walk back. For just a few cents. Wages wasn't nothing in those days. Not too many people had money and those that had it were awfully close with it.

First she got an acre plowed and that became a garden. That's an awful lot of garden, but all of us worked in it. We didn't go to school much but we sure worked around the place. In that garden. Then the next year she got another acre plowed and so forth, and after that I was big enough to drive a team around and I plowed up the rest. I can't remember just where she got the horses. I think she must have borrowed them or maybe rented them, because I know we didn't own them. Horses in them days was expensive. So I was behind the plow. How old was I? Oh, 1905, let me see, I'd be about 10. Yes, I was 10 years old. It must have been quite a sight to see a 10-year-old boy behind a big team of horses plowing. It wasn't good land, it was fair land, some alkali, some sand, and I plowed up the whole shooting match. [pp. 54–55]

The Reality of the Prairies in Song and Verse

Alberta Land (ca. 1913–14)

We've reached the land where we were told
Was chocolate soil and full of gold
And naught was known of storm nor cold,
Alberta Land, Alberta Land.

Chorus

Oh Alberta Land, sweet Alberta Land
As on thy burning soil I stand
I look away across the plains
And wonder why it never rains;
But Foster calls with trumpet sound
And says the rain has passed around.

We have no wheat, we have no oats,
We have no coin to pay our notes,
Our credit's gone and we must pay,
Oh for a harvest how we pray.

Our horses are of bronco race,
Starvation stares us in the face,
We do not live we only stay
And are too poor to get away.

The prairie chickens flip and fly,
They go splendid in a pie
And if you are a man of luck
Perhaps sometime you'll shoot a duck.

The bachelor here lives all alone
In a little sod shack he calls his home;
He darns his sox and bakes his bread
And often wishes he were dead.

The Alberta Homestead (ca. 1920)

1. It was way out west in Alberta
   Where the coyotes howl and sing,
   Where it rained and hailed all summer,
   And we never raised a thing.

2. Oh, I came out here one summer,
   Away out in the west.
   I think I'll turn and go back,
   Or I will starve to death.

3. We travelled through Battle Lake Valley,
   Through muskeg, mud, and mire,
   Till we came where they were surveying
   A road for the C.P.R.

4. I built a little log cabin
   With a roof of natural clay.
   Dear friends, I'm sorry to tell you,
   But I'm bound for the U.S.A.

5. Of money I haven't one dollar,
   And the grubstake she's run mighty low.
   Just as soon as the frog pond froze over,
   It's back to the U.S. I'll go.

6. Farewell to the poor homesteader,
   Farewell to the land so free,
   Farewell to sunny Alberta —
   She's too damn cold for me.

Saskatchewan

Saskatchewan the land of snow
Where winds are always on the blow
Where people sit with frozen toes
And why we stay here no one knows.

Chorus

Saskatchewan Saskatchewan,
There's no place like Saskatchewan;
We sit and gaze across the plains,
And wonder why it never rains,
And Gabriel blows his trumpet sound
He says: "The rain, she's gone around."

Our pigs are dyin' on their feet,
Because they have no feed to eat,
Our horses, though of bronco race,
Starvation stares them in the face.

The milk from cows has ceased to flow,
We've had to ship 'em East, you know,
Our hens are old and lay no eggs,
Our turkeys eat grasshopper legs.

A Literature of Prairie Realism

Wild Geese (1925)
Martha Ostenso

Protest meant only the expenditure of extra effort — the work would
have to be done anyway. Ellen and Charlie hitched the horses to the two
rakes, and Judith and Martin went ahead with the mowing machines.
It was deadening work, so that after a while the spirit forgot to follow
the body behind the horses up and down, up and down, in the bright
heat that rose from the earth and fell from the bare, cloudless sky. The
nostrils began to ache from the sweet, hot, dusty smell of the hay. The
hands grew dry and swollen from the reins, the sun lay like a hot iron
on the shoulders, no matter which way one turned. But presently it was
only the body that was there, enduring; the spirit seemed to have gone
somewhere else, and left an absence of thought, an absence of everything
except attention to the task at hand. [pp. 204–205]

Fruits of the Earth (1933)
F. P. Grove

At last he climbed to the top of his load and started north for the six-
mile trek over open prairie.
A few hundred yards from the Somerville Line, as the east-west road
was called, he reached that flat and unrelieved country which, to the
very horizon, seemed to be a primitive wilderness. North, east, and west,

nothing showed that looked like a settlement, and the impression of an utter loneliness was perhaps even enhanced by the knowledge that somewhere it harboured at least one man by name of Hall, half-crazed with work and isolation, and destined to be Abe's neighbour. As for others, the two who, probably under an impulse to huddle close together in this immensity, had a decade ago filed on the two northern quarters of the same section, they were gone, and having "proved up" on their claims, had vanished again in the outer world.

Abe's brief call at his sister's had somewhat unsettled him. For a year he had mentally lived on that open, flat prairie, planning and adjusting himself. He needed room; he needed a country which would give scope to the powers he felt within him. Forbidding as it looked, this was that country. But Mary's casual remark about the cedars had reawakened in him the vision of the old farm as a place to live in: the house in its cluster of cedars, with the gnarled apple trees in the orchard behind; with the old furniture in the rooms – not very comfortable perhaps, but harmonious in the half-light admitted by the scanty windows half closed with vines: mellowed into unity by being lived in through generations. Here, everything was of necessity new and raw. Ruth in the midst of this? She knew nothing of what she was going into except that Abe was to create some sort of home for her: Ruth, whom a year or so ago he had met casually when buying oranges in a store. . . .

Well, he would conquer this wilderness; he would change it; he would set his own seal upon it! For the moment, one hundred and sixty acres were going to be his, capable of being tilled from line to line!

He would conquer! Yet, as he looked about, he was strangely impressed with this treeless prairie under the afternoon sun. This utterly undiversified country looked flat as a table-top. Differences in level, small as they might be, must exist. Why, otherwise, should there be bare soil here and there, with the smooth and cracked surface of a dried mudhole in clay? Whereas elsewhere the greyish-green, silky prairie grass grew knee-high. Why should the spring floods which he had not yet seen drain away to the east, into the river which carried them to the great lake? Why should it have been observed by those who had preceded him that certain sections of this wilderness dried sooner in spring than others? There must be undulations in the soil.

A year ago, Abe had scanned the district from a purely utilitarian point of view. Apart from the bush land in the far north, this had been almost the last district where free land was still available. Within it he had looked for depth of topsoil, for nearness to possible neighbours, for a convenient distance from a shipping-point.

Nothing but such considerations had had any influence with him a year ago. That the general conformation of a landscape might have to be considered, such an idea he would have laughed at. Yet this prairie seemed suddenly a peculiar country, mysteriously endowed with a power of testing temper and character. But that was exactly what he had wanted: a "clear proposition" as he had expressed it, meaning a piece of land capable of being tilled from line to line, without waste areas, without rocky stretches, without deeply-cut gullies which denied his horses a foothold. He wanted land, not landscape; all the landscape he cared for he would introduce himself.

Yet, half unbeknown to him, there was a dream: of a mansion such as he had seen in Ontario, in the remnants of a colonial estate—a mansion dominating an extensive holding of land, imposed upon that holding as a sort of seigneurial sign-manual. Dominating this prairie.

Had he undertaken more than he could do?

So far he had allowed his horses to idle along the faint trail. At this thought he straightened on top of the tent which covered his household goods. There, just ahead of him, came the turn; so far he had gone north, covering four miles in that direction. Now two miles west; and then look out for the stake which marked his corner.

He shook the lines over the backs of the horses and looked up. There did not seem to be even birds about! But this immense and utter loneliness merely aroused him to protest and contradiction: he would change this prairie, would impose himself upon it, would conquer its spirit! [pp. 21–23]

The prevailing silence—for, apart from man's dwellings, not even the wind finds anything to play its tunes on—is accentuated rather than disturbed by the sibilant hum, in early summer, of the myriads of mosquitoes that haunt the air, bred in stagnant pools, and the shrill notes, in the early autumn, of the swarm of black crickets that literally cover the soil. That silence, like the flat landscape itself, has something haunted about it, something almost furtive. . . .

Abe, now that he was becoming conscious of this landscape at last, and of its significance, could at first hardly understand that he, of all men, should have chosen this district to settle in, though it suited him well enough now. But even that became clear. He had looked down at his feet; had seen nothing but the furrow; had considered the prairie only as a page to write the story of his life upon. His vision had been bounded by the lines of his farm; his farm had been floated on that prairie as the shipwright floats a vessel on the sea, looking not so much at the waves which are to batter it as at the fittings which secure the comfort of those within. But such a vessel may be engulfed by such a sea.

When, these days, he approached his place, the place built to dominate the prairie, he succumbed to the illusion that he who had built it was essentially different from him who had to live in it. More and more the wind-break surrounding his yard seemed to be a rampart which, without knowing it, he had erected to keep out a hostile world. Occasionally the great house seemed nothing less than a mausoleum to enshrine the memory of a child.

Abe felt defeated; at least in so far as he was what he had been; perhaps that defeat would slowly become apparent to the outside world. But the world defeats only him who has already been defeated in his heart. [p. 138]

Settlers of the Marsh (1925)
Frederick Philip Grove

It was not an easy task. To drown one's thought in labour is very difficult on the farm: everything is conducive to contemplation. No high ambitions lead you away from the present; and yet those ambitions which are indispensable, the lowly ones, are really the highest on earth: the desire for peace and harmony in yourself, your surroundings. . . .

But there were no surroundings—there was no little world, no microcosm revolving within the macrocosm. There was the duty to the farm, the country, the world: cold, abstract things devoid of the living blood. . . . [p. 207]

A Field of Wheat (1968)
Sinclair Ross

It was hot—heat so intense and breathless that it weighed like a solid. An ominous darkness came with it, gradual and unnoticed. All at once she turned away from the stove and stood strained, inert. The silence seemed to gather itself, hold its breath. She tried to speak to Nipper and the children, all three sprawled in a heap alongside the house, but the hush over everything was like a raised finger, forbidding her.

A long immobile minute; suddenly a bewildering awareness that the light was choked; and then, muffled, still distant, but charged with resolution, climaxing the stillness, a slow, long brooding heave of thunder.

Martha darted to the door, stumbled down the step and around the corner of the house. To the west there was no sky, only a gulf of blackness, so black that the landscape seemed slipping down the neck of a funnel. Above, almost overhead, a heavy, hard-lined bank of cloud swept its way across the sun-white blue in august, impassive fury. . . .

She stared into the blackness. There it was—the hail again—the same white twisting little cloud against the black one—just as she had seen it four years ago. . . .

She reached the kitchen just as John burst in. With their eyes screwed up against the pommelling roar of the hail they stared at each other. They were deafened, pinioned, crushed. His face was a livid blank, one cheek smeared with blood where a jagged stone had struck him. Taut with fear, her throat aching, she turned away and looked through Joe's legs again. It was like a furious fountain, the stones bouncing high and clashing with those behind them. They had buried the earth, blotted out the horizon; there was nothing but their crazy spew of whiteness. She cowered away, put her hands to her ears. . . .

Nothing but the glitter of sun on hailstones. Nothing but their wheat crushed into little rags of muddy slime. Here and there an isolated straw standing bolt upright in headless defiance. Martha and John walked to the far end of the field. There was no sound but their shoes slipping and rattling on the pebbles of ice. Both of them wanted to speak, to break the atmosphere of calamity that hung over them, but the words they could find were too small for the sparkling serenity of wasted field. Even as waste it was indomitable. It tethered them to itself, so that they could not feel or comprehend. It had come and gone, that was all; before its tremendousness and havoc they were prostrate. They had not yet risen to cry out or protest.

It was when they were nearly back to the house that Martha started to whimper. 'I can't go on any longer; I can't, John. There's no use, we've tried.' With one hand she clutched him and with the other held her apron to her mouth. 'It's driving me out of my mind. I'm so tired — heart-sick of it all. Can't you see?' . . .

Then he left her and she went back to the house. Mounting within her was a resolve, a bravery. It was the warming sunlight, the strength and nearness of John, a feeling of mattering, belonging. Swung far upwards by the rush and swell of recaptured life, she was suddenly as far above the desolation of the storm as a little while ago she had been abject before it. But in the house she was alone; there was no sunlight, only a cold wind through the broken window; and she crumpled again.

She tried to face the kitchen, to get the floor dried and the broken lamps swept up. But it was not the kitchen; it was tomorrow, next week, next year. The going on, the waste of life, the hopelessness. [pp. 73–82]

As For Me and My House (1941)
Sinclair Ross

It's an immense night out there, wheeling and windy. The lights on the street and in the houses are helpless against the black wetness, little unilluminating glints that might be painted on it. The town seems huddled together, cowering on a high, tiny perch, afraid to move lest it topple into the wind. Close to the parsonage is the church, black even against the darkness, towering ominously up through the night and merging with it. There's a soft steady swish of rain on the roof, and a gurgle of eave troughs running over. Above, in the high cold night, the wind goes swinging past, indifferent, liplessly mournful. It frightens me, makes me feel lost, dropped on this little perch of town and abandoned. [p. 5]

I turned once and looked back at Horizon, the huddled little clutter of houses and stores, the five grain elevators, aloof and imperturbable, like ancient obelisks, and behind the dust clouds, lapping at the sky.

It was like one of Philip's drawings. There was the same tension, the same vivid immobility, and behind it all somewhere the same sense of transience.

I walked on, remembering how I used to think that only a great artist could ever paint the prairie, the vacancy and stillness of it, the bare essentials of a landscape, sky and earth . . .

The dust clouds behind the town kept darkening and thinning and swaying, a furtive tirelessness about the way they wavered and merged with one another that reminded me of northern lights in winter. It was like a quivering backdrop, before which was about to be enacted some grim, primeval tragedy. The little town cowered close to earth as if to hide itself. The elevators stood up passive, stoical. All round me ran a hurrying little whisper through the grass. [p. 59]

We've all lived in a little town too long. The wilderness here makes us uneasy. I felt it first the night I walked alone along the river bank—a queer sense of something cold and fearful, something inanimate, yet aware of us. A Main Street is such a self-sufficient little pocket of existence, so smug, compact, that here we feel abashed somehow before the hills, their passiveness, the unheeding way they sleep. We climb them, but they withstand us, remain as serene and unrevealed as ever. The river slips past, unperturbed by our coming and going, stealthily confident. We shrink from our insignificance. The stillness and solitude—we think a force or presence into it—even a hostile presence, deliberate, aligned against us—for we dare not admit an indifferent wilderness, where we may have no meaning at all. [pp. 99–100]

Sketching the Stark Prairies

Robert Hurley, *Winter Scene* **(n.d.)**
Hurley's vision of the prairies.

Robert Hurley, *Untitled* **(ca. 1945)**
Stereotyping the prairie landscape: flat land, railway tracks, telephone poles, and expansive sky.

Robert Hurley, *Sunset* **(1961)**
An uncluttered landscape.

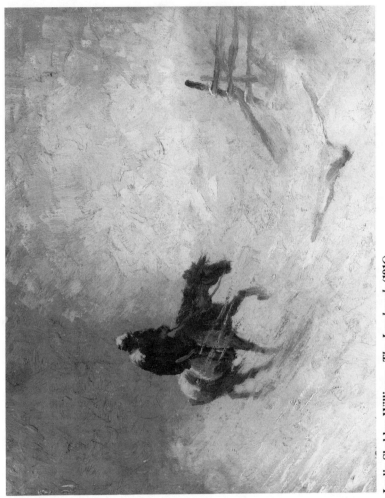

Inglis Sheldon-Williams, *The Landmark* (1916)
A hostile climate; a struggle to survive.

Inglis Sheldon-Williams, *The Fire Guard* **(1923)**
A prairie fire: terror on the prairies.

C. W. Jefferys, *A Prairie Town* **(1925)**
Prairie grain elevators: sentinels of civilization.

C. W. Jefferys, *Wheat Stacks on the Prairies* **(1907)**
Making a go of it on the prairies.

Illingworth Kerr, *Prairie Sky* **(1968)**
A spatial and light landscape.

Illingworth Kerr, *Chinook Country* **(1971)**
Internalizing the prairie landscape.

The Exploited West

Deep Furrows (1918)
Hopkins Moorhouse

He had just delivered his first load of the season's new wheat. Three nights before, by lantern light, he had backed his horses to the wagon and hauled it twenty-five miles to the railway at Indian Head. His stay there had not been conducive to peace of mind.

To reach the rails with a heavy load in favorable weather was simple enough; it merely required time. But many such trips would be necessary before his crop was marketed. Some of the farmers from beyond the Qu'Appelle would be hauling all winter; it was in winter that the haul was long and cruel. Starting at one, two or three o'clock in the morning, it would be impossible to forecast the weather with any degree of accuracy,

So that often they would be overtaken by blizzards. At such times the lack of stopping-places and shelter in the sparsely settled reaches of the trail encompassed the journey with risks every whit as real as pioneer perils of marauding Indians or trailing wolf-packs.

Snow and wind, however, had no place in the thoughts of the lonely farmer at the moment. Such things he had been used to ever since he first homesteaded; this long haul with the products of his toil he had been making for many years. What immediately concerned him was the discouraging prospect of another wheat blockade instead of any improvement in conditions which had become unbearable. With the country as full of wheat as it was this year it required no great gift of prophecy to foretell what would happen.

It was happening already. The railway people were ignoring completely the car-distribution clauses of the Grain Act and thereby playing in with the elevator interests, so that the farmers were going to be just where they were before — at the mercy of the buyers, their legitimate profits filched by excessive dockage, low grades, depressed prices, exorbitant storage charges, even short weights in some cases. All this in spite of the strong agitation which had led to Government action, in spite of the Royal Commission which had investigated the farmers' claims and had recommended the Grain Act, in spite of the legislation on the statutes! Law or no law, the farmer was still to be preyed upon, apparently, without a single weapon left with which——

The eyes of the man in the broad-brimmed hat grew grave. Scoff as he might among the men of the district when the serious ones voiced their fears to him, his own thoughts always came back to those fears. From the Red River Valley to the foothills long-smouldering indignation was glowing like a streak of fire in the prairie grass; a spark or two more and nothing could stop the conflagration that would sweep the plains country. If the law were to fail these red-blooded and long-suffering homesteaders there would be final weapons alright — real weapons! It was no use shutting one's eyes to the danger. Some fool would do something rash, and with the farmers already inflamed and embittered, there was no telling what desperate things might be attempted. [pp. 21–22]

The man who had ridden all day with his thoughts began unconsciously to apply other meanings to the sound, to people the night with dim faces and shapes that came trooping over the edge of the tablelands above — toil-bent figures of old pioneer farmers, careworn faces of women and bright eager faces of little children who were holding out their hands trustfully to the future. There seemed to be a never-ending procession — faces that were apathetic from repeated disappointments, faces that scowled threateningly, brave faces tense with determination and sad faces on which was written the story of struggle hidden within many a lonely wind-buffeted shack on the great bosom of the prairie.

Was it, then, that all the years of toil and hardship were to come to naught for this great company of honest workers, these brave pioneer men and women of the soil? Was all their striving forward to find them merely marking time, shouldered into the backwater while the currents of organized commercialism swept away their opportunities? Were not these producers of the world's bread themselves to partake of the fruits of their labor? [p. 32]

6

THE MYTHIC WEST
1945–1980

In the post-World War II era, the image of the West in literature, art, and historical writing shifted from that of an actual physical landscape — whether depicted as romantic, utopian, or realistic — to a mental landscape, a "region of the mind" shaped by its own mythology. The West became a "mental construct" that took shape in the mind of the beholder based on his or her own perception of the region, often independently of the physical environment itself. As literary critic Dick Harrison writes: "The prairie becomes less a thing 'out there' which must be shaped physically as well as imaginatively and more a territory within the psyche which must be explored and understood."[1] Eli Mandel, another well-known Canadian literary critic and poet, explained it this way:

> It is not a place but attitude, state of mind, that defines the western writer — and that state of mind, I want to suggest, has a good deal to do with a tension between place and culture, a doubleness or duplicity, that makes the writer a man not so much in place as out of place and so, endlessly trying to get back, to find his way home, to return, to write himself into existence, writing west.[2]

This mythic region of the West, like all mythologies, has been a blending of fact and fiction, historical truth and literary creation, physical locale and mental perception so as to create a uniquely prairie outlook.[3] The mythic West has moulded a western Canadian identity in a way that earlier images of the West could not do, because the West has been freed from its restrictions to geographical locale or historical era to become a state of mind where it can take on universal meaning.

In the postwar period, a generation of western Canadian writers, artists, and historians emerged who were born and raised in the West. They have been vitally interested in the region because they were, literally, "children of the West." Historians such as W. L. Morton and George F. G. Stanley, writers such as Margaret Laurence, W. O. Mitchell, Wallace Stegner, Rudy Wiebe, and Robert Kroetsch, and artists such as William Kurelek, Reta Cowley, and Dorothy Knowles have a natural affinity for the West, the source of their own physical and cultural roots. They have wanted to give meaning to a region of which they are a part and which has been very much a part of them. As a result, a western Canadian historical, literary, and artistic tradition has emerged that has produced some of the finest expressions of a regional culture and some of the most vivid images of the West for a national and, indeed, an international audience. These western Canadian cultural expressions reinforce the validity of Northrop Frye's observation that in Canada the best writing has been of a regional nature.[4]

This postwar generation has felt the need, in their quest to create images of the West which have meaning for them, first of all to dispel past images which are unrepresentative of their innate view of the region. Dick Harrison explains what contemporary prairie literary writers have been attempting to do: "Prairie novelists in the 1960's and 1970's have begun to look back, and their desire to re-examine the prairie past is understandable. . . . It is as though they regarded their past as something that must be rediscovered because it has been somehow misrepresented to them."[5]

Current prairie artists, writers, and historians have looked inward, into their own minds, for their images. This inward journey, which has taken the form of self-discovery through a reflection on their own perceptions of the West as children of the region as well as a search for their historical and cultural roots as westerners, has created images of the West which, while mythical, are more "real than reality," because like all images they have governed our perception of the West. Their images have become as much a part of the West as the prairie landscape itself.

Mythologizing the Historical West

Historian W. L. Morton discovered that the history of the West was shaped more by people's perception of themselves than by the region's topography.[6] Past images dictated present perspective. His aim in writing the history of western Canada was to articulate the images of the West — the myths — that moulded the region's historical evolution. In this respect

The historian and the poet had much in common, he noted: "Each is a myth maker, only the historian has neglected his job of making myths in this decadent, analytical age."[7] He described his history of his native province of Manitoba as "a history which informs and shapes our minds."[8]

Morton presented two dominant images (myths) of the West in his historical writings: that of a region that was a hinterland to metropolitan centres outside its borders; and that of an area predominantly rural and agricultural. The two images were interrelated. What had made the West what it was, according to Morton, was the way the region *functioned* as a historical entity within a larger (initially) British imperial and (later) Canadian national context. In both cases — and especially when the West was incorporated into Confederation and took on its own identity — the West functioned as a rural hinterland, and this perception, more than the topography, shaped the region's history. It was a case of mind over matter.

Morton first presented his image of the West as a hinterland and analyzed its effect on the western Canadian psyche in "Clio in Canada: The Interpretation of Canadian History," a paper presented to the Canadian Historical Association in 1946. He accepted the Laurentian thesis, with its assumption that the metropolitan centres of central Canada (the Laurentian Shield region) dominated the rest of the country, as a valid interpretation of Canadian history, but argued that the negative implications of the hinterland-metropolitan relationship for western Canada (in which the West would always be subservient to eastern interests) could only lead to an inferiority complex among its people. This attitude would ultimately be more persuasive in influencing the history of western Canada than the environment. Truth is how an individual perceived it, which in the case of a western Canadian would be that of a second-class citizen of Canada. Morton noted:

> . . . the West was annexed to Confederation as a subordinate region and so remained for sixty years. Such was the historical schooling of the West. It had, therefore, to fight its way up to self-government and equality in Confederation, nor is the process ended. . . . [T]he subordination of the West, when added to its sharp sectionalism, gives it an incisive and cogent character of its own.[9]

Morton elaborated this thesis in "A Century of Plain and Parkland." He noted that the turning point in the historical evolution of the region (what he called the shift from the neo-archaic to the modern West) came in 1870 when the West joined Confederation. With union came an influx of Ontarians who shaped the region's mentality to such an extent that the West adopted values and social structures out of tune with its natural environment. In other words, the West had become, in reality, a hinterland of Ontario, and this association more than anything else shaped the early history of the West:

> Modern civilization came to the plains and parkland in the 1870s, but in a specific form, that of Ontario settlement. The next generation was to be dominated by the introduction of the institutions and mores of Ontario into the prairies. A solid body of agricultural practice, a sharp commercial sense, a rigidly utilitarian approach to life, excessive caution, and a dour self-depreciation—these were new things on the prairies and they were to be the spirit in which the prairies were civilized.[10]

Morton's image of the West has contributed to the region's historical evolution. Westerners came to believe the myth that they had been victimized by eastern (particularly Ontario) interests, and this in turn reinforced their protest tradition. This mythology dated back to the early years of the West's incorporation into Confederation and was evident in early western Canadian protest movements, but Morton contributed to the movement by providing the historical evidence to justify protest (although, ironically, he believed that the West's destiny lay in continued union with the rest of Canada). By emphasizing the constant struggle of western Canada for equality with, and recognition by, the rest of the nation, Morton reinforced the subordinate position of the West that he was trying to dispel. His image became "historical truth" in the minds of many Westerners.

Morton came closest to seeing his mythical West as a fusion of fact and fiction, people and landscape, external reality and internal imagery, in the conclusion to his "Seeing an Unliterary Landscape":

> I think, by way of example, that one fall evening I was rewarded in my search for a landscape in which inner and outer vision were reconciled. It was a late afternoon flight from Winnipeg to Edmonton one October day. The air was clear except for a vast swirl of smoky cloud across the western horizon in which the sun was dying to a glowing ash. The great globe of the prairies rolled majestically below, incised with square stubble and square fallow, engraved by the vast river valleys, gemmed with lapis lazuli of random lakes. The whole was a Renaissance globe wrought for a Medici, turned by the thumb of old Sebastian Cabot, worked in rough bronze burnished to murky gold, fading off in ridge and coulee into smoky purple or darkening over vast plains in dusky amber—the work either of a Cellini or a Durer. It was the west of the drifting buffalo herds, of the island farmsteads, of Butler, Grove and even of Margaret Laurence. It was my west completely envisioned.[11]

Fellow historian George F. G. Stanley, born and raised on the prairies, also created an image of the West in his historical writings. To Stanley, the distinguishing feature of prairie Canada—its "mystique," as he called it in an article of that title—was not its unique topography but its "spirit of independence." That spirit may have germinated in the land and been nurtured in the region's long history of revolt, but it was an innate quality—a state of mind—that westerners possessed and that they carried with them as westerners independently of the physical locale itself. This attitude or image westerners had of themselves as free-spirited people underlay and explained the entire history of western Canada:

> The history of the Canadian West from the earliest days of which we have knowledge by written word or oral tradition, has been one of survival and adaptation to environment. Hence my suggestion that the characteristic spirit of the Westerner is that of independence, self reliance, willingness to strike out on a new path. These are the essence of adaptation and the secret of survival.[12]

Stanley maintained as late as 1969 that this spirit of independence still existed in the West even after the region had become urbanized. "In time," he wrote, "the osmotic action that carried the spirit of independence from the countryside to the urban communities, may cease and we will become as the others are. But that time has not yet come, and the Progressivism of the past is still an effective influence both in our political and in our cultural life."[13]

The West as a Literary Region of Self-Discovery

In the realm of literature, novelists and poets in the post-World War II era have come to believe that the West is an image that has been shaped more by their own literary imagination than by the region's topography.[14] They have created the West and its images in fiction through a fusion of their own personal impressions as children of the region and of the thoughts of others on the West over time, what Wallace Stegner calls a fusion of memory and history. Since both memory and history are mythical—creations of the imagination so as to give order and meaning to the world—then the image of the West is of a mythic region where to be "western" is to be conscious of the roots of one's identity. Contemporary prairie novelists and poets, in searching for their roots, their myths of origin, have often been compared to earlier explorers, charting new territory in this *terra incognita* or "unnamed country," as Harrison describes it, where old images of the West—and even the traditional language—seem inappropriate. They are trying to write themselves, and ultimately their region, into existence through the creation of the right images that will bring the region to life in the mind of the beholder. Novelist and poet Robert Kroetsch expressed the idea this way: "In a sense we haven't got an identity until somebody tells our story. The fiction makes us real."[15]

Margaret Laurence noted in "Sources," a reflective article on her own prairie novels, how much her West was mythic. Her characters—Hagar

Shipley, Rachel, and Morag Gunn—were, she noted, fictional in the true sense of the word; they were creations of her mind through an amalgam of characters she had known from her prairie childhood. Her town of Manawaka was mythical, a fusion of fact and fiction. "In almost every way," she commented, "Manawaka is not so much any one prairie town as an amalgam of many prairie towns. Most of all, I like to think, it is simply itself, a town of the mind, my own private world."[16]

She also noted that the West that she imagined in her novels was a region shaped more by its people than by its topography. She believed that it was the attitudes, beliefs, traditions and values of the West—the mental more than the physical landscape—that shaped the West's unique character and distinctive imagery. In "Sources" she wrote: "When one thinks of the influence of a place on one's writing, two aspects come to mind. First, the physical presence of the place itself—its geography, its appearance. Second, the people. For me, the second aspect of environment is the most important."[17]

The image of the West that emerges in Laurence's personal recollections of her childhood region and in her novels is far from romantic or nostalgic. If anything, it is the image of a prairie that is and was oppressive and stifling rather than liberating and creative—a garrison mentality to escape from rather than a free-spirited region to rejoice in (as George Stanley claimed). In "Where the World Began," an autobiographical sketch of her childhood, she wrote:

> When I was eighteen, I couldn't wait to get out of that town, away from the prairies. I did not know then that I would carry the land and town all my life within my skull, that they would form the mainspring and source of the writing I was to do, wherever and however far away I might live.
> This was my territory in the time of my youth, and in a sense my life since then has been an attempt to look at it, to come to terms with it. Stultifying to mind it certainly could be, and sometimes was, but not to the imagination. . . . [I]n raging against our injustices, our stupidities, I do so as *family*, as I did, and still do in writing, about those aspects of my town which I hated and which are always in some ways aspects of myself.[18]

In her novels, too, Laurence depicts her protagonists as imprisoned by their social environment, with its innate bigotry and self-repression. Her characters are victims of pride and guilt—inherently Judeo-Christian characteristics most strongly personified in the early Ontario-Scottish Calvinists who settled the West and stamped their attitudes on the region. Their qualities of perseverance and repression of self may have enabled an earlier generation of pioneers to survive the harsh elements and the rigour of the land and climate, but their legacy, according to Laurence, was a world of guilt, intolerance, and unemotionalism from which a person must escape to be truly free.

It was appropriate that Laurence should entitle her autobiographical essay "Where the World Began." In that title two images emerge—that of a physical place where she was born and grew up, but equally that of a spiritual region that shaped her outlook and therefore governed, like all myths, what she would see in the world around her. To understand that outlook—to discover her perception of the world—she had first to come to terms with her images of the prairie West. Those images of a place of people, feelings, and attitudes she captured in her essay:

> A strange place it was, that place where the world began. A place of incredible happenings, splendours and revelations, despairs like multitudinous pits of isolated hells. A place of shadow-spookiness, inhabited by the unknowable dead. A place of jubilation and of mourning, horrible and beautiful.
>
> It was, in fact, a small prairie town. . . .
>
> This is where my world began. A world which includes the ancestors—both my own and other people's ancestors who became mine. A world which formed me, and continues to do so, even while I fought it in some of its aspects, and continue to do so. A world which gave me my own lifework to do, because it was here that I learned the sight of my own particular eyes.[19]

In her novels, Laurence has the ability to capture images of the West which came out of her own particular background and experience, but which transcended the particular to take on universal meaning in the minds of her readers. In essence, she captured the West in her own imagination and in that of others; in so doing, she *created* the West. Her images *are* the West in the sense that they have become part of our perception of it, as much a part of the West as the physical landscape itself.

Novelist Wallace Stegner also came to understand the West as a state of mind that moulded his being during his journey of self-discovery—a journey that was both physical, as he returned to his childhood place of Whitemud [Eastend] Saskatchewan, and spiritual, as he came to terms with what it meant to be a western Canadian. As he went back in time to capture his childhood memories, a journey made possible by the smell of "wolf willow," the title of his semi-autobiographical account, he discovered, like Laurence, that this place where his world began was more than his world; it had universal meaning:

> . . . it is a fact that once I have, so to speak, recovered myself as I used to be, I can look at the town, whose childhood was exactly contemporary with my own, with more understanding. It turns out to have been a special sort of town—special not only to me, in that it provided the indispensable sanctuary to match the prairie's exposure, but special in its belated

concentration of Plains history. The successive stages of the Plains frontier flowed like a pageant through these Hills, and there are men still alive who remember almost the whole of it. My own recollections cover only a fragment; and yet it strikes me that this is *my* history. My disjunct, uprooted, cellular family was more typical than otherwise on the frontier. But more than we knew, we had our place in a human movement. What this town and its surrounding prairie grew from, and what they grew into, is the record of my tribe. If I am native to anything, I am native to this.[20]

Wolf Willow, like Margaret Laurence's novels, contains images of the West whose meaning goes beyond those of the author to become a collective imagery that shapes—and creates—the region he imagines. The symbol of his West is "the question mark in the circle"—man "a challenging upright thing" in the midst of a flat surface that encircles him. Writer George Melnyk describes it this way: "The prairie horizon is the perfect metaphor for the furthest boundary, the ultimate reaches of earth-bound consciousness. On the prairie one twists around and around till the straight horizon line turns into its opposite, a circle, and the visual turns visionary."[21]

W. O. Mitchell uses the prairies as a setting in which to present a universal message in *Who Has Seen the Wind* (1947). Through the eyes of a child, Brian O'Connal, Mitchell narrates the story of a boy coming of age in a prairie world with its "realities of birth, hunger, satiety, eternity, death." Young Brian, like every prairie child, is drawn between a life of freedom, as symbolized by the wind on the open prairies and embodied in the youthful Ben, and one of social conformity, as symbolized by the prairie town and embodied in the tyrannical Mrs. Abercrombie, the banker's wife, who wants to dictate the social values of the town. Here the two historical images of the West—the free-spirited West that Stanley talks about and the hinterland, garrisoned region that Morton depicts—are juxtaposed in a life struggle set against a panoramic backdrop of prairie, land, and sky. Mitchell's image of the West is an ambivalent one: a prairie with the power to create but also to destroy, to liberate but also to enslave, a life-force yet a death threat. The two images are intertwined throughout the novel:

> The sunlight bathed the prairie's stooks, haystacks, and fields with subtle light; gray clouds blackened; those near the prairie's edge blushed pink, salmon, rose. A titaree-ing killdeer called in the dusk. . . .
> The night wind had two voices: one that keened along the pulsing wires, the prairie one that throated long and deep. Brian could feel its chill reaching for the very center of him and he hunched his shoulders as he felt the wincing of his very core against it.
> Here and there a farm dog barked; farmhouse windows burned yellow in the night; and, seeing them, the boy felt still more lost and lonely.

He thought of people sheltered in the four-walled wells of houses, content and warm by fizzing gasoline or flickering oil-lamp flames.[22]

Robert Kroetsch, like Laurence, Stegner, and Mitchell, has also explored his inner psyche to discover his images of the West. The most experimental of contemporary prairie novelists, Kroetsch has searched for a literary form and a language appropriate to the West. He rejects earlier literary forms—and their accompanying imagery—as inappropriate for understanding the modern West. Much of his writing is aimed at breaking away from these earlier approaches—to dislodge the reader, so to speak—so as to make him more receptive to modern imagery. This has meant discovering order in chaos or, more precisely, creating that order. As he noted in an interview: "The western landscape is one without boundaries quite often. So you have the experience within a kind of chaos, yet you have to order it somehow to survive. I'm particularly interested in the kinds of orderings we do on that landscape."[23]

To order the prairie landscape—both the physical and mental landscapes—is to create it, for the author imposes a perception on the external world. He sees what he wants and is culturally induced to see. In so doing, the author creates the West, a mythic region which is a fusion of fact and fiction, historical "truth" and literary licence.

A favourite technique of Kroetsch's is to take actual historical events in prairie history and to fictionalize them. In *The Words of My Roaring* (1966), for example, he deals with the historical era of Social Credit in Alberta under its leader William Aberhart, but the event is only a means to express Kroetsch's images of the West. *The Studhorse Man* (1969), is concerned with the historical era of transition from a pre- to a post-technological West, from a pastoral to a mechanized West. But beyond this facade lies a powerful story of what it means to be a western Canadian in a vanishing West, an urban West that is becoming indistinguishable from any other region of the world. *Gone Indian* (1973), the third in his trilogy on the historical West, takes the reader back to an earlier period of time, the era of transition from a pre- to a post-settlement period. All three of these novels deal with a rural, small-town West. The images he evokes are familiar to westerners not only because the rural West has been a recent part of the past for so many of them, but also because that image is one still deeply embedded in the western Canadian psyche. While becoming citified, western Canadians still think of themselves—still have images of themselves—as a rural, agricultural people.[24]

Kroetsch's mythical West is evident in his short story "That Yellow Prairie Sky." He consciously juxtaposes two stories (images) into one so as to bombard the reader with a series of traditional images in an untraditional way. In one descriptive passage, he writes:

> The sky was the garment of love. It was a big sky, freckled with the stars of the universe; a happy sky, shrouding all the pain. It was the time of spring, and spring is love, and in the night sky arrow after arrow of honking geese winged across the yellow moon, driving winter from the world.
>
> Right after the wedding we moved into the shack and really went to work. I was busy from morning till night putting in a big crop, while Julie helped with the chores and looked after her little chicks and put in a big garden. When the crop was in we started on the summer fallow, and before that was done it was haying time.[25]

The need to search for new images of the West and a corresponding new language in which to express that imagery is also characteristic of Robert Kroetsch's poetry, as it is of the poetry of other western poets such as George Bowering, John Newlove, and Sid Marty. These poets are searching within for the words and the images that can express their feelings for the region, and they express those feelings in imagism — images presented in phrases and free verse as opposed to complete statements so as to convey the emotion felt. Literary critic D. G. Jones notes: "To tell it as it is, to name and define a world of inarticulate feeling, to reveal the significance of those elements of their experience that do not conform to conventional ideas of what is significant, the imagist program provides a basic method."[26] Such imagism is particularly appropriate for poems about the past (and many contemporary poets, like their novelist counterparts, are interested in repossessing the actuality of their childhood, of their father's and grandfather's world) because the poet is reconstructing that past in mythical form in his own mind through memory flashes and fleeting images that are a fusion of fact and fiction. In this way, the disjointed poetry with its random imagery conforms to "reality." George Bowering's "Grandfather Bowering" and John Newlove's "The Pride" both present images of a prairie past which combine personal reminiscences and actual historical events.

Sketching the Prairie Landscape of the Mind

Western Canadian art in the postwar era moved in two directions: toward abstraction and toward representational and folk art.[27] In both cases, artists consciously moved away from earlier approaches in that they were searching within their minds rather than in the landscape itself for the images and icons that best expressed their perception of, and feelings for, the West. Rather than reacting to the landscape, as earlier artists had done, current prairie artists have discovered the West within their own psyche (not unlike the journey of self-discovery of current prairie writers) and then imposed that concept onto the landscape through the medium of their art. The West they create is thus purely out of their own imagination. Canadian art historian Douglas Cole explains the trend in postwar western Canadian art in terms of world art in general: "Since roughly Van Gogh, art was becoming increasingly subjective, increasingly seeking to express emotion or spiritual attitude. The subjective artist used painting as an outlet for his own internal moods and responses. The picture became something of a transcript of an inner condition while subject matter became of less importance than the painter's expression or feelings about it."[28] Abstraction and representation have been useful media by which to present this more *conceptual* as opposed to *perceptual* approach to prairie art.

Contemporary prairie artists, like their literary counterparts, have reacted against earlier depictions of the West as unrepresentative of their perception of the region. Pre-World War I artists often recreated European-type scenes and styles on a landscape that did not fit; in essence, they saw the West through eastern eyes. Artists in the realist tradition during the interwar years came closer to capturing images of the West in their use of prairie icons such as barns, fences, telephone poles, and expansive skies. But even these artists were limited by the external landscape; they captured the physical realities of the prairies but were unable to convey its spiritual dimension. That dimension could only come from within, and from artists whose inner being had been formed by living on the prairies. It is this inner prairie – the images in the mind's eye – that current prairie artists have attempted to express on canvas.

One means to do this was through abstraction. Abstract painting is not, of course, a prairie invention, but it could very well have been. It is an art form particularly suited to the prairie landscape. As Illingworth Kerr, one of the West's first abstract painters, concluded: the answer to western space, with its "vast scale and power of mood rather than tangible form,"[29] lay in abstraction. Illingworth Kerr's abstract paintings are indeed visual equivalents of the mood of a prairie landscape; they convey his inner feelings for his native region. He pointed out how the subjects of his abstract landscape paintings usually come from within as opposed to coming from the landscape itself. They "were not sought but were suggested by the imagination (inner self). Old memories and recent impressions introduced surprising contrasts – at least as surprising and disconcerting to me as they may be to you."[30] Literary critic Northrop Frye explained in a different context what the abstract artist was attempting to do:

> The effort of stylizing and simplifying is to bring out more clearly not what the artist sees, but what he experiences in his seeing. Abstraction sets the painter free from the particular experiences, and enables him to paint the essence of his pictorial vision.[31]

The essence or image of the West in many abstract paintings is of an inner solitude, loneliness, stillness, and awe often conveyed through broad bands of colours or in simple divisions of space in Cubist fashion. Light and space are the essence of the two great dimensions of the prairie landscape: earth and sky. In prairie abstract painting, the observer moves beyond the surface, uncluttered as it is by detail, to the inner soul of the artist himself.

Representational and folk art of the prairie region appears to be more akin to conventional art forms of the past than abstraction, in that the viewer sees on canvas traditional prairie icons such as farmsteads, hayfields, and grain elevators. Yet while the medium may appear to be the same (and in many cases that, too, is an illusion), the message is different. Representational and folk artists use familiar icons as a means to convey inner thoughts and feelings; they are commentaries on the region rather than reflections of it. For some, like Dorothy Knowles and Reta Cowley, these icons, which the artists present through a pleasant blending of colours and the use of light strokes, convey a powerful feeling of love and affinity for a landscape that is and has been so much a part of them as "children of the West."[32] Their paintings often evoke childhood memories in other prairie inhabitants, and a love for the land that lies deep in the heart of many prairie dwellers.

For others, familiar icons are allegorical and metaphorical. They are meant to represent more than meets the eye; they contain a hidden message. In George Jenkins's paintings, for example, an empty field or an abandoned farmstead expresses his views on the modern West. As he noted: "A plough in a field can be a landscape but the abandoned field in the background gives the painting social significance and the work takes on an entirely different meaning."[33] As the West has experienced the onslaught of urbanization and industrialization, it has changed. Jenkins's means to comment on that change and the resulting social upheaval is to take familiar images of the West and to present them in an unfamiliar way, thus using past images as a means of presenting new images of the West. His objects, which appear in an unnatural and eerie form, become icons of a past age, a means by which he can come to terms with his past and the ghosts of that past, analogous to Margaret Laurence's search for her roots.

Prairie artists Kenneth Lochhead and Ivan Eyre use human figures on a prairie landscape as a commentary on man's alienation from the land; their figures seem out of place — defying the land about them while at the same time challenging it. The landscape itself is empty, meaningless — a wasteland, of which man does not feel a part. Their paintings express the existentialist view of prairie man found in modern prairie literature.[34]

William Kurelek is the finest of prairie representational and folk artists.[35] Born in Alberta of Ukrainian parents and raised near Stonewall,

Manitoba, Kurelek absorbed almost by osmosis the familiar sights, sounds, and smells of the prairie landscape. They became a part of his being that moulded his view of the world. His paintings capture familiar prairie scenes. They evoke childhood memories and a rural past not unlike the writings of Margaret Laurence and W. O. Mitchell. Kurelek's paintings appeal to a wider audience precisely because they go beyond the particular to capture a world and a feeling that is more than the artist's alone. He was telling, through his art, the story of a boy growing up on a prairie farm in the midst of the Depression. But his story becomes everyone's story to the point where, as Robert Fulford notes, Kurelek "became perhaps the most universally admired artist of his generation as well as the most successful book illustrator in Canada."[36] He had the ability to express on canvas what others could only feel intuitively, and he was conscious of that gift: "No one seems to understand why I am so fascinated by this place not even the local people. Only I it seems can express it though others may feel it inarticulately."[37]

A regional painter, Kurelek is, like the best of regionalists, able to embrace and express a place and its people. Equally, however, a good regionalist is one who is able to be a universalist, using the familiar and particular to express a universal message. When Kurelek's prairie particularism is blended with his fervent Catholic faith, his universal message becomes clear. His paintings of prairie scenes in their simplicity and familiarity can mask the deeper message that lies within. Unfamiliar icons are blended in with the familiar—a picture of Christ on the Cross in a typical prairie homestead, the mushroom cloud of an atomic bomb in the background of a prairie homestead, the Christ-child in a prairie stable.

The pictures are allegorical; they are Kurelek's medium to present his message on the dangers of the secularization of modern society. That process of secularization is most evident to Kurelek on the prairies because it stands juxtaposed to the rural, agricultural, and traditionally religious nature of that region when he was growing up, and also because secularization has occurred so rapidly and so recently on the prairies that the "new West" stands in stark contrast to the old. As Fulford notes: "Kurelek reflected in his work a quality that eastern city-dwellers have often noted in westerners: they are closer to the land, not so much in space as in time. . . . Even in the 1980s the remembered vision of the prairie as virginal and untouched—menacing in its way, and yet conveying enormous promise—is always just on the edge of the conversation."[38] Thus, like Jenkins, Kurelek uses typical and atypical icons to present his image of the West and to convey his message. As Ronald Rees points out: "In psychological terms they [Kurelek's paintings] are good gestalts, perfect microcosms that manage, through the presentation of simple, everyday events, to convey entire worlds."[39]

In the post-World War II era, the prairies have been transformed into a "state of mind." Ceasing to be associated directly with a particular physical locale, the image of the West is of a "landscape of the mind" moulded by the myths and realities of a western Canadian tradition. Yet these myths are a blending of the legends and feelings of the region evoked by its particular geography and unique history. The search for appropriate images of the West continues to be pursued within the traditional framework—the altering image—of the region itself. There continues, therefore, to be a healthy and creative tension between "perception" or "image" and "reality"—what Eli Mandel called "place and culture."[40]

Mythologizing the Historical West

Seeing an Unliterary Landscape (1970)
W. L. Morton

The walking-plough, tipped with its point set to slip into the sod, its mouldboard gleaming a lambent silver polished by miles of turning soil, jerks as the horses lean into their collars, and the furrow rolls.

Such is one of the clearest images of my boyhood memory. It is an image drawn from one of the many skills of old-time farming, the breaking every July of a few acres more of new land from meadow and poplar bush. I look back on it with fondness for something gone forever except in fading memory, and am proud that I was once good at the plough. Indeed, sometimes now I find myself falling into the ploughman's halting plod, taking the weight of the share's twist on the right foot every second stride. I could drive a straight furrow and cover every wisp of grass and trash beneath the gleaming furrows, the soil moist with summer rain and turned for the first time since the waters of Lake Agassiz laid it down deep below the now phantom waves.

The image is one which may, moreover, be opened into many petals, each of entrancing colour. Only consider the meanings of that turning mould. For one thing, what an archaism ploughing it was. It was becoming unusual even in those days half a century ago to break land with the walking-plough; the tractor was taking over. In a sense, however, I was fortunate because I was among the last of millennial generations of men who followed the plough, as I knew even then. So I belonged, to a human labour force, peasant, serf, slave, whose work fed household, village and city, and carried the fabric of civilisation on their sweating shoulders. A strange boast, if you like, but it is a strong, rich memory. [pp. 1–2]

A Century of Plain and Parkland (1969)
W. L. Morton

One hundred years ago the prairies, the lands rolling upward from the Red River to the foothills of the Rockies, were primitive, with little trace of human habitation. No rut scored the sod, no furrow scarred the long roll of the prairie. The 'pitching' tracks of the Indians, the cart trails of the fur freighters were scarcely to be seen. The plains were as thousands of years of geological and climatic change had made them. Men had hardly touched them, for man himself was primitive, in that he had adapted himself to nature, and not nature to himself. The grasses flowed, the prairie fires ran in the wind; the buffalo grazed like cloud shadows in the plain; the buffalo hunt raised a flurry of dust in the diamond summer light; the rivers sought the distant sea unchecked; summer made green, autumn bronze, winter white, spring gray, the august monotony of the plains, *secula seculorum*. What had been wrought, green grass on dry grass, day on night turning, lay unchanged until it became the setting for the last frontier.

Primitive the plains were in 1867, to man at least, although the processed outcome of a majestic evolutionary logic. Yet man, the Indian, the fur trader, and the first farmers had already put the plain and parkland to their uses. But their uses were archaic, adapted to nature, and not imposed upon the orchestral rhythms of plains ecology. The plains tribes of the short grass buffalo plains had created a hunting economy and a civilization based upon the plains' chief product, the sea-like, inexhaustible, ever-renewable buffalo herds. This they had done by means of the pound and the horse, come since 1740 to the Canadian plains, and the buffalo skin teepee, the easy product of the herds. Few men have ever known an ampler adaptation to what nature had prepared; few men have known, in a life of endless challenge, a greater security, a more conscious independence. . . .

The prairies until 1867 therefore remained, at most neo-archaic. They remained, for modern civilization, a virgin *tabula rasa*, a blank sheet with no writing, an unmarked parchment, unscraped, unspoiled, unprepared. [pp. 19–20]

The isolation, however, was ended by 1867. Not only had Lorin Blodget with his *Climatology of North America*, and Hind and Palliser by their expeditions, ended the myth of the sub-arctic character of prairie climate; the new route to St. Paul had since 1844 been drawing the West into the pattern of continental integration. Beyond St. Paul lay the network of rivers, canals, and railways that was making North America a trading unit. The volume of the St. Paul trade, after the admission of free trade in furs throughout the southeastern prairies by the outcome of the Sayer trial in 1849, drew the West towards the American Union and the modern period. Continental integration had begun; the isolation of the prairies was ending; the coming of modern civilization, the railway, the town, agriculture and industry, was inevitable. The already apparent dwindling of the buffalo herds was only an anticipation, historically apt, biologically sad, of what was inevitable.

Such matters were not, however, only economic and ecological; they were also political. The beginning of the integration of the prairies into the continental pattern was one of the principal causes of Confederation. The jarring Canadas and the about to be depressed Maritimes could face the future neither in their existing state, nor even in a united future, unless they had a hinterland for expansion. The lands to the north afforded none; the shorelines and fisheries of the Gulf of St. Lawrence little, only the prairies offered the expansion that was necessary to union. Confederation was, therefore, in part only, but also in essential fact, a prelude and preparation for the annexation of the prairies to the Canadian version of continental integration. [p. 21]

The West as a Literary Region of Self-Discovery

Sources (1970)
Margaret Laurence

When one thinks of the influence of a place on one's writing, two aspects come to mind. First, the physical presence of the place itself— its geography, its appearance. Second, the people. For me, the second aspect of environment is the most important, although in everything I have written which is set in Canada, whether or not it is actually set in Manitoba, somewhere some of my memories of the physical appearance of the prairies come in. I had, as a child and as an adolescent, ambiguous feelings about the prairies, and I still have them, although they no longer bother me. I wanted then to get out of the small town and go far away, and yet I felt the protectiveness of that atmosphere, too. I felt the loneliness and the isolation of the land itself, and yet I always considered southern Manitoba to be very beautiful, and I still do. I doubt if I will ever live there again, but those poplar bluffs and the blackness of that soil and the way in which the sky is open from one side of the horizon to the other—these are things I carry inside my skull for as long as I live, with the vividness of recall that only our first home can really have for us.

Nevertheless, the people were more important than the place. Hagar, in *The Stone Angel*, was not drawn from life, but she incorporates many qualities of my grandparents' generation. Her speech is their speech, and her gods their gods. I think I never recognized until I wrote that novel just how mixed were my own feelings towards that whole generation of pioneers — how difficult they were to live with, how authoritarian, how unbending, how afraid to show love, many of them, and how willing to show anger. And yet — they had inhabited a wildernness and made it fruitful. They were, in the end, great survivors, and for that I love and value them.

The final exploration of this aspect of my background came when I wrote — over the past six or seven years — a number of short stories set in Manawaka and based upon my childhood and my childhood family, the only semi-autobiographical fiction I have ever written. I did not realize until I had finished the final story in the series how much all these stories are dominated by the figure of my maternal grandfather, who came of Irish Protestant stock. I think perhaps it was through writing these stories that I finally came to see my grandfather not only as the repressive authoritarian figure from my childhood, but also as a boy who had had to leave school in Ontario when he was about twelve, after his father's death, and who, as a young man, went to Manitoba by sternwheeler and walked the fifty miles from Winnipeg to Portage la Prairie, where he settled for some years before moving to Neepawa. He was a very hard man in many ways, but he had had a very hard life in many ways, too. I don't think I knew any of this, really knew it, until I had finished these stories. I don't think I ever knew, either, until that moment how much I owed to him. One sentence near the end of the final story may show what I mean. "I had feared and fought the old man, yet he proclaimed himself in my veins." [pp. 82–83]

Where the World Began (1976)
Margaret Laurence

A strange place it was, that place where the world began. A place of incredible happenings, splendours and revelations, despairs like multitudinous pits of isolated hells. A place of shadow-spookiness, inhabited by the unknowable dead. A place of jubilation and of mourning, horrible and beautiful.

It was, in fact, a small prairie town.

Because that settlement and that land were my first and for many years my only real knowledge of this planet, in some profound way they remain my world, my way of viewing. My eyes were formed there. Towns like ours, set in a sea of land, have been described thousands of times as dull, bleak, flat, uninteresting. I have had it said to me that the railway trip across Canada is spectacular, except for the prairies, when it would be desirable to go to sleep for several days, until the ordeal is over. I am always unable to argue this point effectively. All I can say is—well, you really have to live there to know that country. The town of my childhood could be called bizarre, agonizingly repressive or cruel at times, and the land in which it grew could be called harsh in the violence of its seasonal changes. But never merely flat or uninteresting. Never dull.

In winter, we used to hitch rides on the back of the milk sleigh, our moccasins squeaking and slithering on the hard rutted snow of the roads, our hands in ice-bubbled mitts hanging onto the box edge of the sleigh for dear life, while Bert grinned at us through his great frosted moustache and shouted the horse into speed, daring us to stay put. Those mornings, rising, there would be the perpetual fascination of the frost feathers on windows, the ferns and flowers and eerie faces traced there during the night by unseen artists of the wind. Evenings, coming back from skating, the sky would be black but not dark, for you could see a cold glitter of stars from one side of the earth's rim to the other. And then the sometime astonishment when you saw the Northern Lights flaring across the sky, like the scrawled signature of God. After a blizzard, when the snowploughs hadn't yet got through, school would be closed for the day, the assumption being that the town's young could not possibly flounder through five feet of snow in the pursuit of education. We would then gaily don snowshoes and flounder for miles out into the white dazzling deserts, in pursuit of a different kind of knowing. If you came back too close to night, through the woods at the foot of the town hill, the thin black branches of poplar and chokecherry now meringued with frost, sometimes you heard coyotes. Or maybe the banshee wolf-voices were really only inside your head.

Summers were scorching, and when no rain came and the wheat became bleached and dried before it headed, the faces of farmers and townsfolk would not smile much, and you took for granted, because it never seemed to have been any different, the frequent knocking at the back door and the young men standing there, mumbling or thrusting defiantly their requests for a drink of water and a sandwich if you could spare it. They were riding the freights, and you never knew where they had come from, or where they might end up, if anywhere. The Drought and Depression were like evil deities which had been there always. You understood and did not understand. (pp. 213–15]

When I was eighteen, I couldn't wait to get out of that town, away from the prairies. I did not know then that I would carry the land and town all my life within my skull, that they would form the mainspring and source of the writing I was to do, wherever and however far away I might live.

This was my territory in the time of my youth, and in a sense my life since then has been an attempt to look at it, to come to terms with it. Stultifying to the mind it certainly could be, and sometimes was, but not to the imagination. It was many things, but it was never dull. [p. 217]

This is where my world began. A world which includes the ancestors—both my own and other people's ancestors who become mine. A world which formed me, and continues to do so, even while I fought it in some of its aspects, and continue to do so. A world which gave me my own lifework to do, because it was here that I learned the sight of my own particular eyes. [p. 219]

Prairie: Time and Place (1969)
Peter Stevens

We can't comprehend the prairie
flattened into need; we feel it
in the cold testing flesh
tight across our skulls
waiting for the ease of greenness
where bunch-topped aspens lean
in the wind's reach for the sky
struggling to trap in their branches
all the wide horizon.

The sun's clear-edged heat
parches minds to dry bone
but we grope for firmness;
we see brush holding on
huddled in blurred clusters.

A single track stitches towns
along straight lines; above them
white names flake from red walls
thrown black across bleached fields.
Trucks bounce over gravel ruts
through their own dust flying
along all the main streets
banked by wind-skinned snow
melting to mud and dust.

A few speculative images
shyly define our place
trying to embrace our world

the necessarily outrageous flats
pitted against the huge sky.

Saskatchewan (1968)
Edward McCourt

No doubt the political scientist and the sociologist can explain such
goings-on in their own peculiar terms; but whenever any friend of mine
from eastern Canada remarks on the multiplicity of political parties
spawned on the prairies and the maverick tendencies of many of the party
constituents, I am content to tell him the story of Mr. Portingale.

In the old homesteading days of more than half a century ago, Mr.
Portingale was a near neighbour of ours. He was a scruffy little
Englishman born, according to the nomenclature of his time, into the
lower middle class. Mr. Portingale was a staunch imperialist and devout
church-goer; he knew his place in the scheme of things and until he
took to homesteading in the middle of the prairie was content to keep
it. A meek little man (but with no hope of inheriting the earth or any
part thereof), he never dreamt of calling into question the wisdom and
rectitude of either God or the government.

Not, that is, until he had lived—but only barely—through part of a
prairie winter. One day in mid January of his first year on the homestead
he borrowed my father's team and sleigh and hauled a load of grain to
town, thirty miles away. He spent the night in the hotel and next morning,
in defiance of warnings from weather-wise old-timers, started for home.
Ten miles out, a blizzard met him head on. Fortunately the horses,
grizzled old veterans of many a winter storm, took charge of Mr.
Portingale and dragged him several hours later into our yard. My father
dug him out from under about two feet of snow, unwound him from the
horse-blankets he had thoughtfully wrapped himself in, and half-dragged,
half-carried him into our kitchen.

Mother superintended the thawing-out operations. She placed one end
of Mr. Portingale in a tub of cold water (his feet were badly frost-bitten)
and after first clearing a channel through the icicles festooning his scraggy
moustache poured into the other end about a gallon of hot tea generously
laced with ginger.

Within fifteen minutes Mr. Portingale was thawing out all right and
suffering the tortures of the damned. His feet were immersed in a tub
of flaming coals and the tea had peeled most of the skin off the roof
of his mouth. In the ordinary way Mr. Portingale was the humblest, least
aggressive of men, his voice an appropriate piping treble, and the strongest
expletive any of us had heard him use—and then only when greatly

moved – was 'Gryte Scott!' But now those of us gathered in the kitchen were seeing something vastly more significant than the mere restoration of Mr. Portingale's circulatory system to its more or less normal channels; we were awe-stricken witnesses to a striking spiritual phenomenon peculiar to the prairies. For all of a sudden, Mr. Portingale was no longer a humble sheep content to follow the bell-wether of the flock – he was the Stag at Bay. He glared at us out of red-rimmed bloodshot eyes and flung bloated pin-cushion hands aloft.

'The bloodiest absolutely bloodiest climate on the fice of the bloody earth!' Mr. Portingale bawled. 'And by God something's bloody well got to be done abaat it!'

Saskatchewan teems with Mr. Portingales. Men who, lapped in an enervating cloak of eastern smog or rendered soft and pliable by the eternal West Coast rain, would pass through life in meek unquestioning obedience to those placed in authority over them, develop, after a brief spell of prairie living, affinities with the Mau Mau or the I.R.A. Scorched by sun and battered by wind three months of the year and confined in a deep freeze for six, the prairie dweller is soon afflicted by a kind of nervous irritability which impels him to flail out in all directions. Being, as a rule, a religious man – intimate association with nature at its most awesome inclines to make him so – he hesitates to blame the Almighty for his miseries. The next authority – human, fallible, vulnerable – is the government. And something, by God, has got to be done about it! [pp. 8–9]

The Prairie: A State of Mind (1968)
Henry Kreisel

Man, the giant-conqueror, and man, the insignificant dwarf always threatened by defeat, form the two polarities of the state of mind produced by the sheer physical fact of the prairie. [p. 173]

The prairie, like the sea, thus often produces an extraordinary sensation of confinement within a vast and seemingly unlimited space. The isolated farm-houses, the towns and settlements, even the great cities that eventually sprang up on the prairies, become islands in that land-sea, areas of relatively safe refuge from the great and lonely spaces. [p. 175]

To conquer a piece of the continent, to put one's imprint upon virgin land, to say, "Here I am, for that I came," is as much a way of defining oneself, of proving one's existence, as is Descartes's *cogito, ergo sum*. . . .

The conquest of the land itself is by contrast a dominant theme, and the price paid for the conquest by the conqueror or the would-be conqueror is clearly and memorably established. The attempt to conquer the land is a huge gamble. Many lose, and there are everywhere mute emblems testifying to defeat. . . . But into the attempted conquest, whether ultimately successful or not, men pour an awesome, concentrated passion. The breaking of the land becomes a kind of rape, a passionate seduction. The earth is at once a willing and unwilling mistress, accepting and rejecting her seducer, the cause of his frustration and fulfilment, and either way the shaper and controller of his mind, exacting servitude. [p. 176]

The prairie settlements, insecure islands in that vast land-sea, have been austere, intensely puritan societies. Not that puritanism in Canada is confined to the prairie, of course, but on the prairie it has been more solidly entrenched than even in rural Ontario, and can be observed in something very like a distilled form.

It can be argued that in order to tame the land and begin the building, however tentatively, of something approaching a civilization, the men and women who settled on the prairie had to tame themselves, had to curb their passions and contain them within a tight neo-Calvinist framework. But it is not surprising that there should be sudden eruptions and that the passions, long suppressed, should burst violently into the open and threaten the framework that was meant to contain them. [p. 178]

Prairie puritanism is now somewhat beleaguered and shows signs of crumbling, but it remains a potent force still, and the vast land itself has not yet been finally subdued and altered. On a hot summer day it does not take long before, having left the paved streets of the great cities where hundreds of thousands of people now live, one can still see, outlined against the sky, the lonely, giant-appearing figures of men. . . . And on a winter day one can turn off the great superhighways that now cross the prairies and drive along narrow, snow-covered roads, and there it still lies, the great, vast land-sea. [p. 180]

The Pride (1968)
John Newlove

. . .

Those are all stories;
the pride, the grand poem
of our land, of the earth itself,
will come, welcome, and
sought for, and found,

in a line of running verse,
sweating, our pride;

we seize on
what has happened before,
one line only
will be enough,

a single line and
then the sunlit brilliant image suddenly floods us
with understanding, shocks our
attentions, and all desire
stops, stands alone;

we stand alone,
we are no longer lonely
but have roots,
and the rooted words
recur in the mind, mirror, so that
we dwell on nothing else, in nothing else,
touched, repeating them,
at home freely
at last, in amazement;

'the unyielding phrase
in tune with the epoch,'
the thing made up
of our desires,
not of its words, not only
of them, but of something else,
as well, that which we desire
so ardently, that which
will not come when
it is summoned alone,
but grows in us
and idles about and hides
until the moment is due—
the knowledge of
our origins, and where
we are in truth,
whose land this is
and is to be.

. . .

The Prairie
Sid Marty

Now but a bruise on the sidehill,
the sod hut they packed their love into
Little more than desire
kept out the sun and the rain
Not much more than love
did they have
there on the ravished plain

Here is their hard won house
abandoned now
that they built from the roots
coming out of the ground at last
to name every direction they wheeled in
and plant their landmark in the air,
to break the desolate arc
. . . but the name of the house is lost
like them

It is a secret kept by the neighbours
who survived
the politics of wind
and money

They will understand me
knowing how hard it is
to corral the wind

And you strangers
knowing only the highway,
you too
can at least imagine
in that extremity
as any desert
the sole relief of a tree

Hunting grouse
on the old abandoned farm,
we found a crabapple tree
heavy with fruit,
eaten only by deer

How many years ago
did the couple we'll say

were young
windburnt flowers
plant the dozen varieties
of trees

Act of love, to seed the prairie
among the buffalo beans,
the old dream shouldered aside

Sliced the turf, and watered green shoots
from mountain streams flowing
under deep black dirt
under the glacial debris

A thousand beaded pails
carried in the heat of summer
flashing of the metal
by the white alkali sloughs

Crabapples cured by frost taste sweet
tasting of cool nights
moonshine cider,
water, the depths of earth

The flavour of love savoured by strangers
lingers on in red crabapples
Though the passion of this house
has faded like a fiery old woman
hugging the wind in her spaces
beneath the open windows of the sky

In Open Prairie (1979)
Kenneth McRobbie

In prairie open
        to everything
from elsewhere
        which passes, on its

second appearing,
        still as sign
of nothing: an eddy
        of distant dust,

veer of disturbed
    birds, feathery
far smoke—the works
    of other men

come at us
    like random weather,
seasons in sequence,
    or alien missions

whose high vapour-trails
    fume up from the south
simple parabolas
    against heaven.

They exact from us
    no response.
Our wide, dry
    sea affords

no purchase for
    action. We have
got used to
    being overwhelmed.

We assume it all
    will pass, that
there is room
    on either side

and anyway time.
    So we just wait
for what's next,
    and make up the past.

A Prairie Sampler
Dorothy Livesay

The drama of Winnipeg is in its seasons, its weather. The city cannot rely on mountains or hills, even, for variety; nothing but the endless flatness of prairie grass surrounds it, where the streets end. It cannot rely on trees for beauty—they must battle for life. Elms, oaks and maples struggle to grow house high, and evergreens are rare. But summer, with its intense heat, all-powerful sun, ever-deepening blue sky, and the long, cool twilights lasting nearly to midnight, summer pulls the child into its drama. Nights may be lit by the aurora borealis drawing, with phosphorescent fingers, its great designs on the heavens. Or, at evening, the intolerable blanket of heat is suddenly broken by gusts of wind, tearing up dust and leaves. Clouds loom on the horizon terrible as an army with banners, black flying formations that suddenly open up in thunder; and loud as fireworks the rain explodes, great curtains of it rent asunder when the forked lightning pierces; and down the barren street a pelting river of rain sweeps dust and leaves into the gutters.

"Ah-h. That'll clear the air. A wonderful storm. Come out onto the verandah, Dorothy!" Father's high, still markedly south of England voice was always one of command and not (at that age) to be questioned. But I caught some of his excitement, crouched against the door and out of the wet, watching this lashing of the city, this agony of twisted trees, this rush for shelter by anyone caught unawares (umbrellas turned inside out at the first gust), and laughing uproariously with him when a Model-T Ford, dashing for home, was caught in the hurricane, its hood nearly ripped off but still swaying on up the empty roadway, with the black, flapping canvas lifting it along like a full-blown sail. [pp. 85–86]

'The Buffalo Hunt' from Riel
Don Gutteridge

It began with the gathering at Pembina:
One thousand carts drawn from a rim of prairie
Flatness along the straight spokes of the wind
To single hub. It began anew each spring
As if it had not happened before: after
The ploughing and the planting: though it was never
Spoken; only a live excitement swelling
To the eye like an alien sap—pulled
Memory of root and rock; the instincts stirred;
A thousand ploughs abruptly stopped (seed abandoned
To the sun) and one horizon rimmed with clouds
Of the great gathering, as the Métis spirit
Moved with the ancient wind and the ancient ways,
Came like the gray geese across a prairie sky
At the break of winter, their straight V's seeking
A true north, their blood singing through wings of lost
Continents and the turning of seasons unborn
And not to be known by blood or wings' longing.
They came to Pembina, in June, after the plough
And the seed, with remembering in their eyes.

And *he* remembered (with all the clarity
Of ten year old wonder looking up and around)
That one time his mother had let him go, her soft
Palms holding his, pressing them, only letting go
When male voices rang from the roadway just beyond
Their garden and the young wheat not able yet
To stand straight up; he had clambered about the cart
Among the strong smells (old buffalo robes with the smell
Of humans on them now—June nights could be cold—
The gunpowder in gleaming masculine horns,
Tallow, grease, leather) and above all the smell of sky
Drifting forever into roundness of earth
And the wheels turning beneath him in endless
Diminutive repetitions; he watched the days
And nights circle over, under, around him,
And dreamed of the buffalo.

Wolf Willow (1955)
Wallace Stegner

The rest of that country is notable primarily for its weather, which is violent and prolonged; its emptiness, which is almost frighteningly total; and its wind, which blows all the time in a way to stiffen your hair and rattle the eyes in your head.

This is no safety valve for the population explosion, no prize in a latter-day land rush. It has had its land rush, and recovered. If you owned it, you might be able to sell certain parts of it at a few dollars an acre; many parts you couldn't give away. Not many cars raise dust along its lonely roads—it is country people do not much want to cross, much less visit. But that block of country between the Milk River and the main line of the Canadian Pacific, and between approximately the Saskatchewan-Alberta line and Wood Mountain, is the place where I spent my childhood. It is also the place where the Plains, as an ecology, as a native Indian culture, and as a process of white settlement, came to their climax and their end. Viewed personally and historically, that almost featureless prairie glows with more color than it reveals to the appalled and misdirected tourist. As memory, as experience, those Plains are unforgettable; as history, they have the lurid explosiveness of a prairie fire, quickly dangerous, swiftly over. [pp. 3–4]

It is a long way from characterless; "overpowering" would be a better word. For over the segmented circle of earth is domed the biggest sky anywhere, which on days like this sheds down on range and wheat and summer fallow a light to set a painter wild, a light pure, glareless, and transparent. The horizon a dozen miles away is as clean a line as the nearest fence. There is no haze, neither the woolly gray of humid countries nor the blue atmosphere of the mountain West. Across the immense sky move navies of cumuli, fair-weather clouds, their bottoms as even as if they had scraped themselves flat against the flat earth.

The drama of this landscape is in the sky, pouring with light and always moving. The earth is passive. And yet the beauty I am struck by, both as present fact and as revived memory, is a fusion: this sky would not be so spectacular without this earth to change and glow and darken under it. And whatever the sky may do, however the earth is shaken or darkened, the Euclidean perfection abides. The very scale, the hugeness of simple forms, emphasizes stability. It is not hills and mountains which we should call eternal. Nature abhors an elevation as much as it abhors a vacuum; a hill is no sooner elevated than the forces of erosion begin tearing it down. These prairies are quiescent, close to static; looked at for any length of time, they begin to impose their awful perfection on the observer's mind. Eternity is a peneplain. [p. 7]

Desolate? Forbidding? There was never a country that in its good moments was more beautiful. Even in drouth or dust storm or blizzard it is the reverse of monotonous, once you have submitted to it with all the senses. You don't get out of the wind, but learn to lean and squint against it. You don't escape sky and sun, but wear them in your eyeballs and on your back. You become acutely aware of yourself. The world is very large, the sky even larger, and you are very small. But also the world is flat, empty, nearly abstract, and in its flatness you are a challenging upright thing, as sudden as an exclamation mark, as enigmatic as a question mark.

It is a country to breed mystical people, egocentric people, perhaps poetic people. But not humble ones. At noon the total sun pours on your single head; at sunrise or sunset you throw a shadow a hundred yards long. It was not prairie dwellers who invented the indifferent universe or impotent man. Puny you may feel there, and vulnerable, but not unnoticed. This is a land to mark the sparrow's fall. [p. 8]

Who Has Seen the Wind (1947)
W. O. Mitchell

Here was the least common denominator of nature, the skeleton requirements simply, of land and sky—Saskatchewan prairie. It lay wide around the town, stretching tan to the far line of the sky, shimmering under the June sun and waiting for the unfailing visitation of wind, gentle at first, barely stroking the long grasses and giving them life; later, a long hot gusting that would lift the black topsoil and pile it in barrow pits along the roads, or in deep banks against the fences.

Over the prairie, cattle stood listless beside the dried-up slough beds which held no water for them. Where the snow-white of alkali edged the course of the river, a thin trickle of water made its way toward the town low upon the horizon. Silver willow, heavy with dust, grew along the riverbanks, perfuming the air with its honey smell.

Just before the town the river took a wide loop and entered at the eastern edge. Inhabited now by some eighteen hundred souls, it had grown up on either side of the river from the seed of one homesteader's sod hut built in the spring of eighteen seventy-five. It was made up largely of frame buildings with high, peaked roofs, each with an expanse of lawn in front and a garden in the back; they lined avenues with prairie names: Bison, Riel, Qu'Appelle, Blackfoot, Fort. Cement sidewalks extended from First Street to Sixth Street at MacTaggart's Corner; from that point to the prairie a boardwalk ran. [pp. 3–4]

The wind was persistent now, a steady urgency upon his straight back, smoking up the dust from the road along the walk, lifting it and carrying it out to the prairie beyond. Several times Brian stopped: once to look up into the sun's unbearable radiance and then away with the lingering glow stubborn in his eyes; another time when he came upon a fox-red caterpillar making a procession of itself over a crack that snaked along the walk. He squashed it with his foot. Further on he paused at a spider that carried its bead of a body between hurrying thread-legs. Death came for the spider too.

He looked up to find that the street had stopped. Ahead lay the sudden emptiness of the prairie. For the first time in his four years of life he was alone on the prairie. [p. 10]

He had seen it often, from the veranda of his uncle's farmhouse, or at the end of a long street, but till now he had never heard it. The hum of telephone wires along the road, the ring of hidden crickets, the stitching sound of grasshoppers, the sudden relief of a meadow lark's song, were deliciously strange to him. Without hesitation he crossed the road and walked out through the hip-deep grass stirring in the steady wind; the grass clung at his legs; haloed fox-tails bowed before him; grasshoppers sprang from hidden places in the grass, clicketing ahead of him to disappear, then lift again.

A gopher squeaked questioningly as Brian sat down upon a rock warm to the backs of his thighs. He picked a pale blue flax-flower at his feet, stared long at the stripings in its shallow throat, then looked up to see a dragonfly hanging on shimmering wings directly in front of him. The gopher squeaked again, and he saw it a few yards away, sitting up, watching him from its pulpit hole. A suave-winged hawk chose that moment to slip its shadow over the face of the prairie.

And all about him was the wind now, a pervasive sighing through great emptiness, unhampered by the buildings of the town, warm and living against his face and in his hair.

Then for the second time that day he saw a strange boy—one who came from behind him soundlessly, who stood and stared at him with steady gray eyes in a face of remarkable broadness, with cheekbones circling high under a dark and freckled skin. He saw that the boy's hair, bleached as the dead prairie grass itself, lay across his forehead in an all-round cowlick curling under at the edge. His faded blue pants hung open in two tears just below the knees. He was barefooted.

Brian was not startled; he simply accepted the boy's presence out here as he had accepted that of the gopher and the hawk and the dragonfly.

"This is your prairie," Brian said.

The boy did not answer him. He turned and walked as silently as he had come, out over the prairie. His walk was smooth.

After the boy's figure had become just a speck in the distance, Brian looked up into the sky, now filled with a soft expanse of cloud, the higher edges luminous and startling against the blue. It stretched to the prairie's rim. As he stared, the gray underside carded out, and through the cloud's softness was revealed a blue well shot with sunlight. Almost as soon as it had cleared, a whisking of cloud stole over it.

For one moment no wind stirred. A butterfly went pelting past. God, Brian decided, must like the boy's prairie. [pp. 11–12]

Sketching the Prairie Landscape
of the Mind

Ivan Eyre, *Black Sun* **(1966)**
Lost prairie souls.

Otto Rogers, *Sunset Stillness* **(1966)**
Rendering a prairie landscape.

Kenneth Lochhead, *Return to Humanity* **(1955)**
An existential landscape.

Harry Savage, *Partridge Hill Road Series* **(1977)**
Prairie abstraction: light and space.

Maureen Enns, *Sky Hill* **(1977)**
A landscape in the mind's eye.

Dorothy Knowles, *The River* **(1967)**
A majestic landscape.

George Jenkins, *The Old Toal Place* (1969)

William Kurelek, *Dinnertime on the Prairies* (1963)
A Christian message for prairie dwellers.

William Kurelek, *Not Going Back to Pick Up a Cloak* **(1971)**
Rural prairie society confronts modern civilization.

CONCLUSION

Throughout its history, the Canadian West has evoked strong images in the minds of those who visited, settled in, or sometimes simply wrote about, the region. These people saw in the West what they wanted, or were conditioned by their cultural milieu, to see. At different times, they perceived a West that was a wasteland, a pristine wilderness, a source of national greatness and imperial grandeur, a utopia, a harsh and cruel land, or a mythical region shaped by the attitudes and beliefs of its people. Each of these images held sway for a period of time and then gave way to a new image, resulting in changing images of the Canadian West.

The categorizing of these images in this way suggests that they were cut-and-dried. They were not. Ideas or images are fluid, and people could, and did, hold differing images of the West at one and the same time according to their perspective. Thus, for example, Henry Youle Hind could, in the report of his scientific expedition of 1857, depict the West at one point as a wasteland when describing the so-called "desert" conditions in the grasslands of the southern region, and at another point as a great agricultural hinterland for central Canada when thinking about the "fertile belt" to the north of the grasslands. And without skipping a beat, he could evoke images of a pristine wilderness when describing a tranquil prairie scene. Thus, to categorize the West in terms of a particular image at a particular point in time and to fit particular individuals into specific categories, as I have done, is simply one way of looking at the region and a means of bringing order to the variety of responses to the Canadian prairies over three centuries. The categories must be fluid and open, but identifying these dominant images offers a means to appreciate and to understand how, and why, perceptions of the Canadian West have changed over time.

These images have been more than passing commentaries on the region; they have greatly influenced — and sometimes dictated — policies toward the area, and thus profoundly affected the historical evolution of the West. The West remained the home of the native people and virtually unpopulated by the white man for the first two centuries of European exploration — from 1650 to 1850 — because of the image of the area as a wasteland, ill-suited for agriculture. Based on what Europeans believed to be essential for agriculture from their European perspective — namely, a moderate climate and a forested region — they could see no agricultural potential in this barren, cold, desolate, and inhospitable region of the North West. So long as this image predominated, the Hudson's Bay Company was able to control the region almost unchallenged, as a fur trading area, and the native people could continue to see the West as their physical and spiritual homeland.

Only when people were encouraged to look at the North West in terms of its agricultural potential did they "discover" that that potential existed. The image of a bountiful and rich land pre-existed, or at least co-existed with, the "scientific proof" that the region contained a climate and a soil conducive to agricultural production. Indeed, it was the image that persuaded scientists to search for the proof to justify their perception. The incentive to look at the West in terms of its settlement potential came out of the Romanticism of the mid-nineteenth century, with its positive image of the Canadian West as an Edenic wilderness, and out of the British and Canadian imperial and national movements of the late nineteenth century that looked at the North West in terms of its potential as a vast agricultural hinterland for the commercial and political exploits of the Canadian nation and the British Empire.

Equally, the utopian image of a "promised land," which was a logical evolution from the romantic and imperial vision of the West, was the motivating force behind the great immigration scheme at the turn of the century. What attracted hundreds of thousands of eastern and central Canadians, Americans, British, and western and eastern Europeans to the Canadian West was the image of the region as "the last best West," one of the few remaining regions in North America, if not the world, where conditions were right to create the perfect society. Without the image of a better society, people would have no incentive to move there. The immigration propaganda, the booster literature of prairie towns and cities, and the depictions of the region in early western Canadian literature and art created that image. That image, in turn, made the settlement of the Canadian West a possibility at the turn of the century.

It is not surprising that the reality of settlement did not match the ideal in the mind of early settlers. The resulting cultural shock meant the need to adjust or alter the image so as to deal with the reality. Some westerners, particularly those involved in the agrarian protest movements on the prairies in the early twentieth century, attempted to alter the reality to fit the ideal in their minds. They saw protest as a means to change the political, economic, social, and cultural structure of the region so as to create the utopian agricultural community based on agrarian values and a rural social structure. The image of western farmers as "God's Chosen People" and of the family farm as the ideal social unit—the inspiration for western agrarian protest movements—was a logical outgrowth of the utopian image of the West. Other westerners sought a new "realistic" image of the West which was more in tune with what they perceived the region to be like. The new image of a harsh land that exacted its toll from the people who tried to conquer it was essential to bring the area under control and to make it a commercial success. Those who succeeded were precisely those settlers who could confront the harsh realities of their lives in the new land and survive. That such drive and determination might poison their personal relationships was a price that many paid to succeed. That it would also transform the region from a society based on agrarian values and ideals to one based on competitive commercial needs—from agriculture as a way of life to agribusiness—was a fact that few westerners were aware of at the time. It was the realistic image of a harsh land and of a western society dominated by eastern metropolitan forces that provided the mindset necessary to conquer, subdue, and transform the region.

A region becomes over time more than a product of its environment, or even the perception of the environment. It becomes a "mental construct," shaped by the attitudes, beliefs, and stories of its people. This mythology governs what one sees as "reality." In the case of western Canada, it is the stories and historical myths of the past that have taken shape over time, including a fusion of the earlier images of the West— the fact and fiction of the region—that have shaped the mentality of its people and projected the image of the West as a region of the mind. The West becomes its own image.

One image has remained consistent throughout the changing images of the West—the West as a region shaped and affected by outside forces. Throughout its three centuries of exploration and settlement, the West has had an image that has necessitated its people looking at themselves and their region in relation to other areas or regions. Perhaps this is simply stating the obvious, that a region is itself a relational entity. Initially, the image of a wasteland was in terms of the usefulness of the region for European fur trading interests and the limitations of the area for European-style farming. By mid-century the West was seen in terms of its opportunity for those people from populated areas of Britain, the United States, or eastern and central Canada who wanted to escape the ills of urban and industrial society and to commune with God and Nature. The West was viewed from a European Romantic perspective. Others saw the West in terms of its potential for national greatness and imperial grandeur. When population flowed into the West from areas of Europe, Britain, the United States, and other regions of Canada, the West was seen in terms of fulfilling utopian dreams shaped by ideals from elsewhere. External perceptions dictated internal images. Even historians, writers, and artists in the post-World War II era have struggled to find images of the West which are uniquely western, and therefore ones that will distinguish the region from other regions of Canada, North America, or the world. In the attempt to distinguish, the factor of association continues to play a role.

In truth, the West has been many things to many people. It has taken on different images at different times as a result of changing assumptions and cultural values that observers have brought to their perception of the region. Together these images, shaped by outside forces, have fostered a search for a self-generating image within the region itself. Plato's dictum, "Know thyself" is something western Canadians can aspire to achieve, since their region has been the subject of much interest, reflection, and soul searching. That fascination for the region will remain in the future as westerners continue to want to seek their identity through their own images of the West.

NOTES

Chapter One

1. John Snow, *These Mountains are our Sacred Places: The Story of the Stoney Indians* (Toronto, 1977), 12.
2. For a good overview of the history of the Canadian West during the fur trade era see Gerald Friesen, *The Canadian Prairies: A History* (Toronto, 1984); for a personal account see Mary Quayle Innis, *Travellers West* (Toronto, 1956). An excellent study of images of the Canadian West in the nineteenth century from the perspective of expansionists in Canada West (Ontario) is Doug Owram, *Promise of Eden: The Canadian Expansionist Movement and the Idea of the West, 1856–1900* (Toronto, 1980).
3. There has been no attempt to discuss the intellectual perspective of European explorers, fur traders, and artists within the context of the Age of Enlightenment in Canadian historiography, but there has been within the American literature. See, for example, W. H. Truettner, *The Natural Man Observed: A Study of Catlin's Indian Gallery* (Washington, 1979); Paul Rossi and David Hunt, *The Art of the Old West* (New York, 1971); Peter Hassrick, *The Way West: Art of Frontier America* (New York, 1977); and John Logan Allen, *Passage Through the Garden: Lewis and Clark and the Image of the American Northwest* (Urbana, 1975).
4. For information on Henry Kelsey, see A. G. Doughty and C. Martin, eds., *The Kelsey Papers* (Ottawa: Public Archives of Canada, 1929). See also John Warkentin, "Steppe, Desert and Empire," in A. W. Rasporich and H. C. Klassen, eds., *Prairie Perspectives 2* (Toronto, 1973), 102–36 and J. Warkentin, *The Western Interior of Canada: A Record of Geographical Discovery: 1612–1917* (Toronto, 1964).
5. *The Kelsey Papers*, 1–15.
6. L. J. Burpee, ed., *Journals and Letters of Pierre Gaultier de Varennes de la Vérendrye and His Sons* (Toronto, 1927), 7.
7. On Alexander Mackenzie, see W. Kaye Lamb, ed., *The Journals and Letters of Sir Alexander Mackenzie* (Cambridge, 1970). For David Thompson see J. B. Tyrrell, ed., *David Thompson's Narrative of His*

Exploration in Western America, 1784–1812 (Toronto, 1916); and Richard Glover, ed., *David Thompson's Narrative, 1784–1812* (Toronto, 1962). See as well, Warkentin, "Steppe, Desert and Empire"; and his *The Western Interior of Canada.*

8. *The Journals and Letters of Sir Alexander Mackenzie,* 411.

9. Glover, *David Thompson's Narrative, 1784–1812,* xliii.

10. *David Thompson's Narrative,* 222.

11. Daniel W. Harmon, *Sixteen Years in the Indian Country, The Journals of Daniel Williams Harmon 1800–1816,* ed. W. K. Lamb (Toronto, 1957), 238.

12. Wreford Watson, "The Role of Illusion in North American Geography: A Note on the Geography of North American Settlement," *The Canadian Geographer* 13 (Spring, 1969), 16.

13. Quoted in John Warkentin, "The Desert Goes North," in Brian Blouet and M. Lawson, eds., *Images of the Plains: The Role of Human Nature in Settlement* (Lincoln, 1975), 149–63; see as well his "The Geography of Franklin and Long: A Comparison," in C. Berger and R. Cook, eds., *The West and the Nation* (Toronto, 1976), 33–71. On the American image of the West in the era of exploration and fur trade, see Allen, *Passage Through the Garden*; and his "To Unite the Discoveries: The American Response to the Early Exploration of Rupert's Land," in Richard Davies, ed., *Rupert's Land: A Cultural Tapestry* (Waterloo, 1988), 79–96.

14. On John Palliser see Irene Spy, Introduction to *The Papers of the Palliser Expedition, 1857–1860* (Toronto, 1968); for Henry Youle Hind see W. L. Morton, *Henry Youle Hind: 1823–1908* (Toronto, 1980).

15. H. Y. Hind, *Narrative of the Canadian Red River Exploring Expedition of 1857 and of the Assiniboine and Saskatchewan Exploring Expedition of 1858.* Reprint. (Edmonton, 1971), 222.

16. Walter Prescott Webb, *The Great Plains* (New York, 1931).

17. Spry, *The Papers of the Palliser Expedition,* 9.

18. On Arthur Dobbs, see D. W. Moodie, "Early British Images of Rupert's Land," in R. Allen, ed., *Man and Nature on the Prairies* (Regina, 1976), 1–20.

19. Earl of Selkirk, "Prospectus," in John Strachan, *A Letter to the Right Honourable the Earl of Selkirk on His Settlement at Red River* (London, 1816), 69.

20. Strachan, *Letter to the Right Honourable the Earl of Selkirk,* 10.

21. See Owram, *The Promise of Eden,* 7–10.

22. Thomas Simpson, *Narrative of the Discoveries on The North Coast of America: Effected by the Officers of the Hudson's Bay Company During the Years 1836–39* (London, 1843), 15.

23. Sir George Simpson, *Narrative of a Journey Round the World During the Years 1841 and 1842,* Volume I (London, 1847), 55–56.

24. *Report from the Select Committee on the Hudson's Bay Company* (London, 1857), 45.

25. Captain H. Warre, *Sketches in North America and the Oregon Territory,* Introduction by A. Hanna (Barre, Massachusetts, 1970), 15.

26. On missionaries in the North West see John Webster Grant, *Moon of Wintertime: Missionaries and the Indians of Canada in Encounter since*

1534 (Toronto, 1984); see as well Owram, *The Promise of Eden*, 23ff.

27. John West, *The Substance of a Journey During a Residence at the Red River Colony, British North America* (London, 1824), 43, 28.

28. Pierre Jean de Smet, *Life and Travels Among the North American Indians*, ed. H. M. Chittenden and A. T. Richardson (New York, 1905), 515–16.

29. Sarah Tucker, *The Rainbow in the North: A Short Account of the First Establishment of Christianity in Rupert's Land by the Church Missionary Society* (London, 1850), 4, 35.

30. Quoted in Friesen, *The Canadian Prairies*, 106.

31. On Peter Rindisbacher, see Alvin M. Josephy, Jr., *The Artist Was a Young Man: The Life Story of Peter Rindisbacher* (Fort Worth, 1970). See as well Ronald Rees, *Land of Earth and Sky: Landscape Painting of Western Canada* (Saskatoon, 1984); and Clifford Wilson, "Peter Rindisbacher, first Western artist," *Canadian Art, XX*, 1 (January/February, 1963), 50–53.

32. Quoted in Josephy, *The Artist was a Young Man*, 63.

33. Robert Montgomery Martin, *The Hudson's Bay Territories and Vancouver's Island, with an Exposition of the Chartered Rights, Conduct and Policy of the Honourable Hudson's Bay Corporation* (London, 1849), 6.

Chapter Two

1. William Francis Butler, *The Great Lone Land* (London, 1872), 199–200.

2. For a detailed discussion of William Butler and his image of the West see Susan Jackel, "Images of the Canadian West, 1872–1911," (Ph.D. dissertation, University of Alberta, 1977); see also Edward McCourt, *Remember Butler: The Story of Sir William Butler* (London, 1967).

3. On the Romantic tradition as it relates to the American West see William Goetzmann, *Exploration and Empire: The Explorer and the Scientist in the Winning of the American West* (New York, 1966); and Hugh Honour, *The New Golden Land: European Images of America from the Discoveries to the Present Times* (New York, 1975); on the Canadian west, see Gerald Friesen, *The Canadian Prairies: A History* (Toronto, 1984), 104ff; and Doug Owram, *Promise of Eden: The Canadian Expansionist Movement and the Idea of the West 1856–1900* (Toronto, 1980), 16–19, although Owram tends to play down the romantic image of the West and even to see it in negative terms with regard to its impact on the development of the West.

4. Quoted in Susan Jackel, "Images of the Canadian West, 1872–1911," 49.

5. Butler, *Great Lone Land*, 351.

6. Mary Quayle Innis provides an excellent account of the Victorian traveller, with chapters on the Earl of Southesk and on Viscount Milton and Dr. Cheadle, in her *Travellers West* (Toronto, 1956).

7. P. F. Tytler, *The Northern Coast of America and the Hudson Bay's Territories* (London, 1853), 314–15.

8. H. Y. Hind, *Narrative of the Canadian Red River Exploring Expedition of 1857 and of the Assiniboine and Saskatchewan Exploring Expedition of 1858.* Reprint. (Edmonton, 1971), 134–35.

9. Earl of Southesk, *Saskatchewan and the Rocky Mountains* (Edinburgh, 1875), 283, 13.

10. Viscount Milton and W. B. Cheadle, *The North-West Passage by Land* (London, 1867), 51–52.

11. George J. Mountain, *Songs of the Wilderness* (n.p., 1846), 107.

12. For a discussion of this question see Barbara Novak, *Nature and Culture: American Landscape and Painting, 1825–1875* (New York, 1980).

13. John Ryerson, *Hudson's Bay or A Missionary Tour in The Territory of the Hon. Hudson's Bay Company* (Toronto, 1855), 143, 155.

14. Alexander Sutherland, *A Summer in Prairie Land* (Toronto, 1881), 103.

15. For a discussion of the views of late nineteenth century Protestant missionaries see John W. Grant, *Moon of Wintertime* (Toronto, 1984), 143–66.

16. For a discussion of Romanticism and art in the Canadian and American West see W. H. Goetzmann and J. C. Porter, *The West as Romantic Horizon* (Nebraska, 1981); W. H. Truettner, *The Natural Man Observed: A Study of Catlin's Indian Gallery* (Washington, 1979); Peter Hassrick, *The Way West: Art of Frontier America* (New York, 1977); and Ann Davis and Robert Thacker, "Pictures and Prose: Romantic Sensibility and the Great Plains in Catlin, Kane, and Miller," *Great Plains Quarterly* 6 (Winter 1986), 3–20.

17. On Paul Kane see Ronald Rees, *Land of Earth and Sky: Landscape Painting of Western Canada* (Saskatoon, 1984), 11–14; J. Russell Harper, *Paul Kane's Frontier* (Austin, 1971); and Ann Davis, *A Distant Harmony: Comparisons on the Painting of Canada and the United States of America* (Winnipeg, 1982), 33–68.

18. Paul Kane, *Wanderings of an Artist Among the Indians of North America*, Second Edition (Toronto, 1925), lii.

19. Harper, *Paul Kane's Frontier*, 18.

20. J. Russell Harper, *Painting in Canada: a History*, Second Edition (Toronto, 1977), 123.

21. *Ibid*. On Frederick Verner see Joan Murray, *The Last Buffalo: The Story of Frederick Arthur Verner, Painter of the Canadian West* (Toronto, 1984); and Ronald Rees, *Land of Earth and Sky*, 14–15.

22. See Eric Quayle, *Ballantyne the Brave: A Victorian Writer and His Family* (London, 1967), and his "R. M. Ballantyne in Rupert's Land," *Queen's Quarterly*, 75, 1 (Spring 1968), 62–71; see as well Dick Harrison, *Unnamed Country: The Struggle for a Canadian Prairie Fiction* (Edmonton, 1977).

23. R. M. Ballantyne, *Snowflakes and Sunbeams* (London, 1863), 97.

24. Quayle, "R. M. Ballantyne in Rupert's Land," 70.

25. George F. Crofton, "A Poet in Scarlet," *Alberta Historical Review*, 15 (1967), 17.

26. For a discussion of Henri Julien and other travelling artists in the late nineteenth century see Paul Holgarth, *Artists on Horseback: The Old West in Illustrated Journalism, 1847–1900* (New York, 1972).

27. Henri Julien, "Expedition to the North West," ed. Hugh Dempsey, *Alberta Historical Review*, 9, 1 (Winter, 1961), 10–11.

28. Harrison discusses Edmund Collins in "The Beginnings of Prairie Fiction," *Journal of Canadian Fiction*, IV, I (1975), 162–64.

29. J. E. Collins, *Annette, The Métis Spy* (Toronto, 1886), 142–43.

30. See Eli Mandel, "Images of Prairie Man," in R. Allen, ed., *A Region of the Mind* (Regina, 1973), 201–9.

31. George M. Grant, *Ocean to Ocean*. Reprint (Edmonton, 1963), 74.

32. George M. Grant, *Picturesque Canada* (Toronto, 1882), 282.

33. Thomas Rawlings, *The Confederation of the British North American Provinces including British Columbia and the Hudson's Bay Territory* (London, 1865), 98–99.

Chapter Three

1. Charles Mair, "The New Canada: Its Resources and Productions," in *The Canadian Monthly and National Review*, 8 (November, 1875), 163.

2. For an excellent discussion of the image of the West in the lexicon of nationalism see Doug Owram, *Promise of Eden: The Canadian Expansionist Movement and the Idea of the West, 1856–1900* (Toronto, 1980); see as well Gerald Friesen, *The Canadian Prairies: A History* (Toronto, 1984), 104–10.

3. Dawn Glanz, *How the West was Drawn: American Art and the Settling of the Frontier* (Ann Arbor, 1978), 112.

4. See Owram, *Promise of Eden*, 125–48.

5. For a discussion of imperialism and Canadian nationalism see Carl Berger, *The Sense of Power* (Toronto, 1970).

6. Alexander Morris, *Nova Britannia* (Toronto, 1884), 59.

7. For an analysis of George Brown's views of the West in his *Globe* see Frank H. Underhill, "Some Aspects of Upper Canadian Radical Opinion in the Decade Before Confederation," Canadian Historical Association Annual *Report* (1927), 46–61.

8. Owram, *Promise of Eden*, 48.

9. Quoted in *ibid.*, 46.

10. Lorin Blodget, *Climatology of the United States, and of the Temperate Latitudes of the North American Continent* (Philadelphia, 1857), 529. For a discussion of Blodgett's views see John Warkentin, "Steppe, Desert and Empire," in A. W. Rasporich and H. C. Klassen, eds., *Prairie Perspectives 2* (Toronto, 1973), 102–36.

11. James Edward Fitzgerald, *An Examination of the Charter and Proceedings of the Hudson's Bay Company* (London, 1849), 114, 117.

12. John McLean, *Notes of a 25 Year Service in the Hudson's Bay Company* (London, 1849), 308, 309.

13. Henry Youle Hind, *Narrative of the Canadian Red River Exploring Expedition of 1857 and of the Assiniboine and Saskatchewan Exploring Expedition of 1858* II (London, 1860), 234.

14. On Humphrey Lloyd Hime see A. J. Birrell, *Into the Silent Land: Survey Photography in the Canadian West, 1858–1900* (Ottawa, 1975); and Ralph Greenhill, "Early Canadian Photographer, Humphrey Lloyd Hime," *Image*, 11, 3 (1962), 9–11.

15. Edward Cavell, *Journeys to the Far West* (Toronto, 1979), vii.

16. On Benjamin Baltzly and Charles George Horetzky, see *Into the Silent Land*.

17. On William G. R. Hind the artist, see J. Russell Harper, *William G. R. Hind, 1833–1889,* Canadian Artists Series (Ottawa, 1976); *Image of Canada* (Ottawa, 1972); and Ronald Rees, *Land of Earth and Sky: Landscape Painting of Western Canada* (Saskatoon, 1984); and his "Images of the Prairie: Landscape Painting and Perception in the Western Interior of Canada," *Canadian Geographer*, xx, 3 (1976), 259–78.

18. James W. Taylor, *Northwest British America and Its Relations to the State of Minnesota* (St. Paul, 1860), 12.

19. On American, and especially Minnesotan, expansionist ambitions in the North West, see Alvin C. Gluek, *Minnesota and the Manifest Destiny of the Canadian Northwest: A Study in Canadian-American Relations* (Toronto, 1965).

20. Mair, "The New Canada," 161.

21. Quoted in Owram, *Promise of Eden*, 49.

22. Thomas Keefer, *Philosophy of Railroads*. Reprint. (Toronto, 1972), x.

23. F. A. Wilson and A. B. Richards, *Britain Redeemed and Canada Preserved* (London, 1850), 172.

24. R. Carmichael-Smyth, *Letter to the Right Honourable Earl Grey* (London, 1850), 10.

25. Millington Henry Synge, *Great Britain One Empire* (London, 1852), 56.

26. *Prospectus issued by the International Financial Society Ltd., July, 1863* in J. M. Bumsted, ed., *Documentary Problems in Canadian History*, I (Georgetown, 1969), 226.

27. Margaret MacLeod, *Songs of Old Manitoba* (Toronto, 1959), 93.

28. Mary Quayle Innis, *Travellers West* (Toronto, 1956), 219–335 provides an excellent overview of both the context and the nature of George Grant's and Sandford Fleming's overland trip in 1872. Also very good on early visitors to the West, including Grant and Fleming, is Irene Spry "Early Visitors to the Canadian Prairies," in Brian Blouet and M. Lawson, eds. *Images of the Plains: The Role of Human Nature in Settlement* (Nebraska, 1975), 165–80.

29. George M. Grant, *Ocean to Ocean*. Reprint. (Edmonton, 1967), 97.

30. On the national artists associated with the Canadian Pacific Railway Company, see Dennis Reid, *"Our Own Country:" Being an Account of the National Aspirations of the Principal Landscape Artists in Montreal and Toronto, 1860–1890* (Ottawa, 1979); see as well Elizabeth Brown, *A Wilderness for All: Landscapes of Canada's Mountain Parks, 1885–1960* (Banff, 1985); on photography, see M. T. Hodley, "Photography and the Landscape of Travel: Western Canada, 1884–1914," (M. A. Thesis, University of Calgary, 1984). For the American context, see William H. Truettner, *National Parks and the American Landscape* (Washington, 1972).

31. Edward Cavell and Dennis Reid, *When Winter Was King* (Banff, 1988), 71.

32. Quoted in Reid, *"Our Own Country,"* 418.

33. Lord Dufferin, *My Canadian Journal: 1872–78* (New York, 1891), 396.

34. Marquis of Lorne, *The Canadian North-West: Speech Delivered at Winnipeg* (Ottawa, 1882), 9.

35. On the artistic depictions of the Marquis of Lorne's tour of western Canada in the 1880s see Paul Hogarth, *Artists on Horseback: The Old West in Illustrated Journalism, 1857–1900* (New York, 1972), 133–65; and Ronald Rees, *Land of Earth and Sky*, 19–21.

36. Alexander Begg, *The Great North-West of Canada: A Paper Read at Conference, Indian and Colonial Exhibition.* (London, 1886), 9–11.

Chapter Four

1. Nicholas Flood Davin, ed., *Homes for Millions: The Great Canadian North-West: Its Resources Fully Described* (Ottawa, 1891), 6.

2. R. J. C. Stead, "The Plough," in *The Empire Builders* (Toronto, 1923), 31–32.

3. For a discussion of the immigration propaganda see Klaus Peter Stich, "'Canada's Century': The Rhetoric of Propaganda," *Prairie Forum*, 1 (April 1976), 19–30; Bruce Peel, "The Lure of the West," Papers of the Bibliographical Society of Canada, 5 (1966), 19–29; James Hedges, *Building the Canadian West: The Land and Colonization Policies of the Canadian Pacific Railway* (New York, 1939), 94–125; Harold M. Troper, *Only Farmers Need Apply: Official Government Encouragement of Immigration from the United States, 1896–1911* (Toronto, 1972), passim; and Pierre Berton, *The Promised Land: Settling the West, 1896–1914* (Toronto, 1984), 13–18. A good study of the American immigration propaganda is David M. Emmons, *Garden in the Grasslands: Boomer Literature of the Central Great Plains* (Lincoln, 1971).

4. Canada, Department of the Interior, *Canada West* (Ottawa, 1913), 4.

5. Bruce Peel, "The Lure of the West," Papers of the Bibliographical Society of Canada (1966), 29.

6. George Livingstone Dodds, *The Last West: The Latest Gift of The Lady Bountiful* (Winnipeg, 1906), 26.

7. See Carl Berger, "The True North Strong and Free," in Peter Russell, ed., *Nationalism in Canada* (Toronto, 1966), 3–26.

8. Thomas Spence, *The Prairie Lands of Canada* (Montreal, 1880), 6.

9. Isaac Cowie, *The Western Plains of Canada Rediscovered* (n.p., 1903), 22.

10. Charles Mair, "General Description of the North-West," in N. F. Davin, ed., *Homes for Millions*, 11.

11. Canada, Department of the Interior, *Western Canada: The Granary of the British Empire* (Ottawa, 1906), 79–80.

12. Canada, Department of the Interior, *Read this Pamphlet on Manitoba, the N.W.T., Provinces of Ontario and Quebec* (Ottawa, 1883), 20.

13. George Grant, *Picturesque Canada*, I (Toronto, 1882), 324.

14. *Ibid.*, 339.

15. Alexander Begg, *The Great Canadian North West: Its Past History, Present Conditions and Glorious Prospects* (Montreal, 1881), 109.

16. George Bryce, *Manitoba: Its Infancy, Growth and Present Condition* (London, 1882), 333–34.

17. For John Macoun's views of the Canadian West see William A. Waiser, "Macoun and the Great North-West," (M. A. Thesis, University of Saskatchewan, 1976); see as well Doug Owram, *Promise of Eden: The Canadian Expansionist Movement and the Idea of the West, 1856–1960* (Toronto, 1980), 149–67.

18. John Macoun, *Manitoba and the Great North West* (Guelph, 1882), 103.

19. Quoted in Mary Quayle Innis, *Travellers West* (Toronto, 1956), 226.

20. Spence, *The Prairie Lands*, 26.

21. Quoted in *ibid.*, 21.

22. On utopian settlements on the Prairies see Anthony Rasporich, "Utopian Ideals and Community Settlements in Western Canada, 1880–1914," in H. Klassen, ed., *The Canadian West: Social Change and Economic Development* (Calgary, 1977), 37–62; and his "Utopia, Sect and Millennium in Western Canada, 1870–1940," *Prairie Forum*, 12, 1 (Fall, 1987), 217–43; Benjamin G. Smillie, *Visions of the New Jerusalem: Religious Settlement on the Prairies* (Edmonton, 1983).

23. Rasporich, "Utopian Ideals and Community Settlements," 38.

24. A. E. M. Hewlett, "Old Cannington Manor, Assiniboia, N.W.T." in Cannington Manor, Hewlett Papers, Saskatchewan Archives, 1.

25. *Ibid.*, 4.

26. Quoted in Rasporich, "Utopian Ideals and Community Settlements," 342–43.

27. On the Parry Sounders see R. Douglas Francis, "The Establishment of the Parry Sound Colony," *Alberta History*, 29 (Winter, 1980), 23–29.

28. W. C. Pollard, *Pioneering in the Prairie West* (Toronto, 1926), 87.

29. On the Barr Colony, see Pierre Berton, *The Promised Land* (Toronto, 1984), 102–35.

30. On religious communities see Smillie, *Visions of the New Jerusalem.*

31. E. A. Partridge, *War on Poverty* (Winnipeg, 1925), 134.

32. On the subject of boosterism and western Canadian urban centres, see Alan F. J. Artibise, "Boosterism and the Development of Prairie Cities, 1871–1913," in A. F. J. Artibise, ed., *Town and City: Aspects of Western Canadian Urban Development* (Regina, 1981), 206–36; and his "City-Building in the Canadian West: From Boosterism to Corporatism," *Journal of Canadian Studies*, 17, 3 (Fall, 1982), 35–44.

33. Quoted in Artibise, *Town and City*, 220.

34. Quotations are taken from the following "booster" pamphlets: Wolseley Board of Trade, *Wheat Wealthy Wolseley: The Grain Golden City of the Central West*. (n.d.), Alix Board of Trade, *Alix: The Centre of Alberta, the Garden of the West* (1911); Saskatoon Board of Trade, *Saskatoon* (1908); T. W. Sheffelds, *Facts and Opportunities in Regina and Saskatchewan* (1911).

35. On the subject of western Canadian literature and imagery at the turn of the century, see Patricia Roome, "Images of the West: Social Themes in Prairie Literature, 1898–1930," (M.A. Thesis, University of Calgary, 1976); Gerald Friesen, "Three generations of fiction: an introduction to prairie cultural history," in D. J. Bercuson and P. Buckner, eds., *Eastern and Western Perspectives* (Toronto, 1981), 183–96; Dick Harrison,

Unnamed Country: The Struggle for a Canadian Prairie Fiction
(Edmonton, 1977), 72–100; and Frank Watt, "Western Myth: The World
of Ralph Connor," in D. G. Stephens, ed., *Writers of the Prairies*
(Vancouver, 1973), 26–36.

36. Friesen, "Three generations," 186.
37. Emily Murphy, *Janey Canuck in the West.* Reprint. (Toronto, 1975), 27, 138.
38. Ralph Connor, *The Sky Pilot* (Toronto, 1899), 161–62.
39. Nellie McClung, *Clearing in the West* (Toronto, 1935), 56.
40. For a discussion of western Canadian folk songs see Leonora M. Pauls,
    "The English Language Folk and Traditional Songs of Alberta: Collection
    and Analysis for Teaching Purposes" (M. Music Thesis, University of
    Calgary, 1981).
41. Margaret A. MacLeod, *Songs of Old Manitoba* (Toronto, 1959), 76–77.
42. *Ibid.*, 81.
43. *Ibid.*, 90.
44. On images in Canadian art at the turn of the century see Ronald Rees,
    Land of Earth and Sky: Landscape Painting of Western Canada (Saskatoon,
    1984), 27–42; and his "Images of the Prairie: Landscape Painting and
    Perception in the Western Interior of Canada," *Canadian Geographer*, xx,
    3 (1976), 259–78; on Inglis Sheldon-Williams see Patricia Ainslie, *Inglis
    Sheldon-Williams* (Calgary, 1982).
45. Quoted in Rees, *Land of Earth and Sky*, 35.
46. Friesen, "Three Generations of Fiction," 186.
47. R. J. C. Stead, *The Cowpuncher* (Toronto, 1918), 49.
48. Arthur Stringer, *The Prairie Wife* (New York, 1915), 58–59.
49. Murphy, *Janey Canuck*, 114.
50. *Ibid.*, 11, 213.
51. Connor, *The Sky Pilot*, 12.
52. R. J. C. Stead, "The Homesteader," in *The Empire Builders* (Toronto,
    1923), 34.
53. Quoted in Rees, *Land of Earth and Sky*, 29–30.
54. Ralph Connor [C. W. Gordon], *The Foreigner: A Tale of Saskatchewan*
    (Toronto, 1909), 378.
55. Connor, *The Sky Pilot*, 27.
56. Nellie McClung, *Sowing Seeds in Danny* (Toronto, 1939), 40.

Chapter Five

1. R. Douglas Francis, "The Ideal and the Real: The Image of the Canadian
   West in the Settlement Period," in R. Davies, ed., *Rupert's Land: A Cultural
   Tapestry* (Waterloo, 1988), 253–73. See as well R. Rees, *New and Naked
   Land: Making the Prairies Home* (Saskatoon, 1988); and his "Nostalgic
   Reaction and the Canadian Prairie Landscape," *Great Plains Quarterly*,
   II, 3 (Summer, 1982), 157–67.
2. Public Archives of Canada [PAC], MG 29 C 38, "My Four Years
   Experience in the North West of America: Roughing it in the Far West"
   (unpublished manuscript), 1–2.

3. Adam Shortt, "Some Observations on the Great North-West"
    Part I : "Immigration and Transportation," *Queen's Quarterly*, II, 3
    (January, 1895), 183–97.
    Part II: "Social and Economic Conditions," *Queen's Quarterly*, III,
    (July, 1895), 11–22.
4. See Rees, *New and Naked Land*.
5. Lewis G. Thomas, "Associations and Communications," Presidential
    Address, Canadian Historical Association *Historical Papers* (1973), 8.
6. Adele Wiseman, "A Brief Anatomy of an Honest Attempt at a Pithy
    Statement about the Impact of the Manitoba Environment on My
    Development as an Artist," *Mosaic*, 3, 3 (Spring, 1970), 101.
7. PAC, MG 30, C16, vol. 6.
8. Evan Davies and Aled Vaughan, *Beyond the Old Bone Trail* (London,
    1960), 35.
9. Quoted in Jorgen Dahlie, "Scandinavian Experiences on the Prairies,
    1890–1920: The Frederiksens of Nokomis," in H. Palmer, ed., *Settlement
    of the Canadian West* (Calgary, 1977), 106.
10. John Donkin, *Trooper and Redskin in the Far North-West* (London, 1889),
    196–97, 253.
11. On folk songs see Leonora M. Pauls, "The English Language Folk and
    Traditional Songs of Alberta: Collection and Analysis for Teaching
    Purposes," (M.Mus. Thesis, University of Calgary, 1981); and J. B. Rogers
    and P. J. Rogers, "Some Folk Songs from the Thirties," in R. D. Francis
    and H. Ganzevoort, eds., *The Dirty Thirties in Prairie Canada* (Vancouver,
    1980), 141–55.
12. Pauls, "The English Language Folk and Traditional Songs of Alberta," 151.
13. *Ibid.*, 252.
14. *Ibid.*, 142, 255.
15. *Ibid.*, 144.
16. *Ibid.*, 251.
17. On the "realistic" tradition in prairie literature see Dick Harrison, *Unnamed
    Country: The Struggle for a Canadian Prairie Fiction* (Edmonton, 1977),
    100–153; and his "Fiction of the 1930s" in Francis and Ganzevoort, eds.,
    The Dirty Thirties, 77–87; Gerald Friesen, "Three generations of fiction:
    an introduction to prairie cultural history," in D. J. Bercuson and P.
    Buckner, eds., *Eastern and Western Perspectives* (Toronto, 1981), 183–96;
    and Patricia Roome, "Images of the West: Social Themes in Prairie
    Literature, 1898–1930" (M. A. Thesis, University of Calgary, 1976).
18. Martha Ostenso, *Wild Geese* (Toronto, 1925), 60–61.
19. F. P. Grove, *Fruits of the Earth*. Reprint. (Toronto, 1965), 21–22, 23.
20. F. P. Grove, "Snow," in D. Pacey, ed., *Tales from the Margin: The Selected
    Short Stories of F. P. Grove* (Toronto, 1971), 267, 269.
21. Quoted in "Introduction" to F. P. Grove, *Fruits of the Earth*, edited by
    M. G. Parks (Toronto, 1965), viii–ix.
22. Ostenso, *Wild Geese*, 35–36.
23. F. P. Grove, *Settlers of the Marsh*. Reprint. (Toronto, 1966), 45.
24. Grove, *Fruits of the Earth*, 38.
25. Arthur Stringer, *The Prairie Child* (New York, 1922), 225.

26. Sinclair Ross, "A Field of Wheat," in Ken Mitchell, ed., *Horizon* (Toronto, 1977), 151, 152.

27. Sinclair Ross, *As For Me and My House*. Reprint. (Toronto, 1970), 99–100.

28. Harrison, *Unnamed Country*, 131.

29. On the religious nature of the agrarian protest movements in western Canada see Richard Allen, "The Social Gospel as the Religion of the Agrarian Revolt," in C. Berger and R. Cook, eds., *The West and the Nation* (Toronto, 1976), 174–86.

30. Robert Stead, *The Smoking Flax* (Toronto, 1924), 7.

31. *Ibid.*, 122.

32. Robert Stead, *Grain*. Reprint. (Toronto, 1963), 54.

33. On realism in prairie art see Ronald Rees, *Land of Earth and Sky: Landscape Painting of Western Canada* (Saskatoon, 1984); *Watercolour Painting in Saskatchewan, 1905–1980*, Exhibition Catalogue (Saskatoon, 1980); and Patricia Bovey, "Prairie Painting in the Thirties," in Francis and Ganzevoort, eds., *The Dirty Thirties*, 111–24.

34. Quoted in Rees, *Land of Earth and Sky*, 38. On Jefferys, see Robert Stacey, *C. W. Jefferys* (Ottawa, 1985).

35. Stacey, *C. W. Jefferys*, 8.

36. On Hurley see Jean Swanson, *Sky Painter: The Story of Robert Newton Hurley* (Saskatoon, 1973); on Fitzgerald, see F. Eckhardt, "The Technique of L. L. Fitzgerald," *Canadian Art*, xv, 2 (April, 1958), 114–18; on Kerr, see *Harvest of the Spirit: Illingworth Kerr Retrospective*, Exhibition Catalogue (Edmonton, 1985), and his *Paint and Circumstance* (Calgary, 1987); on Phillips see Douglas Cole, "Out of the Mainstream: Walter J. Phillips and the Context of Canadian Art," *Manitoba History*, No. 3 (Spring 1982), 2–7.

37. Rees, *Land of Earth and Sky*, 46.

38. Quoted in *ibid.*, 49.

39. Swanson, *Sky Painter*, 95.

40. Percy H. Wright, "The Robert Hurley Vogue," Saskatoon *Star Phoenix*, February 1, 1952.

41. On the metropolitan-hinterland relationship see J. M. S. Careless, "Frontierism, Metropolitanism, and Canadian History," in C. Berger, ed., *Approaches to Canadian History* (Toronto, 1967), 63–83; Brenton M. Barr and John C. Lehr, "The Western Interior: The Transformation of a Hinterland Region," in L. D. McCann, ed., *Heartland and Hinterland: A Geography of Canada* (Scarborough, 1982), 251–93; and J. Howard Richards, "The Prairie Region," in John Warkentin, ed., *Canada: A Geographical Interpretation* (Agincourt, 1968), 396–437.

42. Careless, "Frontierism, Metropolitanism, and Canadian History," 78.

43. Hopkins Moorehouse, *Deep Furrows* (Toronto, 1918), 276.

Chapter Six

1. Dick Harrison, *Unnamed Country: The Struggle for a Canadian Prairie Fiction* (Edmonton, 1977), 189.

2. Eli Mandel, "Writing West: On the Road to Wood Mountain," *Canadian Forum*, LVII (June-July, 1977), 28.

3. For a good discussion on the mythic West in the American tradition see Robert G. Athearn, *The Mythic West in Twentieth-Century America* (Lawrence, 1986); and his "The American West: an enduring mirage?" in *Inventing the West* (Sun Valley, 1982), 4-7.

4. Northrop Frye, *The Bush Garden* (Toronto, 1971), ii–iii.

5. Harrison, *Unnamed Country*, 183.

6. See Carl Berger, *The Writing of Canadian History: Aspects of English-Canadian Historical Writing since 1900* (Toronto, 1976), 238-58, for a good overview of Morton's views of western Canadian history.

7. Quoted in *ibid.*, 252.

8. W. L. Morton, *Manitoba: A History* (Toronto, 1957), viii.

9. W. L. Morton, "Clio in Canada: The Interpretation of Canadian History," in C. Berger, ed., *Approaches to Canadian History* (Toronto, 1967), 47, 48.

10. W. L. Morton, "A Century of Plain and Parkland," in R. D. Francis and H. Palmer, eds., *The Prairie West: Historical Readings* (Edmonton, 1985), 22.

11. W. L. Morton, "Seeing an Unliterary Landscape," *Mosaic,* III, 3 (Spring, 1970), 11.

12. George F. G. Stanley, "The Western Canadian Mystique," in D. Gagan, ed., *Prairie Perspectives* (Toronto, 1970), 23.

13. *Ibid.*, 25.

14. On western Canadian literature in the post-World War II era, see Harrison, *Unnamed Country*, 183-213; Gerald Friesen, "Three generations of fiction: an introduction to prairie cultural history," in D. J. Bercuson and P. Buckner, eds., *Eastern and Western Perspectives* (Toronto, 1981), 183-96; W. H. New, *Articulating West: Essays on Purpose and Form in Modern Canadian Literature* (Toronto, 1972); Eli Mandel, "Images of Prairie Man," in R. Allen, ed., *A Region of the Mind* (Regina, 1973), 201-9; and his "Romance and Realism in Western Canadian Fiction," in A. W. Rasporich and H. C. Klassen, eds., *Prairie Perspectives 2* (Toronto, 1973), 197-211.

15. Robert Kroetsch, ed., *Creation* (Toronto, 1970), 63.

16. Margaret Laurence, "Sources," *Mosaic,* III, 3 (Spring, 1970), 82.

17. *Ibid.*

18. Margaret Laurence, "Where the World Began," in *Heart of a Stranger* (Toronto, 1976), 217, 218.

19. *Ibid.*, 213, 219.

20. Wallace Stegner, *Wolf Willow* (Toronto, 1955), 19-20.

21. George Melnyk, *Radical Regionalism* (Edmonton, 1981), 37.

22. W. O. Mitchell, *Who Has Seen the Wind* (Toronto, 1947), 233.

23. Russell Brown, "An Interview with Robert Kroetsch," *The University of Windsor Review,* VII (Spring, 1972), 2.

24. For a discussion of the theme of ruralism in the post-World War II Canadian West, see R. Douglas Francis, "The Mythic West," (unpublished paper), London Conference for Canadian Studies, November 24, 1987.

25. Kroetsch, "That Yellow Prairie Sky," *Creation*, 22.

26. D. G. Jones, *Butterfly on Rock: A Study of Themes and Images in Canadian Literature* (Toronto, 1970), 168.

27. On western Canadian art in the postwar period see Ronald Rees, *Land of Earth and Sky: Landscape Painting of Western Canada* (Saskatoon, 1984), 50–58; J. R. Harper, *Painting in Canada* (Toronto, 1966), 314–29; and Suzanne Devonshire Baker, *Artists of Alberta* (Edmonton, 1980).

28. Douglas Cole, "Out of the Mainstream: Walter J. Phillips and the Context of Canadian Art," *Manitoba History*, No. 3 (Spring, 1982), 6.

29. Illingworth Kerr, *Fifty Years a Painter*, Exhibition Catalogue (1973).

30. *Ibid.*

31. Northrop Frye, "Lawren Harris: An Introduction," in *The Bush Garden* (Toronto, 1971), 210.

32. On Reta Cowley and Dorothy Knowles see *Reta Cowley*, Exhibition Catalogue (Regina, 1975); *Dorothy Knowles Paintings, 1964–1982*, Exhibition Catalogue (Edmonton, 1983).

33. Quoted in Rees, *Land of Earth and Sky*, 55.

34. On Eyre see Joan Murray, *Ivan Eyre Exposition*, Exhibition Catalogue, (Oshawa, 1980).

35. On William Kurelek see Ramsay Cook, "William Kurelek: A Prairie Boy's Visions," *Journal of Ukrainian Studies*, 5 (Spring, 1980), 33–48; Joan Murray, *Kurelek's Vision of Canada* (Edmonton, 1983); and Ron Stanaitis, "The People's Painter: William Kurelek 1927–1977," *Golden West*, XII, 1 (January, 1978), 22–30.

36. Robert Fulford, "Foreword," to *Canada: A Landscape Portrait*, ed. J. A. Kraulis, (Edmonton, 1982), 11.

37. Quoted in Cook, "William Kurelek," 37.

38. Fulford, "Foreword," 11.

39. Rees, *Land of Earth and Sky*, 57.

40. Mandel, "Writing West," 28.

BIBLIOGRAPHY
OF PRIMARY SOURCES

Ballantyne, R. M. *The Dog Crusoe and His Master: A Tale of the Western Prairies.* London, n.d.

——. *Snowflakes and Sunbeams, or The Young Fur-Trader: A Tale of the Far North.* London, 1863.

——. *Hudson's Bay; or Everyday Life in the Wilds of North America.* London, 1848. Reprint Edmonton, 1972.

——. *The Pioneers: A Tale of the Western Wilderness: Illustration of the Adventures and Discoveries of Sir Alexander Mackenzie.* London, 1872.

Begg, Alexander. *The Great Canadian North West: Its Past History, Present Conditions and Glorious Prospects.* Montreal, 1881.

——. *The Great North-West of Canada: A Paper Read at Conference, Indian and Colonial Exhibition.* London, 1886.

Blodget, Lorin. *Climatology of the United States, and of the Temperate Latitudes of the North American Continent.* Philadelphia, 1857.

Brunson, Alfred. "Missionary Intelligence. The North Red River Settlement." New York: *Christian Advocate,* September 15, 1837.

Bryce, George. *Manitoba: Its Infancy, Growth and Present Condition.* London, 1882.

Butler, William F. *The Wild North Land: Being the Story of a Winter Journey, with Dogs, Across Northern North America.* London, 1873. Reprint Edmonton, 1968.

——. *The Great Lone Land: A Narrative of Travel and Adventure in the North-West of America.* London, 1872.

Carmichael-Smyth, R. *Letter to the Right Honourable Earl Grey, on the Subject of Transportation and Emigration as Connected With an Imperial Railway Communication Between the Atlantic and Pacific.* London, 1850.

Collins, Edmund. *Annette; the Métis Spy. A Heroine of the North West Rebellion.* Toronto, 1886.

Connor, Ralph [Charles Gordon]. *The Sky Pilot: A Tale of the Foothills.* New York, 1899.

——. *The Prospector.* New York, 1904.

Cowie, Isaac. *The Western Plains of Canada Rediscovered.* n.p., 1903.

Crofton, George F. "A Poet in Scarlet." *Alberta Historical Review* 15 (1967): 17–19.

Curwood, James Oliver. *The River's End: A New Story of God's Country.* New York, 1919.

——. *The Flaming Forest: A Novel of the Canadian Northwest.* Toronto, 1923.

Dahlie, Jorgen. "Scandinavian Experiences on the Prairies, 1890–1920: The Frederiksens of Nokomis." *Settlement of the West.* Ed. H. Palmer. Calgary, 1977: 102–13, 254–58.

Davin, Nicholas Flood, ed. *Homes for Millions: The Great Canadian North-West; Its Resources Fully Described.* Ottawa, 1891.

Department of the Interior (Canada). *Read this Pamphlet on Manitoba, the N.W.T., Provinces of Ontario and Quebec.* Ottawa, 1883.

——. *Farming and Ranching in Western Canada: Manitoba, Assiniboia, Alberta, Saskatchewan.* Ottawa, 1890.

——. *Western Canada: Manitoba and the Northwest Territories.* Ottawa, 1899.

——. *Western Canada: How to Get There; How to Select Lands; How to Make a Home.* Ottawa, 1902.

de Smet, Pierre Jean. *Life, Letters, and Travels Among the North American Indians.* Eds. H. M. Chittenden and A. T. Richardson. New York, 1905.

Dodds, George Livingstone. *The Last West: The Latest Gift of The Lady Bountiful.* Winnipeg, 1906.

Donkin, John G. *Trooper and Redskin in the Far North West: Recollection of Life in the North West Mounted Police, Canada, 1884–1888.* London, 1889.

Dorothy Knowles Paintings, 1964–1982. Edmonton, 1983.

Dufferin and Ava, Marchioness of. *My Canadian Journal: 1872–8. Extracts from my Letters Home Written While Lord Dufferin was Governor-General.* New York, 1891.

Fitzgerald, James Edward. *An Examination of the Charter and Proceedings of the Hudson's Bay Company, with Reference to the Grant of Vancouver's Island.* London, 1849.

Grant, George M. *Ocean to Ocean: Sandford Fleming's Expedition through Canada in 1872.* Toronto, 1873. Reprint Edmonton, 1967.

——. *Picturesque Canada.* Toronto, 1882.

Grove, Frederick Philip. *Settlers of the Marsh.* Toronto, 1925. Reprint Toronto, 1966.

——. *Fruits of the Earth.* Toronto, 1933. Reprint Toronto, 1965.

Gutteridge, Don. "'The Buffalo Hunt' from Riel." *Mosaic* 3 (Spring, 1970): 118–22.

Hamilton, J. C. *The Prairie Province; Sketches of Travel from Lake Ontario to Lake Winnipeg.* Toronto, 1876.

Hewlett, A. E. M. "Old Cannington Manor, Assiniboine, N.W.T." Cannington Manor, Hewlett Papers, Saskatchewan Archives.

Hiemstra, Mary. "Prairie Settlers." *Horizon: Writings of the Canadian Prairies.* Ed. Ken Mitchell. Toronto, 1977: 50–54.

Hind, Henry Youle. *Narrative of the Canadian Red River Exploring Expedition of 1857 and of the Assiniboine and Saskatchewan Exploring Expedition of 1858.* London, 1860. Reprint Edmonton, 1971.

Journals and Letters of Pierre Gaultier de Varennes de la Vérendrye and His Sons. Ed. Lawrence J. Burpee. Toronto, 1927.

Kane, Paul. *Wanderings of an Artist Among the Indians of North America.* London, 1859. Reprinted in *Paul Kane's Frontier.* Edited with an introduction by J. Russell Harper. Austin, 1971.

Kelsey, Henry. *The Kelsey Papers* [1690–92]. Ottawa, 1929.

Kerr, Illingworth. *Paint and Circumstance.* Calgary, 1987.

Kreisel, Henry. "The Prairie: A State of Mind." *Transactions of the Royal Society of Canada* 6, Series 4 (June, 1968): 171–80.

Kroetsch, Robert, ed. *Creation.* Toronto, 1970.

Land, A Living and Wealth: The Story of Farming and Social Conditions in Western Canada. Grand Trunk Pacific Railway, 1913.

Laurence, Margaret. "Sources." *Mosaic* 3 (Spring, 1970): 80–84.

——. "Where the World Began." *Heart of a Stranger.* Ed. M. Laurence. Toronto, 1976.

Livesay, Dorothy. "A Prairie Sampler." *Mosaic* 3 (Spring, 1970): 85–92.

Lorne, Marquis of. *The Canadian North-West: Speech Delivered at Winnipeg.* Ottawa, 1882.

——. *Canadian Pictures.* Third Edition. London, 1892.

McClung, Nellie. *Sowing Seeds in Danny.* Toronto, 1908. Reprint Toronto, 1939.

——. *Clearing in the West: My Own Story.* Toronto, 1935.

McCourt, Edward. *Saskatchewan.* Toronto, 1968.

Mackenzie, Alexander. *Voyages from Montreal, on the River St. Lawrence, through the Continent of North America to the Frozen and Pacific Oceans; in the Years 1789 and 1793, with a Preliminary Account of the Rise, Progress, and Present State of the Fur Trade of that Country.* London, 1801.

McLean, John. *Notes of a 25 year Service in the Hudson's Bay Company.* London, 1849.

Macoun, John. *Manitoba and the Great North West.* Guelph, 1882.

McRobbie, Kenneth. "In Open Prairie." *First Ghost to Canada.* Winnipeg, 1979.

Mair, Charles. "The New Canada: Its Resources and Production." *The Canadian Monthly and National Review* 8, 2 (August, 1875): 156–64.

——. "The Buffalo Plains." *Songs of the Great Dominion: Voices from the Forests and Waters, The Settlements and Cities of Canada.* Ed. W. D. Lighthall. London, 1889.

Martin, Robert Montgomery. *The Hudson's Bay Territories and Vancouver's Island, with an Exposition of the Chartered Rights, Conduct and Policy of the Honourable Hudson's Bay Corporation.* London, 1849.

Martin, S. and R. Hall, eds. *Rupert Brooke in Canada.* Toronto, 1978.

Marty, Sid. "The Prairie." *Horizon: Writings of the Canadian Prairies.* Ed. Ken Mitchell. Toronto, 1977.

Mélançon, Claude. "The Creation of Man." *Horizon: Writings of the Canadian Prairies.* Ed. Ken Mitchell. Toronto, 1977.

Milton, Viscount and W. B. Cheadle. *The North-West Passage by Land; Being the Narrative of an Expedition from the Atlantic to the Pacific.* London, 1867.

Mitchell, W. O. *Who Has Seen the Wind.* Toronto, 1947.

Moorhouse, Hopkins [Herbert Joseph]. *Deep Furrows: Which Tells of Pioneer*

Trails Along Which the Farmers of Western Canada Fought Their Way to Great Achievements in Co-operation. Toronto, 1918.

Morris, Alexander. *The Hudson's Bay and Pacific Territories*. Toronto, 1859.

——. *Nova Britannia; Or Our New Canadian Dominion Foreshadowed, Being a Series of Lectures, Speeches and Addresses*. Toronto, 1884.

Morton, W. L. "Clio in Canada: the Interpretation of Canadian History." *University of Toronto Quarterly* 15, 3 (April, 1946): 227–34.

——. "Seeing an Unliterary Landscape." *Mosaic* 3 (Spring, 1970): 1–11.

——. "A Century of Plain and Parkland." *The Prairie West: Historical Readings*. Eds. R. D. Francis and H. Palmer. Edmonton, 1985.

Mountain, George J. *Songs of the Wilderness: Being a Collection of Poems*. n.p., 1846.

Murphy, Emily. *Janey Canuck in the West*. London, 1910. Edited with an introduction by Isabel Bassett. Toronto, 1975.

Narrative of an Expedition to the Source of St. Peter's River, Lake Winnepeek, Lake of the Woods, etc. Performed in the Year 1823. Ed. W. H. Keating. London, 1825.

Newlove, John. "The Pride." *Black Night Window*. Toronto, 1968.

"Not a Penny in the World." *Horizon: Writings of the Canadian Prairie*. Ed. Ken Mitchell. Toronto, 1977: 54–55.

Ostenso, Martha. *Wild Geese*. Toronto, 1925.

Pacey, D., ed. *Tales from the Margin: The Selected Short Stories of F. P. Grove*. Toronto, 1971.

Palliser, John. *The Papers of the Palliser Expedition 1857–1860*. Ed. Irene Spry. Toronto, 1968.

Parlby, Mrs. Walter. "Canada–The Hope of the World: An English Lady's Opinion of the Opportunities of the West." In "Why Go to Canada," supplement to the Calgary *Daily Herald* (June, 1910).

Partridge, E. A. *War on Poverty: The One War that Can End War*. Winnipeg, 1926.

Pollard, W. C. *Pioneering in the Prairie West: A Sketch of the Parry Sound Colonies that Settled near Edmonton, N.W.T. in the Early Nineties*. Toronto, 1926.

Prospectus issued by the International Financial Society, Ltd., July 1863, for the sale of new capital stock of the Hudson's Bay Company, Canada and British Columbia. Return to an Address of the Honourable The House of Commons. London, 1863.

Rawlings, Thomas. *The Confederation of the British North American Provinces; Their Past History and Future Prospects, Including Also British Columbia and Hudson's Bay Territory*. London, 1865.

Rendell, Alice. "Letter from a Barr Colonist" [1904]. *Alberta Historical Review* 2 (Winter, 1963): 24–26.

Report from the Select Committee on the Hudson's Bay Company. London, 1857.

Rich, E. E., ed. *James Isham's Observations on Hudson's Bay, 1743, and Notes and Observations on a Book Entitled 'A Voyage to Hudson's Bay in the Dobbs Gallery, 1749.'* London, 1749.

Ross, Sinclair. *As For Me and My House*. Toronto, 1941. Reprint Toronto, 1965.

——. "A Field of Wheat." *The Lamp at Noon and Other Stories*. Toronto, 1968: 73–82.

Ryerson, John. *Hudson's Bay; or A Missionary Tour in the Territory of the Hon. Hudson's Bay Company*. Toronto, 1855.

Saskatoon Board of Trade. "The Psychology of Saskatoon." *Saskatoon*. Saskatoon: Phoenix Job Print, 1908.

——. *Saskatoonlets*. Saskatoon: Saturday Press, 1911.

Shortt, Adam. "Some Observations on the Great North-West. Part I: Immigration and Transportation." *Queen's Quarterly* 2 (January, 1895): 183–97.

——. "Some Observations on the Great North-West. Part II: Social and Economic Conditions." *Queen's Quarterly* 3 (July, 1895): 11–22.

Simpson, Sir George. *Narrative of a Journey Round the World During the Years 1841 and 1842*. Volume 1. London, 1847.

Simpson, Thomas. *Narrative of the Discoveries on the North Coast of America, Effected by the Officers of the Hudson's Bay Company During the Years 1836–39*. London, 1843.

Southesk, Earl of. *Saskatchewan and the Rocky Mountains*. Edinburgh, 1875.

Spence, Thomas. *The Prairie Lands of Canada: Presented to the World as a New and Inviting Field of Enterprise for the Capitalist and New Superior Attractions and Advantages as a Home for Immigrants*. Montreal, 1880.

Stanley, George F. G. "The Western Canadian Mystique." *Prairie Perspectives*. Ed. David Gagan. Toronto, 1970: 6–27.

Stead, R. J. C. *Prairie Born and Other Poems*. Toronto, 1911.

——. *The Homesteaders: A Novel of the Canadian West*. Toronto, 1916.

——. *The Cowpuncher*. Toronto, 1918.

——. "The Plough." *The Empire Builders*. Toronto, 1923.

——. *The Smoking Flax*. Toronto, 1924.

——. *Grain*. Toronto, 1926. Reprint Toronto, 1963.

Stegner, Wallace. *Wolf Willow: A History, a Story and a Memory of the Last Prairie Frontier*. Toronto, 1955.

Stevens, Peter. "Prairie: Time and Place." *Nothing But Spoons*. Montreal, 1969.

Strachan, John. *Letter to the Right Honourable the Earl of Selkirk on his Settlement at the Red River*. London, 1816.

Stringer, Arthur. *The Prairie Wife*. New York, 1915.

——. *The Prairie Mother*. New York, 1920.

——. *The Prairie Child*. New York, 1922.

Sutherland, Reverend Alexander. *A Summer in Prairie-Land: Notes of a Tour through the North-West Territory*. Toronto, 1881.

Synge, Millington Henry. *Great Britain One Empire: On the Union of the Dominions of Great Britain by Inter-Communication with the Pacific and the East Via British North America*. London, 1852.

Taylor, James W. *Northwest British America and Its Relations to the State of Minnesota*. Minnesota, 1860.

Thompson, David. *David Thompson's Narrative of His Explorations in Western America 1784–1812*. Ed. J. B. Tyrrell. Toronto, 1916, in *The Western Interior of Canada*. Ed. J. Warkentin. Toronto, 1964: 91–105.

Toronto *Globe*. "Lake Superior and the Northern Country." November 12, 1850.

——. "The Great North West." December 10, 1856.

——. "The North West." January 26, 1863.

Tucker, Sarah. *The Rainbow in the North: A Short Account of the First Establishment of Christianity in Rupert's Land by the Church Missionary Society.* London, 1850.

Tytler, P. F. *The Northern Coasts of America and the Hudson Bay's Territories: A Narrative of Discovery and Adventure.* London, 1853.

Van Waeterstadt, Frans. "Into the World: Letter from an Emigrant." *Leeuwarder Nieuwsblad*, April 4, 1927. Translated by Herman Ganzevoort.

Warre, Captain Henry. *Sketches in North America and the Oregon Territory.* Ed. A. Hanna. Barre, Massachusetts, 1970.

West, John. *The Substance of a Journey During a Residence at the Red River Colony, British North America.* London, 1824.

SELECT BIBLIOGRAPHY
OF SECONDARY SOURCES

Ainslie, Patricia. *Inglis Sheldon-Williams*. Calgary: Glenbow Museum, 1982.

Allen, John Logan. *Passage Through the Garden: Lewis and Clark and the Image of the American Northwest*. Urbana: University of Illinois Press, 1975.

——. "To Unite the Discoverers: The American Response to the Early Exploration of Rupert's Land." *Rupert's Land: A Cultural Tapestry*. Ed. Richard Davies. Waterloo: Wilfrid Laurier Press, 1988: 79–96.

Allen, Richard, ed. *A Region of the Mind: Interpreting the Western Canadian Plains*. Regina: Canadian Plains Study Center, 1973.

——. *Man and Nature on the Prairies*. Regina: Canadian Plains Research Center, 1976.

——. "The Social Gospel as the Religion of the Agrarian Revolt." *The West and the Nation*. Eds. C. Berger and R. Cook. Toronto: McClelland and Stewart, 1976: 174–86.

Artibise, A. F. J. "Boosterism and the Development of Prairie Cities, 1871–1913." *Town and City: Aspects of Western Canadian Urban Development*. Ed. A. F. J. Artibise. Regina: Canadian Plains Research Center, 1981: 209–36.

——. "City-Building in the Canadian West: From Boosterism to Corporatism." *Journal of Canadian Studies* 17, 3 (Fall, 1982): 35-44.

Athearn, Robert G. "The American West: an enduring mirage?" *Inventing the West*. Sun Valley: Institute of the American West, 1982: 4–7.

——. *The Mythic West in Twentieth-Century America*. Lawrence, Kansas: University Press of Kansas, 1986.

Baker, Suzanne Devonshire. *Artists of Alberta*. Edmonton: University of Alberta Press, 1980.

Barr, Brenton M. and John C. Lehr. "The Western Interior: The Transformation of a Hinterland Region." *Heartland and Hinterland: A Geography of Canada*. Ed. L. D. McCann. Scarborough: Prentice-Hall Canada Inc., 1982: 250–93.

Bell, Michael. *Painters in a New World*. Toronto: McClelland and Stewart, 1973.

Berger, Carl. *The Sense of Power: Studies in the Ideas of Canadian Imperialism, 1867-1914*. Toronto: University of Toronto Press, 1970.

——. *The Writing of Canadian History: Aspects of English-Canadian Historical Writing Since 1900.* Toronto: Oxford, 1976.

Berry, Virginia. *Vistas of Promise: Manitoba 1874–1919.* Exhibition Catalogue. Winnipeg: Winnipeg Art Gallery, 1987.

Berton, Pierre. *The Promised Land: Settling the West 1896–1914.* Toronto: McClelland and Stewart, 1984.

Billington, Ray Allen. *Land of Savagery; Land of Promise: The European Image of the American Frontier in the Nineteenth Century.* New York: W. W. Norton and Co., 1981.

Birrell, A. J. *Into the Silent Land: Survey Photography in the Canadian West, 1858–1900.* Ottawa: Public Archives, 1975.

Blodgett, Edward. "The Concept of the 'Prairie' in Canadian Fiction." *Proceedings of the 7th Congress of the International Comparative Literature Association,* Vol. I. Stuttgart, Budapest, 1979: 121–26.

Bovey, Pat. "Prairie Paintings in the 1930s." *The Dirty Thirties in Prairie Canada.* Eds. R. D. Francis and H. Ganzevoort. Vancouver: Tantalus Research Ltd., 1980: 111–24.

Bowden, Martyn J. "The Great American Desert and the American Frontier, 1800–1882: Popular Images of the Plains." *Anonymous Americans: Explorations in Nineteenth-Century Social History.* Ed. Tamara K. Hareven. New Jersey: Prentice-Hall Inc., 1971: 48–79.

Brown, Elizabeth. *Landscapes of Canada's Mountain Parks, 1885–1960.* Banff: Whyte Museum of the Canadian Rockies, 1985.

Careless, J. M. S. "Frontierism, Metropolitanism, and Canadian History." *Approaches to Canadian History.* Ed. C. Berger. Toronto: University of Toronto Press, 1967: 63–83.

Cavell, Edward. *Journeys to the Far West.* Toronto: Lorimer, 1979.

Cavell, E. and D. Reid. *When Winter Was King.* Banff: Altitude Publishing, 1988.

Chalmers, John W. "Myself the Wanderer: Canada's Literate Artist, Paul Kane." *Montana* 20, 4 (October, 1970): 36–49.

Cole, Douglas. "Out of the Mainstream: Walter J. Phillips and the Context of Canadian Art." *Manitoba History* 3 (Spring, 1982): 2–7.

Cook, Ramsay. "William Kurelek: A Prairie Boy's Vision." *Journal of Ukrainian Studies* 5 (Spring, 1980): 33–48.

Crozier, Lorna and Gary Hyland, eds. *A Sudden Radiance: Saskatchewan Poetry.* Regina: Coteau Books, 1987.

Davidson, Marshall. *History of the Artists' America.* New York: American Heritage Publishing Co., 1973.

Davis, Ann. *A Distant Harmony: Comparisons in the Painting of Canada and the United States of America.* Winnipeg: Winnipeg Art Gallery, 1982.

Davis, Ann and Robert Thacker. "Pictures and Prose: Romantic Sensibility and the Great Plains of Catlin, Kane, and Miller." *Great Plains Quarterly* 6 (Winter, 1986): 3–20.

Doyle, James. "American Literary Images of the Canadian Prairies, 1860–1910" *Great Plains Quarterly.* III (Winter, 1983): 30–38.

Dunae, Patrick. "'Making Good': The Canadian West in British Boys Literature, 1890–1914." *Prairie Forum* 4, 2 (Fall, 1979): 165–81.

Dunbar, G. S. "Isotherms and Politics: Perception of the Northwest in the

1850s." *Prairie Perspectives 2*. Eds. A. W. Rasporich and H. C. Klassen. Toronto: Holt, Rinehart and Winston, 1973: 80–101.

Dyck, E. F., ed. *Essays on Saskatchewan Writing*. Regina, Saskatchewan Writers Guild, 1986.

Emmons, David M. *Garden in the Grasslands: Boomer Literature of the Central Great Plains*. Nebraska: University of Nebraska Press, 1971.

Fowke, Edith, ed. *Canadian Vibrations*. Toronto: Macmillan, 1972.

Fowke, Edith and Richard Johnston. *Folks Songs of Canada*. Waterloo: Waterloo Music, 1954.

——. *More Folk Songs of Canada*. Waterloo: Waterloo Music, 1964.

Fowke, Edith, A. Mills and H. Blume. *Canada's Story in Song*. Toronto: W. J. Gage Ltd., 1965.

Francis, R. Douglas. "Changing Images of the West." *Journal of Canadian Studies* 17, 3 (Fall, 1982): 5–19.

——. "From Wasteland to Utopia: Changing Images of the Canadian West in the Nineteenth Century." *Great Plains Quarterly* 7, 3 (Summer, 1987): 178–94.

——. "The Ideal and the Real: The Image of the Canadian West in the Settlement Period." *Rupert's Land: A Cultural Tapestry*. Ed. R. Davies. Waterloo: Wilfrid Laurier Press, 1988: 253–73.

Friesen, Gerald. "The Western Canadian Identity." Canadian Historical Association Annual *Report* (1973): 13–19.

——. *The Canadian Prairies: A History*. Toronto: University of Toronto Press, 1984.

——. "Three generations of fiction: an introduction to prairie cultural history." *Eastern and Western Perspectives*. Eds. D. J. Bercuson and P. Buckner. Toronto: University of Toronto Press, 1981: 183–96.

Fulford, Robert. "Foreword." *Canada: A Landscape Portrait*. J. A. Kraulis, Ed. Edmonton: Hurtig, 1982.

Fry, Philip. "Prairie Space Drawings." *Artscanada* 29, 3 (1972): 40–57.

Glanz, Dawn. *How the West was Drawn: American Art and the Settling of the Frontier*. Michigan: UMI Research Press, 1978.

Gluek, Alvin C. *Minnesota and the Manifest Destiny of the Canadian Northwest: A Study in Canadian-American Relations*. Toronto: University of Toronto Press, 1965.

Goetzmann, William. *Exploration and Empire: The Explorer and the Scientist in the Winning of the American West*. New York: W. W. Norton and Co., 1966.

Goetzmann, William H. and Joseph C. Porter. *The West as Romantic Horizon*. Nebraska: Center for Western Studies, Joslyn Art Museum, 1981.

Grant, John Webster. *Moon of Wintertime: Missionaries and the Indians of Canada in Encounter Since 1534*. Toronto: University of Toronto Press, 1984.

Hadley, H. T. "Photography and the Landscape of Travel: Western Canada, 1884–1914." M.A. Thesis. University of Calgary, 1984.

Harper, J. Russell. *Painting in Canada: a History*. Second Edition. Toronto: University of Toronto Press, 1966.

——. *Paul Kane's Frontier including Wanderings of an Artist among the Indians of North America*. Austin: University of Texas Press for the Amon Carter Museum and the National Gallery of Canada, Ottawa, 1971.

——. *William G. R. Hind: 1883–1889*. Ottawa: National Museum of Canada, 1976.

Harrison, Dick. "The Beginnings of Prairie Fiction." *Journal of Canadian Fiction* 4, 1 (1975): 159–77.

——. *Unnamed Country: The Struggle for a Canadian Prairie Fiction*. Edmonton: University of Alberta Press, 1977.

Harvest of the Spirit: Illingworth Kerr Retrospective. Exhibition Catalogue. Edmonton: Edmonton Art Gallery, 1985.

Hassrick, Peter. *The Way West: Art of Frontier America*. New York: Harry N. Abrams, Inc., 1977.

Hedges, James, B. *Building the Canadian West: The Land and Colonization Policies of the Canadian Pacific Railway*. New York: Russell and Russell, 1939.

Hogarth, Paul. *Artists on Horseback: The Old West in Illustrated Journalism 1857–1900*. New York: Watson-Guptill Publications, 1972.

Honour, Hugh. *The New Golden Land: European Images of America from the Discoveries to the Present Times*. New York: Pantheon Books, 1975.

Hunt, David C. *The Artists' Legacy of the West*. Nebraska: Center for Western Studies, Joslyn Art Museum, 1982.

Innis, Mary Quayle. *Travellers West*. Toronto: Clarke, Irwin and Co., 1956.

Jackel, Susan. "Images of the Canadian West 1872–1911." Ph.D. dissertation. University of Alberta, 1977.

Jones, D. G. *Butterfly on Rock: A Study of Themes and Images in Canadian Literature*. Toronto: University of Toronto Press, 1970.

Josephy, Alvin M. *The Artist was a Young Man: The Life Story of Peter Rindisbacher*. Fort Worth: Amon Carter Museum, 1970.

Kaye, B. and D. W. Moodie. "Geographical Perspectives on the Canadian Plains." *A Region of the Mind*. Ed. R. Allen. Regina: Canadian Plains Study Centre, 1973: 17–46.

Kraulis, J. A., ed. *Canada: A Landscape Portrait*. Edmonton: Hurtig Publishers, 1982.

McCann, L. D., ed. *Heartland and Hinterland: A Geography of Canada*. Scarborough: Prentice-Hall Canada Inc., 1982.

McCourt, Edward. *Remember Butler: The Story of Sir William Butler*. London: Routledge and Kegan Paul, 1967.

——. *The Canadian West in Fiction*. Revised Edition. Toronto: The Ryerson Press, 1970.

MacLeod, Margaret. *Songs of Old Manitoba*. Toronto: Ryerson Press, 1959.

Mandel, Eli. "Images of Prairie Man." *A Region of the Mind*. Ed. R. Allen. Regina: Canadian Plains Study Centre, 1973: 201–9.

——. "Romance and Realism in Western Canadian Fiction." *Prairie Perspectives* 2. Eds. A. W. Rasporich and H. C. Klassen. Toronto: Holt, Rinehart and Winston, 1973: 197–211.

——. "Writing West: On the Road to Wood Mountain." *Canadian Forum* 57 (June-July, 1977): 25–29.

Melnyk, George. *Radical Regionalism*. Edmonton: NeWest Press, 1981.

Mitchell, Ken, ed. *Horizon: Writings of the Canadian Prairies*. Toronto: Oxford, 1977.

Moodie, D. W. "Early British Images of Rupert's Land." *Man and Nature on the Prairies.* Ed. Richard Allen. Regina: Canadian Plains Studies Centre, 1976: 1–20.

Morton, W. L. "The Bias of Prairie Politics." *Transactions of the Royal Society of Canada* 49, Series 3, Section 2 (June, 1955): 57–66.

——. *Henry Youle Hind: 1823–1908.* Canadian Biographical Studies Series. Toronto: University of Toronto Press, 1980.

Murray, Joan. *Ivan Eyre: Exposition.* Exhibition Catalogue. Oshawa: Robert McLaughlin Gallery, 1980.

——. *Kurelek's Vision of Canada.* Edmonton: Hurtig Publishers, 1983.

——. *The Last Buffalo: The Story of Frederick Arthur Verner, Painter of the Canadian West.* Toronto: The Pagurian Press, 1984.

New, W. H. *Articulating West: Essays on Purpose and Form in Modern Canadian Literature.* Toronto: New Press, 1972.

Novak, Barbara. *Nature and Culture: American Landscape and Painting, 1825–1875.* New York: Oxford University Press, 1980.

Novotny, Fritz. *Painting and Sculpture in Europe 1780 to 1880.* London: Pelican Books, 1960.

Owram, Doug. *Promise of Eden: The Canadian Expansionist Movement and the Idea of the West, 1856–1900.* Toronto: University of Toronto Press, 1980.

Painchaud, Robert. "French-Canadian Historiography and Franco-Catholic Settlement in Western Canada, 1870–1915." *Canadian Historical Review* 59, 4 (December, 1978): 447–66.

Pauls, Leonora M. "The English Language Folk and Traditional Songs of Alberta: Collection and Analysis for Teaching Purposes." M. Mus. Thesis. University of Calgary, 1981.

Peel, Bruce. "The Lure of the West." Papers of the Bibliographical Society of Canada 5 (Toronto, 1966): 19–29.

Quayle, Eric. *Ballantyne the Brave: A Victorian Writer and His Family.* London: Rupert Hart-Davis, 1967.

——. "R. M. Ballantyne in Rupert's Land." *Queen's Quarterly* 75 (Spring, 1968): 62–71.

Rasky, Frank. *The Taming of the Canadian West.* Toronto: McClelland and Stewart, 1967.

Rasporich, Anthony. "Utopian Ideals and Community Settlements in Western Canada 1880–1914." *The Canadian West: Social Change and Economic Development.* Ed. H. Klassen. Calgary: Comprint Publishing Company, 1977: 37–62.

——. "Utopia, Sect and Millennium in Western Canada, 1870–1940." *Prairie Forum* 12, 2 (Fall, 1987): 217–43.

Rea, J. E. "The Roots of Prairie Society." *Prairie Perspectives.* Ed. D. Gagan. Toronto: Holt, Rinehart and Winston, 1970: 46–57.

——. "Images of the West." *Western Perspectives 1.* Ed. D. J. Bercuson. Toronto: Holt, Rinehart and Winston, 1974: 4–9.

Rees, Ronald. "Images of the Prairie: Landscape Painting and Perception in the Western Interior of Canada." *Canadian Geographer* 20, 3 (1976): 259–78.

——. *Images of the Prairie.* Saskatoon: Saskatoon Gallery and Conservatory Corporation, 1979.

——. "Nostalgic Reaction and the Canadian Prairie Landscape." *Great Plains Quarterly* 2, 3 (Summer, 1982): 157–67.

——. *Land of Earth and Sky: Landscape Painting of Western Canada.* Saskatoon: Western Producer Prairie Books, 1984.

——. *New and Naked Land: Making the Prairies Home.* Saskatoon: Western Producer Prairie Books, 1988.

Reid, Dennis. *"Our Own Country Canada": Being an Account of the National Aspirations of the Principal Landscape Artists in Montreal and Toronto 1860–1890.* Ottawa: National Museums of Canada, 1979.

Render, Lorne. *The Mountain and the Sky.* Calgary: Glenbow-Alberta Institute and McClelland and Stewart West, 1974.

Richards, J. Howard. "The Prairie Region." *Canada: A Geographical Interpretation.* Ed. John Warkentin. Agincourt: Methuen Publications, 1968: 396–437.

Ricou, Lawrence. *Vertical Man/Horizontal World: Man and Landscape in Canadian Prairie Fiction.* Vancouver: University of British Columbia Press, 1973.

Rogers, T. B. and P. J. Rogers. "Some Folk Songs from the Thirties." *The Dirty Thirties in Prairie Canada.* Eds. R. D. Francis and H. Ganzevoort. Vancouver: Tantalus Research Limited, 1980: 141–55.

Rogers, T. B. "'The Strawberry Roan' in Alberta: An Expression of Regional Identity." *Prairie Forum* 12, 1 (Spring, 1987): 75–93.

Roome, Patricia. "Images of the West: Social Themes in Prairie Literature, 1898–1930." M.A. Thesis. University of Calgary, 1976.

Rosenberg, Bruce A. *The Code of the West.* Bloomington: Indiana University Press, 1982.

Rossi, Paul A. and David C. Hunt. *The Art of the Old West.* New York: Alfred A. Knopf, Inc., 1971.

Ruggles, Richard I. "The West of Canada in 1763: Imagination and Reality." *Canadian Geographer* 15, 4 (1971): 235–61.

Rutherford, Paul. "The Western Press and Regionalism." *Canadian Historical Review* 53 (September, 1971): 287–305.

Silver, Arthur. "French Canada and the Prairie Frontier, 1870–1890." *Canadian Historical Review* 50 (March, 1969): 11–36.

Smillie, Benjamin, ed., *Visions of the New Jerusalem: Religious Settlement on the Prairies.* Edmonton: NeWest Press, 1983.

Smith, Henry Nash. *Virgin Land: The American West as Symbol and Myth.* New York: Alfred A. Knopf, Inc. 1950.

Snow, Chief John. *These Mountains are our Sacred Places: The Story of the Stoney Indians.* Toronto and Sarasota: Samuel Stevens, 1977.

Spry, Irene. "Introduction." *The Papers of the Palliser Expedition 1857–60.* Toronto: Champlain Society, 1968.

——. "Early Visitors to the Canadian Prairies." *Images of the Plains: The Role of Human Nature in Settlement.* Eds. B. Blouet and M. Lawson. Lincoln: University of Nebraska Press, 1975: 165–80.

Stacey, Robert. *C. W. Jefferys.* Canadian Artists Series. Ottawa: National Gallery of Canada, 1985.

Stanaitis, R. "The People's Painter." *Golden West* 13, 1 (January, 1978): 22–30.

Stephens, D. G., ed. *Writers of the Prairies.* Canadian Literature Series, No. 5. Vancouver: University of British Columbia Press, 1973.

Stich, Klaus Peter. "'Canada's Century': The Rhetoric of Propaganda." *Prairie Forum* 1 (April, 1976): 19-30.

Swainson, D. "Canada Annexes the West: Colonial Status Confirmed." *Federalism in Canada and Australia: The Early Years.* Eds. B. Hodgins, D. Wright and W. Heick. Waterloo: Wilfrid Laurier Press, 1978: 137-57.

Swanson, Jean. *Sky Painter: The Story of Robert Newton Hurley.* Saskatoon: Western Producer Book Service, 1973.

Thacker, Robert. "The Plains Landscape and Descriptive Technique." *Great Plains Quarterly* 2 (Summer, 1982): 146-56.

Thomas, Greg and Ian Clarke. "The Garrison Mentality and the Canadian West." *Prairie Forum* 4 (Spring, 1979): 83-104.

Thomas, Lewis G. "Associations and Communications." Presidential Address, Canadian Historical Association *Historical Papers* (1973): 1-12.

Thomas, L. H. "Mid-Century Debate on the Future of the Northwest." *Documentary Problems in Canadian History,* Vol. 1. Ed. J. M. Bumsted. Georgetown: Irwin-Dorsey Ltd., 1969: 207-27.

——. "British Visitors' Perception of the West: 1885-1914." *Prairie Perspectives* 2. Eds. A. W. Rasporich and H. C. Klassen. Toronto: Holt, Rinehart and Winston, 1973: 181-96.

Thomas, Philip J. *Songs of the Pacific Northwest.* North Vancouver: Hancock, 1979.

Tippett, Maria and Douglas Cole. *From Desolation to Splendour: Changing Perceptions of the British Columbia Landscape.* Toronto: Clarke, Irwin and Co. Ltd., 1977.

Troper, Harold M. *Only Farmers Need Apply: Official Government Encouragement of Immigration from the United States, 1896-1911.* Toronto: Griffin House, 1972.

Truettner, William H. *National Parks and the American Landscape.* Washington: Smithsonian Institute Press, 1972.

——. *The Natural Man Observed: A Study of Catlin's Indian Gallery.* Washington: Smithsonian Institute Press, 1979.

Underhill, F. H. "Some Aspects of Upper Canadian Radical Opinion in the Decade Before Confederation." Canadian Historical Association Annual *Report* (1927): 46-61.

Voisey, Paul. *Vulcan: The Making of a Prairie Community.* Toronto: University of Toronto Press, 1988.

Waiser, W. A. "Macoun and the Great North-West." M.A. Thesis. University of Saskatchewan, 1976.

Warkentin, John. "Steppe, Desert and Empire." *Prairie Perspectives* 2. Eds. A. W. Rasporich and H. C. Klassen. Toronto: Holt, Rinehart and Winston, 1973: 102-36.

——. "The Desert Goes North." *Images of the Plains: The Role of Human Nature in Settlement.* Eds. Brian Blouet and M. Lawson. Lincoln: University of Nebraska Press, 1975: 149-63.

——. "The Geography of Franklin and Long: A Comparison." *The West and the Nation.* Eds. C. Berger and R. Cook. Toronto: McClelland and Stewart, 1976: 33-71.

Watercolour Painting in Saskatchewan 1905–1980, Exhibition Catalogue. Saskatoon: Mendel Art Gallery, 1980.

Watson, J. Wreford. "The Role of Illusion in North American Geography. A Note on the Geography of North American Settlement." *Canadian Geographer* 13, 1 (Spring, 1969): 10–27.

Watt, Frank, "Western Myth: The World of Ralph Connor." *Writers of the Prairies*. Ed. Donald G. Stephens. Vancouver: University of British Columbia Press, 1973: 26–36.

Williams, Raymond. *The Country and the City*. London: Chatto and Windus, 1973.

Wilson, Clifford. "Peter Rindisbacher, first Western artist." *Canadian Art* 20, 1 (January/February, 1963): 50–53.

Woodcock, George. *The Meeting of Time and Space: Regionalism in Canadian Literature*. Edmonton: NeWest Institute for Western Canadian Studies Inc., 1981.

INDEX